Whatsoever a man soweth, that shall he also reap.
Gallations, VI, 7

For as you sow, ye are like to reap.
Samuel Butler (1600-1680), *Hudibras*,
Part II, Canto II

AS YE SOW

The Story of An American Rural Community

Researched and written by
Louis V. Kovi

Flemington, New Jersey
THE HUNTERDON COUNTY BOARD OF AGRICULTURE
1981

Copyright © 1981 by The Hunterdon County Board of Agriculture

All rights reserved. No part of this book may be reproduced in any form, except for review purposes, without written permission from the publisher.

Library of Congress catalog card number: 81-81992

ISBN 0-9606584-0-8

Printed in the United States of America at the Democrat Press, Flemington, New Jersey.

Preface

As Ye Sow is a history of the Hunterdon County Board of Agriculture, featuring the wide-ranging activities of the group from its reorganization in 1915 to the present. It tells how one region survived and prospered through nearly a century of massive changes in American life. While the emphasis is on agriculture, the book is often tied to the many other events and challenges that confronted the entire nation in the early years of this century. The story is told as a narrative, and includes rare photographs and dramatic quotes from some of those who "were there." These help to bring the variety of experiences to life. As historian John T. Cunningham writes in the Foreword: "*As Ye Sow* fills many blanks that have confronted historians seeking to tell the story of the importance of agriculture in New Jersey. Most important, it combines the dry stuff of minutes with general agricultural and social history."

As Ye Sow is presented in two parts — *The Board* and *The Community*. In the first, the Board's history is traced chronologically, with the first chapter covering its early history to 1927, the second 1927 - 1934, the third 1934 - 1940, the fourth 1940 - 1950, and the fifth from 1950 to the present. In the second part, six chapters treat the varying kinds of Hunterdon farming, as well as the number of auxiliary forces at work in the community. Here the effort is to go beyond description and evaluate the impact of Hunterdon people and products on the county, the state, and the nation.

A variety of information supportive of the narrative is in the back of the book. The reader will find lists of Board members who served as officers over the years, Hunterdon members of the State Board, and county residents who have been recognized for unusual service to the industry. Also, there is a chronological guide to historic events and people, as well as several charts and graphs on New Jersey and Hunterdon agricultural production and a selecitve bibliography of references used in the book's preparation. Last, but clearly not of least importance, are the sponsors who contributed money in the spirit of community service to help underwrite the cost of publication. Their support, without which *As Ye Sow* would still be a dream, is gratefully acknowledged and greatly appreciated.

Many people have had a hand in the making of this volume. Some, like the members of the Board of Agriculture, worked from its inception several years ago. Others, like the archivists, librarians, researchers, writers, and editors, joined the work when the book began to take shape two years ago. Along the way, the project became a true community effort. Various other individuals and groups in the county contributed their professional expertise, historical information, family photo albums and scrapbooks, and personal reminiscences, largely on a volunteer basis.

The idea for a book that would chronicle the history and development of Hunterdon's Board, as well as the decision to expand the book to include the history of the rural community in general, came from the Board itself. As with any such effort, a few individuals persevered, including the officers of the Board and Arthur Danberry, Wesley Lance, John Middleton, Kenneth Myers, William McIntyre, Melda Snyder, Seeley Thomas, Lloyd Wescott, and Calvin Wettstein.

As is also so often the case, a group of inexperienced laymen with enthusiasm and dedication needs professional leadership to accomplish its goal. This came in a most remarkable way from Edward J. Mack, editor of the Hunterdon Countv *Democrat*, a weekly newspaper that covers the county, and Richard F. Hixson, a county resident and journalism professor at Rutgers University. They gave the project direction, guidance and know-how.

Mrs. Snyder and Wescott provided inspiration as well as information, and both read and re-read, edited and re-edited the manuscript. Myers, local author and historian and president of the Hunterdon County Historical Society, was a persistent watchdog over accuracy. McIntyre, for many years the county's agricultural extension agent, and Wettstein, his successor and current agent, supplied the wealth of facts and figures on Hunterdon farming, or knew where to find the information.

Lance, a former state senator and long a practicing attorney in the county, and Middleton, once Board president and longtime member of its Executive Committee, insisted that all aspects of Hunterdon's rich agricultural history be included. They reminded their colleagues, for example, that horse farming has become a major New Jersey and Hunterdon industry. Thomas, publisher of the Hunterdon County *Democrat*, made numerous valuable suggestions regarding the printing and publishing of such a major work. Danberry, whose family has been synonymous with Hunterdon rural life for generations, died as the book neared completion. It is the hope of the Board that *As Ye Sow* will become a lasting memorial to all of the farmers who, like Arthur Danberry, played so important a role in the history of Hunterdon County.

When it came to the final research and writing, the services of Louis V. Kovi of Ringoes, a journalist and author whose family has farmed in Hunterdon for more than half a century, proved invaluable. They were made possible through a public service employment project granted to the Board by the federal Comprehensive Employment and Training Act (CETA), Clarence Bodine, Hunterdon County director. Kovi interviewed dozens of key farm officials in the county and the state, including State Secretary of Agriculture Phillip Alampi and John Olsen, state executive director of the Agriculture Stabilization and Conservation Service, a resident of Sergeantsville. He also combed the archives of the Hunterdon County Democrat and the Hunterdon County Historical Society, and talked to farmers whose families have operated in the county for many years.

Kovi's assignment was the most demanding. For the better part of a year he collated on a full time basis the many facts and opinions and then, in the quiet of his farmhouse study, weaved the disparate pieces into a narrative that is both scholarly and entertaining. A farm boy in the best sense of the phrase, he brought to the task the unique perception of a Hunterdon native. He knew instinctively, for example, what information was important and he understood the special lingo of farmers without the aid of an interpreter. Rarely is an author so endowed with first-hand knowledge of the subject he must explain to others. The Board deeply appreciates Kovi's fine work.

Dereck Williamson of Bethlehem Township, journalist and newpaper columnist, was consulted at the outset on writing style and research, and Ria Peale of Tewksbury Township applied her deft editor's pencil to much of the manuscript. Janet Finley Deissig of the *Democrat* staff and resident of Readington Township researched and wrote the chapter on horse farming. She received valuable suggestions and background information from Donald Alpaugh, Richard Fear, Pat Herrmann, Dr. Welling Howell, Richard Mannon, Georgia Rogers, and Robert Tucker. Many of the book's photographs were donated by Kenneth Stryker, whose collection of old and rare prints and negatives is indeed a goldmine. Photographer Kurt Herrmann and *Democrat* photographers Richard Rawlins and Gigi McBrien also applied their craft on several occasions.

No book of this nature is possible without the unselfish help and guidance of archivists and reference librarians. Margot Seigel of the Hunterdon County Library and Roxanne Carkhuff of the County Historical Society, and Kathie Schreiner of the *Democrat* contributed countless hours assisting Kovi and the others in digging through books, manuscrips, newspapers, letters, and other relevant documents. Jane Griffin, the Board of Agriculture secretary in 1980, was always cooperative, as were Nancy B. Crutchfield, county home economist, and Extension Service secretaries Lillian Snyder, Silvia Cohen, Diana Mack, and Lillian Chilmonik. Glenn Brown of Rosemont, a partner in the advertising, marketing and sales promotion firm of Brown & Kosa, designed the dustjacket. Abraham Mittelmark of Califon, an artist whose photo-retouching skills were used to the utmost, designed the book pages. His work, like that of Kovi's, was supported by a project granted by CETA. Always patient and cooperative was the entire workforce at the Democrat Press, particularly Denis Quinlan, who prepared the various charts and graphs, and Jacqueline Holcombe, who set the type and quietly suffered through the many revisions. Cynthia M. Hixson of Clinton Township compiled the index.

Among the many Hunterdon residents who were interviewed by Kovi, the following are noteworthy: Frank Burd of Sergeantsville, Paul Wirtz of Clinton Township, Mr. and Mrs. Robert Manners of Ringoes, James Weisel and Charles Cane of Rosemont, Clayton H. Stains and the late Oscar Grossman of Frenchtown, Mrs. Jacob Oster of Three Bridges, George Lachenmayr of Whitehouse Station, the late Raymond Bastedo, former county detective, of rural Clinton, Mr. and Mrs. Horace Smith of Ringoes, and Mrs. Beth Perry of Whitehouse Station.

Also Jack Rinehart of Hamden and Arthur Rinehart of Clinton, Mrs. Beatrice Aten of Reaville, Earl Hartpence of Stanton, Mr. and Mrs. Terrence Hoffman of Califon, Stanley Douglass of Pittstown, Howard Case of Three Bridges, Mr. and Mrs. James Bowers of Pittstown, Mr. and Mrs. Herman C. Schick of Milford, Mr. and Mrs. Karl J. Nielsen Sr. of Pittstown, Mr. and Mrs. Margin Stout of Milford, Mrs. Peter Kovi and Mr. and Mrs. Louis S. Kovi of Ringoes.

Kovi had access to a number of oral tapes that were made in 1972 of the following individuals: William Phillips, Fred Totten, Mrs. Eloise Schomp, Edwin Gauntt, the first county agent, Mrs. Almena Crane, Arthur West of the New Jersey Farm Bureau, B. F. Ramsburg, former 4-H agent, Mrs. Anne Stevenson Hageman, Edward Quick, Harold Everitt, William McIntyre, Arthur Danberry, Wesley Lance, Mrs. Blanche Hoffman, Alvah Haver, Rev. Edward H. Dunbar, Miss Ruth E. Ent, former extension service secretary, and John Middleton.

All contributed immeasurably to making *As Ye Sow* a vivid narrative of living history.

Finally, John T. Cunningham, New Jersey's leading popular historian, contributed the Foreword. He has written 17 books on New Jersey, the first of which, *This Is New Jersey*, has become a regional bestseller. Cunningham was one of the founders of the New Jersey Historical Commission and served six years as its chairman. He is a past president of the New Jersey Historical Society. Phillip Alampi, New Jersey's Secretary of Agriculture since 1956, contributed the Afterword. Raised on a fruit and vegetable farm in Williamstown, New Jersey, Alampi earned two degrees from Rutgers University, which also awarded him an honorary doctor of laws degree. For a number of years he taught vocational agriculture and coached athletics at Woodstown, New Jersey, high school. Prior to his appointment as secretary of agriculture, Alampi and his wife Ruth conducted farm and garden radio and television shows in New York. He has served in the governor's cabinet longer than any other member in the state's history.

— History Book Committee,
Hunterdon County Board of Agriculture

Flemington, New Jersey
August, 1981

Contents

Preface		v
Foreword by John T. Cunningham		xi
The General Farm: *A Prologue*		1

THE BOARD

I	Bearing Fruit	11
II	Faith and Cooperation	28
III	Changing Times	44
IV	War and Peace	56
V	Population Shifts	67

THE COMMUNITY

VI	Poultry Grade AA	83
VII	Dairy Farming	108
VIII	Crop Farming	126
IX	The Auxiliary Forces	154
X	**Marketing the Product**	178
XI	Horses in Hunterdon	188

Afterword by Phillip Alampi	204
Officers of the Hunterdon County Board of Agriculture	206
New Jersey and Hunterdon County: *A Chronology*	208
Graphs and Charts	210
Bibliography	212
Index	215
Sponsors	220

Foreword
By John T. Cunningham

Hunterdon County, bucolic, "picture postcard country" — the words seem like synonyms, as if nature had decreed that this rich rolling countryside must always be host to those who farm for life.

Yet Hunterdon is changing. Slowly some of the best farm land is being swallowed up for homesites, where substantial houses are plunked into the middle of three to five acres of prime fields once planted in wheat or corn. Chicken ranches are disappearing; statistics that still show substantial numbers of hens on farms are relevant only in awareness that 190,000 of those hens are on but two farms.

Those who might bewail the "disappearance" of farmers or rue the transformations sweeping across Hunterdon might take some small measure of comfort in the fact that change has always been part of the county's agricultural picture.

Chickens themselves, once a robust part of the Hunterdon County farm income, resulted from change wrought by Joseph Wilson of Stockton, who in 1892 made the first known shipment of incubated chicks in the world. Soon Hunterdon led the nation in hatching baby chicks.

Equally, after the sudden rush of railroads to power in the middle of the 19th century shifted most wheat and beef cattle westward, many Hunterdon farmers turned to dairy farming. That accounts for the "picture postcard" look of the dairy farms that are yet in many areas of the county.

Change has not been all man-made. Probably no natural agricultural disaster in New Jersey has been worse than the San Jose Scale scourge that struck Hunterdon's two million peach trees early in the 1890's. A prosperous enterprise quickly disppeared under the sound of axes felling ruined peach orchards.

Change is a major element in this engaging history of the Hunterdon County Board of Agriculture. Surprisingly perhaps, innovation has not come by farmers (much less their Board) thinking and acting as one concerted force.

Indeed, much of *As Ye Sow* revolves around the inability and unwillingness of farmers to cooperate — even in their own best interest.

It is important to recognize this ever-present split in the ranks, for it is basic to understanding both Hunterdon County agriculture and the county's Board of Agriculture. Farmers are not all the same; they represent as many thoughts and as many notions as the diversity of their harvests.

The strength of *As Ye Sow* stems chiefly from the fact that it does not gloss over those differences of opinion. This is one of those rare books commissioned by an organization that does not spend all its pages heaping lavish praise on the sponsors. Consequently what has emerged is a document that is enlightening, important, and readable.

The wrangling of Hunterdon farmers over the appointment of the first County Extension Agent is Exhibit A.

It seems inconceivable — in retrospect — that most Hunterdon County farmers should have fought so stubbornly against the county agent movement, unquestionably one of the significant forces for good in modern American agricultural history. However, retrospection is a poor way to *judge* the past; it is useful only in trying to *understand* the times that created what in hindsight seems monumental foolishness.

New Jersey welcomed its first farm agent in 1912, chiefly because the Lackawanna Railroad acted as co-sponsor and the Sussex County Farm Bureau appointed the agent. Federal and state monies became available in 1914 for partial support of farm agents. Seething hostility toward even the idea of a county agent kept the Hunterdon County Board of Chosen Freeholders from considering the concept until 1916. By then much of the rest of rural New Jersey was pleased with its bright young agents.

Hunterdon's freeholders, goaded by conservative farmers, looked askance at any notion of a "college boy" coming in to teach farmers. Farmers felt their lot was tough enough without having scientific theory compounding their difficulties. A 1922 referendum on the question showed far more support for a county agent among town dwellers than among farmers!

So, as farmers elsewhere laughingly dubbed Hunterdon "the China of New Jersey" (as a symbol of backwardness), the county's recalcitrant men of the soil and their freeholders successfully fought the bad fight from 1916 until 1927. Even decidedly non-rural Essex County had hired a county agent in 1918, nine years before an agent trod the fields of Hunterdon.

This extended tale of arch-conservatism in opposition to good governmental support is not a pleasant recounting (keeping in mind the power of retrospection), yet it is true. To the lasting credit of today's Hunterdon County Board of Agriculture the foot-dragging is recounted in intriguing detail.

Such negativism serves to underscore the power of those farmers who were progressive. Their perseverance in the face of opposition that would have repelled lesser men is a saga worth knowing.

Such a progressive, for example, was Clifford Snyder who was "in the eyes of the arch-conservatives" a "dubious revolutionary — he had gone to college." He had in fact gone to two colleges, M.I.T. and Cornell, but his efforts to make the feed cooperative work in Hunterdon met with bitter opposition among most farmers.

Enough of conservativism.

Against that thread weaving through this tapestry of Hunterdon County farmers and farming, there is also the story of stubborn and prevailing progressivism.

Two examples prove the point.

In 1930, a pair of young hatchery owners founded the Flemington Auction Market for eggs, battling the inevitable army of scoffers to create and to make successful the first such auction market in the nation and perhaps in the world.

Then, in 1938, world history was made in Hunterdon County by the start of the first artificial insemination of dairy cattle in a cooperative association. "Scientific" farming had triumphed on an undreamed-of scale — and in conservative Hunterdon County at that!

The Hunterdon County Board of Agriculture also showed rare insight in 1940 by encouraging a young Rutgers University professor, Hubert Schmidt, in a scholarly study that eventually became the book *Rural Hunterdon*, the first one-county study of agriculture in New Jersey. That book in reality was the prologue for this newest Board-supported history.

Farmers naturally have been pre-eminent in Hunterdon County political and social history. That is also a proper part of *As Ye Sow*.

Interestingly, the progressive farmers who were asked in 1946 to help lead the drive for the Hunterdon County Medical Center initially expressed great doubt that the county could or would ever support such a center. They did sign on despite their openly expressed concern that the county's few wealthy people who might support the center never would use it.

The result became good history. As farmers (and non-farmers, too, in utmost fairness) worked, they caught the vision of good rural hospital care. Hunterdon County Medical Center was opened in 1953, a landmark for farm counties everywhere.

As Ye Sow fills many blanks that have confronted historians seeking to tell the story of the importance on agriculture in New Jersey. This study of the Hunterdon Board of Agriculture reflects a painstaking sifting through the Board minutes (board minutes are never stimulating). Most important, it combines the dry stuff of minutes with general agricultural and social history.

Thus, there exists now a solid, stimulating look at one county's farmers faced with disease in the fields, depression in the markets, stubbornness at the ballot box. It offers a seldom-found glimpse at farmers in the awesome depression of the 1930's — a time that has for most people faded into the forgotten mists of time.

There is every reason to read this narrative with pleasure, for it far transcends the dusty minutes of the meetings or the social gatherings where gentle farm folk are said to have frolicked. It sets farmers — progressive and conservative — against their times and lets the reader make whatever judgments might be pertinent.

Yet the book can teach those who would till the soil, tend the crops, gather the eggs, or milk the cows. The lesson is simple. Nature is omnipresent, ready to do whatever it wills. If mere mortals are to succeed in farming, they must know every scientific and rational weapon to use in the struggle with a relentless, unceasing foe.

If *As Ye Sow* has heroes, it is the farmers themselves. Rich or poor, progressive or conservative, they have stuck to the land — to the eternal good of those who would push them out.

"The history of Hunterdon County could be written in terms of its religious, educational, cultural, and institutional growth; but this would not tell the fundamental story. In order to understand the development of Hunterdon, it is necessary to know the detailed history of its agriculture and the detailed history of its economy, which has been based upon its agriculture, for Hunterdon is rural."

Hubert G. Schmidt,
*Rural Hunterdon:
An Agricultural History.*

The General Farm
A Prologue

They worked together and shared the bounty. If a farmer needed help in operating his grain thresher, he called on his neighbors. On the top row, left to right, are William Pyatt, Russell Cripps, George Pyatt, and Harold Pyatt. On the bottom are Bert Trimmer, Ernie Fredericks, and George Oehme. They're sitting on the thresher, surrounded by straw and bags of threshed grain.

There is a 2,000-year-old essay on leadership that concludes: "And the best leader is the one who, when the work is done, the people say, 'We did it ourselves!' "

In a community where the people are obstinate and too independent to take orders kindly, only the best type of "leader" can lead at all. This is the kind of farming community Hunterdon County was as the 20th century began. This book is the story of the individuals who made up the "modern" Board of Agriculture, organized in 1915. It tells of how they came to understand that an obstinate love of independence can be turned into a grand experiment in cooperation. It is also the story of what happened as this cooperation was applied to problems in times of great turmoil and change in American life in general.

However, in order to understand the achievements of the 20th century it is necessary to look back, for the organizations of the previous 200 years were neither as complex nor as large or bureaucratic as those of our own time.

Historians, as well as old-timers still living in the area, tell us that Hunterdon County has always been farmland, from the time of the original inhabitants, the Leni-Lenape Indians, or "Original People." How and when the Lenape reached New Jersey are still open questions, but archeological evidence suggests that the area has been inhabited for at least 5,000 years. According to Indian legend, the Lenape migrated from Canada through western New York to Ohio, then traveled eastward to the Atlantic, arriving in New Jersey only a few hundred years before the European colonists.

The Lenape, in effect, were the original Hunterdon farmers, what one might call subsistance agriculturalists who paved the way for the white settlers who began arriving around 1700, and, in turn, cleared the woodlands, built modest dwellings, and planted their crops, mainly for subsistance. For the most part these early foreigners were English, Scotch-Irish, Dutch, Rhineland German, and French. Their farms were self-contained, known as the "general farm," but by 1770 they were able to market their surplus wheat, beef, and pork and use their new purchasing power to acquire not only necessities but luxury goods as well from traders and merchants. Hunterdon thus remained a region of general farming for 200 years, with little specialization until the latter part of the 19th century.

Geographically, Hunterdon County is situated on the western side of New Jersey, with the Delaware and Musconetcong rivers providing the natural limits on its southwestern and northwestern borders. Its other borders are more erratic, surrounded by Warren and Morris counties to the north, Somerset to the east, and Mercer to the south. The county covers 279,680 acres, and today is one of the largest rural areas in the state. Despite the farming done by the Lenape, the white settlers found the county mostly untouched wilderness.

An outcropping of the Appalachians, known as the Highlands, penetrates the northern part of the county, while the remainder to the south is part of the Piedmont belt. Sourland Mountain, in the south, has a backbone of diabase or trap rock, as do Round Mountain and Cushetunk near the center of the county, the latter in the shape of a horseshoe that encloses the red shale area called Round Valley. West of Flemington is the Hunterdon Plateau, which rises from 500 to 700 feet above sea level. Cushetunk Mountain is 834 feet and the ridges of the Highlands are even higher. Two ridges, one near West Portal and the other near Anthony, rise to a height of 1,073 feet and are the highest in the county.

John Reading, one of Hunterdon's first settlers, established residence near present-day Stockton around 1703 and called his plantation Mount Amwell, after his home village of Amwell in Hertfordshire, England. The name Amwell was adopted by the new township that was formed in the southern part of the county in 1708. When Hunterdon was set off from Burlington County in 1713 Amwell Township became a township of the new county.

Along with Reading and others, two groups of early pioneers, one largely Anglo-Saxon, the other mostly Dutch, settled in the central part of the county. They were soon followed by English Quakers and later Germans from Pennsylvania. In 1726 a census taker reported 3,236 whites and 141 blacks in the county, though it is likely that only a small percentage of those lived in present Hunterdon. An election return in 1738 named 165 voters in Amwell Township. Kingwood Township was created in 1728 and Readington in 1730 from Amwell, the three municipalities containing all of the territory now in the county.

Most of the settlers coming from Monmouth and Burlington counties and other districts to the south were of English, Scotch, and Scotch-Irish extraction. There were English Baptist groups on Spruce Run in 1738, at Baptistown in 1741, and at Flemington by about 1768. English Quakers from Burlington County settled in the area of what is now Quakertown about 1730. Followers of the Church of England were living in the Ringoes area and in the region where the boundaries of Alexandria, Kingwood, and Franklin townships now intersect. Others took up residence in what is now High Bridge before 1730, in Kingwood and Bethlehem townships by about 1735, and at Mt. Pleasant by about 1750.

Holland Dutch formed another basic element of Hunterdon's early population, settling first at Headquarters, at Baptistown, and in Bethlehem Township, then, in following years, Readington Township became an outpost of the large Dutch settlement of Somerset County. Present-day mailboxes bear dramatic witness to the Dutch influence: Ten Eyck, Van Horn, Van Fleet, Van Etta, Van Doren, Van Sicklen, Voorhees, Stull, Lott, Hall, Fisher, Louw, Wyckoff, Suydam, Latourette, Convenhoven (Conover), Devore, Montfert, Lequear, Dubois, De Witt, Hoagland, Jansen, Johnson, Messler, Smock, Brokaw, Nevius, Farlee, Quick, Melick, Sutphin, and Schenck.

Germans comprised another large early group. One story is that in 1707 a shipload of German refugees, driven off course en route over the Atlantic to New York, were put off at Philadelphia. Determined to join other countrymen in New York, they journeyed overland but changed their minds when they came to the beautiful rolling country that today is Tewksbury Township. To the south, in Ringoes, by 1747 there were 30 members of the German Reformed faith in that area. Their settlement was spread out, as Johann Adam Boellisfeldt (John Belis), one of the pillars of the church, lived at Copper Hill, where he had settled about 1730. Others settled in the Sand Brook region, in Rockaway (Potterstown), at Lelyland (Whitehouse), and at Fuchsenberg (Fox Hill). Still others made their home in the Spruce Run valley, Lebanon, Fairmount, and the Mt. Pleasant-Everittstown region.

Later came the Italians, Hungarians, Czechs, Slovaks, and Poles, most of whom arrived after World War I, and several hundred immigrants from Russia, many of whom were Jewish. The local census taker for West Amwell Township in 1930 reported people from 17 European countries. Evidence of quick Americanization is the fact that only two families were unable to speak English. One other component of Hunterdon's population, the blacks, never were large in numbers; in 1790 one-fifteenth of the county's population was black.

Despite changes in farming methods over the centuries, the crops grown in Hunterdon have not varied greatly since those early days. Pioneers spoke of growing wheat, rye, barley, oats, Indian corn, Indian beans, melons, squash, pumpkins, and hemp, in addition to the varieties of vegetables and flowers grown in the country today. Then, as now, wheat and corn were especially important, followed by rye, a hardy crop, and oats.

Before the manufacture of commercial fertilizer, the early farmers used animal manure or simply wore out the land and moved on. In the 1790s they started using lime from kilns in Bucks County across the Delaware, and several years later they began experimenting with "green manure," crops that were plowed under to enrich and restore the soil. Commercial fertilizer came into use late in the century.

Corn was one of the first crops grown, and it remains the leading field crop today. With the exception of buckwheat, the grains grown in Hunterdon are the same as those grown in colonial days. Of course the varieties have been improved and today produce much higher yields. The first hay was native grass, but timothy and clover were grown by early settlers. Alfalfa was tried in the county about 1795, but with little success until it was promoted by the County Board of Agriculture and the Rutgers University Experiment Station. Soybeans, which are good for rebuilding the soil, were first tried in the late 1800s.

Potatoes started to be grown in the early years of the 19th century, though they never really became a popular and especially remunerative venture for all Hunterdon farmers. Flax has been grown in the county, at least enough for farm household use if not for wide commercial purposes. Turnips, hops, and cabbage are crops more important years ago than they are today in Hunterdon. Tomatoes, once believed to be poisonous, have consistently been grown here, though not as commercial produce until 1900 in the New York market. Several canneries were established to sell to New York and Philadelphia consumers. Fruit growers have also prospered, and one of the most interesting developments in the county's economic history was the half-century-long commercial production of peaches.

Domestic animals, like the crops, have not changed much in Hunterdon over the years — cattle for dairy products, meat, and leather; oxen for work; sheep for wool; swine for the winter meat supply; and poultry for both eggs and meat. Horses were used for travel and as draft animals. From the days of the earliest settlers, cattle has played an important part in the county's agricultural economy, as has poultry raising in general and egg production in particular.

Thus, agriculture was, and is, the chief occupation of the people of Hunterdon County. Over the years there has been increasing specialization in dairy cattle, and poultry and vegetables are thoroughly commercial, too. Improvements in transportation have made possible the carrying of farm products rapidly to their markets, and farmers' cooperatives, fruit exchanges, and dairymen's leagues have all enhanced the farm community.

The Hunterdon County Board of Agriculture, whose members were the catalyst for these changes and improvements, was founded on November 15, 1885, by a group of men and women who called themselves "Patrons of Husbandry," more familiarly known as the Grange. But it was not until the early years of the 20th century that the Board became a substantial force in county affairs. It helped in the establishment of 4-H clubs, following passage of the Board-endorsed Smith-Hughes Bill in 1916, the Cooperative Association for the milling of grain for feed, and, finally, it led in the long-fought struggle for a county extension agent. Through its increasing involvement in common agriculture problems, the Board's various programs helped local farmers survive the nationwide agricultural depression, 1920-1924, the aftermath of World War I. As the 20s drew to a close, the Board could look with pride at increased yields in wheat and corn and improvements in milk production. During the 20s the number of county residents increased by six percent over the previous decade; there were 2,000 new Hunterdon citizens.

Today, Hunterdon agriculture is mechanized, specialized, and commercialized. Promoted by scientific feeding, selective breeding, milk testing, artificial insemination of cattle, cooperative buying and selling, effective use of the newest machinery, and employment of technical advice have all contributed to help make Hunterdon agriculture more efficient.

* * *

In the family since 1785, the John Alfred Rinehart farm home in Oldwick looked like this when the general farm was at its peak in Hunterdon. Great-grandparents Mr. and Mrs. John Rinehart are in the picture with other members of the family. Like most farm houses in the county, the building was constructed with care, quality, and simplicity. The farm home was the nucleus of farm life and it reflected the values of its occupants.

There were 409 square miles of farms in Hunterdon County at the turn of the century. With 100 acres a good general size for a farm, that meant over 2,000 farm families. The majority of the county's 34,000 residents lived on farms. The rest lived in the towns. Most of these were in businesses that served the farm population or passed its produce on to the rest of the country.

The early 1900s were good times in many ways, but different. There was no electricty, no indoor toilets and plumbing, no central heating, no telephone, no cars. If people needed light, they got up with the sun at four, five, or six in the morning. The toilet was a sturdy outhouse, perhaps with a bucket of lime and a Sears catalogue. The kitchen sink usually had a hand pump that ran to a cistern or hand dug well.

In the winter people slept under a down or feather quilt. There was a chamber pot in the room and a washstand. Children might run downstairs with clothes in hand on winter mornings and get dressed in front of the ever-burning kitchen wood stove.

Friends and neighbors provided the fast-news network. And without cars, if one needed to go somewhere fast, it was probably on the back of a horse. Farm wagons had big wheels, so when they sank in the muddy dirt roads in the spring, the hubs didn't get mired so easily.

There were other things missing, too. There were almost no taxes, no road departments, no police, but, yes, there were schools, and the community was always proud of them. On the farm there were carefully tended fields that produced corn, oats, wheat, several kinds of hay, buckwheat, peaches, apples, potatoes, tomatoes, anything that would grow and be sold at market or used to feed the animals. In the barn and the sheds, there were horses, cows, bulls, chickens, goats, pigs, guinea hens, geese, ducks, and other small livestock.

For the past 50 years and more, adventurous people had been opening the expanding frontier, producing food and sending it back to compete with local production. But Hunterdon farmers had the advantage of Philadelphia and New York nearby, with 11 trains a day stopping in Flemington Junction, for example.

As farmers in rapidly changing times, Hunterdon men served those city markets with different items and were prepared to switch if new developments in transportation brought cheap western products east and took their market away. Some specialized, too, in peaches, for example, but most were also always ready to diversify.

Frank E. Burd of Sergeantsville was a boy in those days and he tells the story succinctly:

"I was born in the summer of 1890. My first vivid recollection of public issues was of McKinley running against Bryan in 1896 for President on the Free Silver platform. I remember that campaign and, election night in Flemington. I never saw so many people drunk in my life, after the polls closed at 8 o'clock or whenever it was. There were no fights or riots or anything, but everybody just got high."

That's a strange scene for a farming community, but politics and government have always meant a lot to farmers — especially in terms of what they got paid for their produce. It was maybe one percent of a farmer's life, but it wasn't neglected, and the kids went into town on election day, too.

"When I was a kid, the first work I did was for my mother's uncle next door, Bill Scott, and his brother, Charley. I was about five years old, and I dropped corn on the hills that they marked out with a furrowing plow. You dropped the corn by hand, and covered it with a hoe. Then they came along with a bag of compost over their shoulder and put that on the hill. When the corn got a little size to it, if it got a little weedy, we went in with hoes. We not only hoed it, but sometimes we got down on our hands and knees and pulled the weeds out.

"These old men I worked for, they were old-fashioned. They had what they called Kugler corn plows (for plowing weeds). They're made like a frame with handles and have four shares. They'd plow that corn twice, this way from the rows, and that way from the rows. It was nice to see Uncle Bill straddling that corn row. He'd have to walk straddling the row, holding those plow handles and guiding his team all at the same time. Uncle Bill and Charley used to put in 12 to 15 acres of corn.

"When the corn got big, they cut it in seven hill squares, seven hills each way. The men usually cut corn together. One would cut three rows and tie the shocks, and the other would cut four rows. You would husk it by hand and after you got the corn husked, you would tie your stalks into good-sized bundles that could be easily

Weeding the corn, Chester Smith of Ringoes toils quietly with a mechanical cultivator. Only two or three acres a day might be done with horses, but it was much faster than the old way — getting down on hands and knees and pulling out the weeds one by one.

handled. Then you'd draw four shocks together into a big shock, and in the middle you had your heap of husked corn.

"When Uncle Bill and Charley were hauling in corn, they would come out with a farm wagon, pick it up with two bushel baskets and haul it into the cribs. When they saw a nice big ear, well-filled and nice grain, very often they would throw it to one side, keep it separate and next year they would shell that one by hand. That was their seed corn. They would shell it by hand because the little tip of the kernel was where the germ was. They didn't want to destroy it. You'd never shell seed corn with a sheller. I think some of them partly improved the quality of their corn by carefully selecting seed from year to year. They used to raise immense ears, big long ears.

"There was something I think they had.

Prosperity was always an issue on Hunterdon farms. A family emigrating to the United States might start out with an unpainted and meager dwelling, and work their way up to something better. Happiness was usually reflected in progress toward that goal. (Hunterdon County *Democrat*.))

Maybe it's not gone, but it's disappeared a little — pride in workmanship. They'd pride themselves on being good workers. Why, when farmers would go to hire a man, they'd say 'Oh, I'd like to get him, he's an awful good worker.' That is to say they did the work neatly, they weren't sloppy about what they did, and they gave the farmer a full day's work.

"I can remember, around 1900, a young man would get married, he'd work what they called 'work by the year.' They furnished him a house, kept him a horse — which he sometimes put in to work to make an extra horse — they kept him a cow, he could have some pigs, he could have a few chickens, had a chicken yard, and he got maybe $180 a year. If he burned wood, he got his firewood found. He didn't have much. Unless he smoked he didn't have much to spend for groceries that he couldn't raise.

"I've known several cases where these fellows did very well, and after a few years had some money together and could go to renting their own farm, usually on shares, they called it. And he'd get his equipment together, he'd buy some second-hand machinery, probably he'd got a good, used mowing machine then for around $25 to $30. He didn't think about getting a binder. Maybe, he'd hire somebody to cut his grain for a year or two. He'd buy plows, old plows went for maybe $4 to $5 apiece, a spring tooth harrow for maybe $5. And he got stocked up, and his whole outlay wouldn't be maybe $500.

"He would then save his money and farm on shares for a few years. Somebody would have a farm for sale and he would buy a farm of his own. I know one man in particular who became quite well-to-do. He started to work right next door to us farming. He saved his money, got somebody to back him financially because they knew he was honest. And he paid off his notes on time, established good credit, and he bought his own farm. When he died, he wasn't fabulously rich, but he was what we called in those days, 'well-to-do.'

"When I was a boy, the farms of about 50 to 60 and maybe 75 acres were very desirable, they were about the right size. A man ideally would keep about three horses. He had two for a team, one for the wife to go to the creamery with, and the other to run errands with and use for the hay fork and so on. If they had a binder, he would need a third horse.

"If you were fortunate like some farmers, you'd have a boy or two coming along to help out, so you wouldn't have to hire very much help and spend money. And you could make money.

Straight from the producer to the consumer in this scene depicting the old-fashioned way of milking a cow. The cat is not a pet, but a working farm animal whose assignment was to keep vermin away from the feed. In return the cats lived in the warm hay lofts and had fresh milk twice a day.

"In my day farmers often ran a small dairy. The regulations weren't strict, and most of the farmers up around Quakertown would have six or seven cows. They'd go to the creamery and receive a check every month. That gave them a little loose money. Those farms were very desirable in my day.

"Uncle Bill and his brother, Charley, had at least half their 87-acre farm set out in peaches. They continued with the peach business into the early 1900s, when the scale came along. The trees died and the stumps had to be pulled out. I heard Uncle Bill say one Sunday morning, when he was out in the shop washing eggs, that he thought they'd have been just as well off if they never had a peach tree on the place.

"You see, when the peach trees are set out, until they get a little size, buckwheat or corn was planted among them. After a year or two, when the trees got any size, the ground was out of production for anything except peaches. They couldn't corn it, they couldn't put wheat there, they couldn't get in with a binder to cut it. It wouldn't raise grass nor hay.

"In the spring, farmers used to plow around the peach trees, then they would cultivate between the rows of trees to keep the weeds down. If the weeds got high as your backside, you couldn't pick peaches very well or move a peach ladder. When you figure what they lost on the corn and wheat they might have raised, plus the oats, buckwheat, and hay they might have been able to sell, Uncle Bill figured they'd maybe have been just as well off if they'd never had a peach orchard.

"That didn't mean that some years they didn't hit it good. Peaches sometimes went up to $2 a basket, but usually a dollar a basket. Of course, as old Charley Scott used to say, when you had a good crop, everybody else had peaches and peaches were low, and when peaches were high, nobody had any peaches to sell.

"But a few people made a little money on it, had one or two good years. And the Scotts had one or two good years. I know they did. That's when they cleaned up. Then the poor years would offset that. Thing is, farming used to be a bit more diversified than it is now. On the small farms, it was pretty hard years ago to starve a farmer out, if he was any good. He had his milk check. He had some hogs. He had some eggs to sell, take to the store, trade for groceries. He had some fruit to sell, too. He had hay, corn, wheat, oats — now not all of that is going to be a failure. When you're a one-crop farmer, you've got all your eggs in one basket. If somebody kicks over

Before horses became readily available, male steers, called oxen, were a common means of transportation, surviving into the late 19th century. While horses required complex leather harnessing, oxen pulled with the more primitive U-shaped bent-wood yoke. The white-bearded gentleman on the cart is the only man in the picture not sporting a large mustache.

the peach basket, well . . .

"The Scotts were typical. They didn't have any dairy, didn't want to be bothered with it. Dairy farming is confining. You have to milk twice a day at the same time for the good of the cow. Uncle Bill used to sell eggs. He also sold hay on the side. He'd get around $20 a ton, good prime hay with no weeds in it. And he'd sell maybe 10, 15, 20 tons of timothy hay. He used to sell a little seed wheat, what you call beardless wheat. Maybe they'd sell a little corn also, but not much.

"Uncle Bill and Charley didn't make much money. They didn't get hold of much money, but then they also avoided spending much money. We kind of look back at that and poke fun at it, say they were tight-fisted, but if they wanted to stay in business they had to be like that.

"The Scotts had a thresher that had belonged to their father, who died in 1859. They had harness, sets of harness. God knows whether they got it new, but they used it for years. They farmed up there for 49 years and three months before one of them died. So they used it for 50 years. They used two farm wagons which they had when they started the farm. Maybe they weren't even new then. When they finished using the wagon, it had to go inside. The mower and hay rake stood outside during the summer haying season. But just as soon as the hay season was over, presto! it was taken up and put away. It was that way with everything. They had sleds that they called Buck sleds, which they had them for years and years. After the snow was done, the sleds went right under cover.

"I tell you I think the oldtime farmers — maybe the younger farmers have got it, I'm not sure — but I know the old farmers had it, the quality I call 'patience.' If they had a poor year, well, they'd do without something they wanted. They'd put it off. If they didn't get it this year, they waited till next year, and maybe not get it even then.

"I'll tell you something else. Uncle Charley was very profane, and used to swear a good deal. But, if they had a lot of hay to cut down or a lot of wheat out and a big shower came up, they never stood around and cursed about the rain coming and spoiling the crop. They just said, well, when it stops raining we'll have to get out there and turn that hay over and get it dry. That's patience. I think you might say that farmers did produce something else. There wasn't any market for it, but it was the quality of patience. It was a very great asset.

"If their corn didn't come up — cutworms, nasty, cold wet spring and the cutworm cut off the corn what did they do? Stand around and cuss the damn cutworms? No, they got busy and planted the corn again. Of the several byproducts of farming, one was patience. The farmer had to have patience. Think of all his animals. I've seen farmers mess around with horses that were nasty. Oh, they were patient with them. They put up with them. If it was a good horse once you got the harness put on him, it was a good horse. Uncle Charley was like that. He had a brown horse. I was always a little afraid of him. And if they had a cow, for instance, that was an independent creature, they would put up with it. Patience. They didn't walk out and say, 'Well I'm going to sell the damn cow, I'm getting rid of her right away.' She may have been a good milker.

"I remember once I was over at the farm and it had been raining for hours and we were sitting around. I got impatient, nothing to do, and I said, 'I wish this rain would stop. It's gone on for hours.' Uncle Charley says to me, 'Well, there has been only one rain in the history of the world that never stopped.' I said, 'When?' And he said, 'Now.'"

That was the Hunterdon general farm. Each one was different, but most followed the basic principles Burd described. There was independence and happiness that went with it. There was a freedom to associate openly with the rest of the community or stay at home and farm. The key was frugality and not having to deal with money. The coming years would sweep those ideals away like the waters of a dam breaking. Farmers would have to learn to deal with money, and go from gambling on Mother Nature to gambling on the kindness of their fellow men. To keep their farms, they had to be willing to make changes, changes stunning in their immensity.

Lloyd Wescott of Rosemont is the descendant of one of the adventurous farmers who went west, but wound up himself coming back to farm in the east. He compares his childhood to his adult years: "It has been like going from the banks of the Nile to the Space Age." Several thousand years in one man's lifetime, a rich and eventful time for Hunterdon County, New Jersey, too.

Herman L. Schick (above) of rural Milford stands by a row of pigs butchered one day in 1919. Farming was not always a sentimental pastoral scene, for after having raised an animal from birth, the farmer then killed it himself and did his own butchering on the spot.

Slaughtering was messy but straightforward. A pig would be struck on the head with a sledgehammer or shot with a rifle, its throat cut to bleed the carcass, then slit open and the innards removed. The carcass was dipped in boiling water to loosen the hair (right top). In the other photo (right) amidst steam from the boiling tank, are, left to right, Lester Wilson of Everittstown, Arthur Cronce, Hugh Laire, Russell Sperling, and Harold Wilson. The photos were taken in the 1930s.

How fast can you eat a piece of homemade pie without using your hands? The adults smile good-naturedly as the kids compete. The only way for a farmer to avoid overworking was to have a picnic now and then and bring the entire family. This one, at Butler Park in August, 1938, was sponsored by the Hunterdon County Poultryman's Association.

Typical of an earlier day in Hunterdon is the farmstead of William Phillips near Milford, a symbol of both hard work and paradise.

I
Bearing Fruit

During its early years, from 1886 to 1915, the Hunterdon County Board of Agriculture exposed the farming community to the educational and political influences of the state and region in a way that was sometimes valuable and effective. At other times, it failed in its aims.

Around 1915, dramatic changes began to take place. The men who engineered these changes on the Board were the older farm leaders of the day. By the time the changed Board was mature in 1922, these older men had retired and the next generation assumed the reins of leadership.

Many members of this group were to devote most of their lives to this task and to take the Board into the 1950s.

They took the initiatives begun by their fathers and adapted them to the 20th century with a success that would make Hunterdon a leading agricultural county in the state. This would give farmers, both poor and prosperous, old and young, a fighting chance to live a good life in their chosen vocation.

The names of four men stand out, not because they alone did valuable things but because they formed the core of the farm leadership for so many years:

Clifford E. Snyder of Pittstown, president of the Board, 1921-1959; Theodore H. (Dory) Dilts of Three Bridges, vice-president 1923, 1925-1947; Richard S. Schomp of Stanton, secretary, 1921-1952; and John Hudnett of Neshanic Station, treasurer, 1932-1962. Hudnett was preceded by John Tine of Stanton, treasurer, 1921-1931.

The reorganization of the Board that put these men in office was not a unique local development, but a logical continuation of state and national events as well.

Though the Board was and is largely a male organization, it was founded by a group of men and women who called themselves the 'Patrons of Husbandry,' more familiarly known as the Grange:

"Our county board was organized Nov. 15, 1885, by the Hunterdon County Pomona Grange . . . at the meeting held in the hall of Locktown Grange No. 88 in August. We had quite a fair exhibit (of produce), and the committee was requested to do what it could among the members to collect and bring a good exhibit to the next meeting in October, which was held at the hall of Ringoes Grange No. 12. We had one of the grandest exhibits in point of variety and quality that we have seen in our county in many years, including grain, fruit and vegetables . . ."

The five Granges in existence during those early years were "everything" organizations for farmers. They were nationally organized and had secret rituals, yet any farmer and farm wife were welcome to join. They took a strong interest in politics, but were nonpartisan, and were devoted to their community, a philosophy that continues to this day. And they provided a place for farm families, isolated by the horse and buggy and dirt roads, to socialize.

The 1880s and 1890s were years of national political ferment over farm issues that often bore no fruit. In 1893 the Board reported that a Farmers Alliance picnic and fair drew about 5,000 people. The Alliances, scattered over the nation, were created with lightning-like rapidity during these years to promote the political voice of farmers. And they were disbanded just as rapidly when they didn't work.

Thus, a year after the big picnic the Board reported: "There seems to be little if any more interest of a practical nature taken in farmers' organizations than formerly and quite a number of Alliances have been abandoned. A few of our Granges, however, show substantial gains . . ." The Granges survived this period because of their all-encompassing nature.

Persistence was the backbone of the Board. Its most frequent criticism was that it was hard to get farmers to show a coherent and abiding interest in the Board's constructive nature — which consisted of collecting statistics about local agriculture, and sponsoring "institutes" at which experts talked on the best current prospects in agriculture and the most scientific ways of responding to them.

Empty fields were more common than the farm community liked. The advertisement suggests why, even as late as 1920, when it appeared in the Hunterdon *Democrat*. (Kenneth Stryker Collection.)

Innovative and scientific farming takes a great deal of added labor and energy to establish, the Board maintained, and it appeared farmers had been distracted into neglecting this vital area by their unsuccessful political efforts of the time.

The result was demoralizing, and in 1897, Board president V.R. Mathews of Ringoes summarized this discouragement in a speech in which he claimed that the hardship of a farmer came entirely from wasting time dabbling in politics or business or whiskey.

Let those who will, try for reform, Mathews said, but the farmer interested in improving his difficult lot had better join others and "try to do a little reform work on his own farm by stopping some leaks and giving more time and attention to those departments that yield a better profit."

Mathews claimed that following his advice would make Hunterdon's farmlands a rich cornucopia of productivity, "while on our waste lands we can grow enough persimmons to stop the mouths of all the croakers!" Apparently this was the impassioned speech of a farm leader who saw his community being distracted from conserving its vital energies in hard times. And they were hard times, indeed, provoked by the opening of new lands to the west and the creation of keener competition. Because of the popularity of new land, Hunterdon's farmland values started dropping after the Civil War, not to pick up again until around 1910.

It took 20 years for Mathews' vision of the organized, scientific farmer to be realized and result in the modern Board of Agriculture. Perhaps the early warnings and exhortations of such men helped.

But good crops cannot be grown even by the best farmer unless the sun, rain, and the attitude of farmers to their world and their role in it are right. Not until the period from 1900 to 1920 was that attitude right for progressive farming all over the nation.

A look at some of the items listed in the chronological chart (See Appendix) can give a feeling for what was happening as the recognition of the importance of education began to take hold in American farm life.

The creation of the "county agent" was a major item. Cornell University is credited with starting that initiative in 1901, and by the beginning of World War I, in 1914, almost every farm county in the United States had a county agent.

Hunterdon certainly did not have one, and yet the agent was the crucial person who could make a reality of the dream that scientific agriculture could produce prosperous lives for all farmers. The agent was the librarian and technical expert who had all the data and information on new and, presumably, better farming methods. He could be a direct route to this data for anybody who needed help fast on Hunterdon's 2,000-plus farms. The telephone was beginning to spread, and mail service frequently took less than a day within the county. New cars could send a man speeding round the county during good weather.

But for Hunterdon, with its leaders and officers on the State Board of Agriculture since 1890, the times weren't right. Then, in 1910, a "golden era" in agriculture emerged and lasted till 1919. During that time prices were fairly adequate, so farmers felt more comfortable and outgoing.

State legislation in 1912 enabled Rutgers College, New Jersey's land-grant institution since 1864, to organize its Agricultural Extension Service, which trained county agents and provided them with expert back-up from the agricultural college. The traditional lecture "institutes" were still offered, as were the newer "demonstrations," where actual work was done that farmers could watch.

The Board had written to its political leaders in Washington, asking them to back the Smith-Lever Act for the support of county agents at the federal level. The measure became law in 1914 and New Jersey began offering to pay half of the $4,000 yearly expense of a county agent.

Bearing Fruit

In 1915, the State Board reorganized along more efficient lines — deliberately choosing a nonpolitical relationship to the rest of state government. On the county level there was enough energy left for the leaders to try to revitalize their own Board.

Opportunities that could be applied directly to Hunterdon's farm prosperity were springing up like mushrooms in the cow pasture after a heavy summer's rain. Or so it appeared to some hopeful men.

Herman C. Schick of Milford remembers the late David Agans telling him how he got his start in those days — a start that took him from Three Bridges to the state Assembly and Senate, presidency of the State Grange, and a life devoted to farm leadership. Agans was out in the field with his one-horse walking plow one day. The work routine was simple. There was plenty of time to think of the farm problems of the day, wondering what farmers could do that would work. They'd tried so many things that did not. Finally, the simple answer came to him: organize. Farmers just had to try to work together and organize.

That answer had been tried unsuccessfully on a national scale for decades, and here it was being rediscovered. Agans wound up sitting on the County Board's Executive Committee and helping rewrite the bylaws during these years of reformation.

Egbert T. Bush of Stockton was one of young Agans more mature colleagues. He served as Board president in 1915, 1916, and 1917, the first three years of the new Board. Bush was an unusual man — a school teacher, a scholar, a writer of novels, a philosopher, a farmer. He was not the kind of man to be a strong central leader, his friends reported, yet he was the kind of man to start something with ideas and visions.

Bush seemed poised between two ages, when many things were dying and others were being born. The first year of his term the Chestnut blight reached New Jersey, and a beautiful tree that made fine fence rails became part of history. The last year he served, 1917, the United States entered World War I.

Hay is slowly gathered, one forkful at a time, by this team of two men and a boy. (Hunterdon County Extension Service.)

Bearing Fruit

The Little York-Mount Pleasant Road, now macadamized, as it looked in 1919. (Photo by Sherman Tharp. Herman Schick Scrapbook.)

The oldest extant minutes of the Board date from Bush's first year in 1915 and are written in the terse, hurried handwriting of Roscoe DeMott, secretary.

The traditional four meetings a year were held, starting with the annual organizational session in March. On April 24, "talks were given by wide-awake farmers of our county," including Bush's report of a state-level institute he had attended.

The next day-long meeting in August was the big Fall Social, at which "The Whitehouse Grange ladies served a generous and very tasty lunch." John Tunis Cox of Readington Township, vice President of the State Board of Agriculture from 1901 to 1916, spoke on the reorganization of that Board. Professor Alva Agee from the three-year-old Rutgers Extension Service gave a talk on "the advisability of keeping farms well sodded" to avoid the age-old loss of soils through erosion, which had damaged so much Hunterdon land over the years.

The last meeting on December 11, at which officers were reelected for 1916, the Board delegated Hiram E. Deats of Flemington to attend the State Board annual meeting, and heard Jason Hoffman, the county superintendent of school, discuss the new Smith-Hughes Bill before Congress. It would provide federal aid for agricultural education in high schools.

The Board then voted a resolution favoring the bill and sent it to national representatives. Hoffman led the Board to Flemington High School, where exhibits of county-wide grade school students were on display and were to be judged for quality.

The year 1916 was conventional — the Grange ladies cooking, the "experts" speaking and resolutions to national leaders formulated. So conventional was the year that there are almost no minute entries, except for an intriguing one: "On April 29 it was resolved to request each Grange to elect two delegates to attend the August meeting to co-operate for the betterment of agricultural interests."

What happened? "A motion was made, seconded and carried, that a committee in conjunction with the Pomona Grange be appointed to ask for an appropriation for funds for farm demonstration."

J.S. Cray, W.H. Kuhn and President Bush were going to ask the freeholders to put up $2,000 to be matched by $2,000 from the state for a county agent.

When it came to money, Hunterdon was a notoriously conservative county. Between 1910 and 1915 the freeholders had gone into debt to the tune of $315,000 to improve the road system that farmers had complained about for so long. Another $2,000 wasn't going to kill them, but the forces of conservatism and frugality prevailed for the next 11 years in the effort to fund a county agent.

Without an agent, the programs of the County Board and of other farm groups would be reduced to a fraction of their effectiveness.

The quiet, persistant initiatives of the preceding two years bore fruit in January of 1916 when the Board blitzed the county with experts. Day-long farmers' institutes were held at the Ringoes Grange Hall, the Lebanon Reformed Church, the Sergeantsville Grange, the Pattenburg School, and Lambertville. Among the speakers were Extension Service experts, successful farmers from other counties, and Rutgers Agricultural College professors talking on such topics as:

"Some of My Experience in Commercial Poultry Farming."

"Alfalfa, a Profitable Crop for Hunterdon County Farms."

"Modern Methods In Dairy Farming."

"Renovating an Old Apple Orchard."

"Practical Methods In Hog Raising."

"Very practical" wrote secretary pro-tem W.E. Rittenhouse reporting on these activities. He didn't forget to enter that Rev. Alphonse Dare of Haddonfield spoke on "The County Church and its Relation to Agriculture," and "Miss Anna Hauser of the State Agricultural College talked on 'Home Decorations,' a good subject, ably handled."

"Mr. F.J. Espelle of Sergeantsville Grange read an editorial claiming that city boys will be the future scientific farmers. This was followed by a lively discussion, which was ably closed by Prof. Alexis L. Clark on the proper education of the county boys and girls."

These talks of church, home, and children were the heart of the institute for the distaff side of the family, and they were being wooed by the Board. Although farm wives' names rarely appeared in newsprint or on meeting rosters, their role in the running of the farm was as strong as the man's.

Bush and his colleagues used the institutes to stir the imagination of the whole farm community, and to encourage the idea that Hunterdon's farmers were strong, valuable people. People who could sit and listen to an expert could also go home and imitate the prosperity-producing methods he spoke about so easily. The Board of Agriculture was staking its reputation on the average farmer and his ability to learn and innovate successfully. And it was inviting the whole county to call its bluff.

Things kept on moving after the big splash of institutes. The Board resolved: "That the County Board of Agriculture work through the Granges of the county as far as possible to organize the county into community organizations for the purpose of developing better agriculture and to help meet the present National Crisis."

Grange committees were revitalized, and 17 men volunteered to cover regional areas of the county and keep communications with non-Grangers open. In May the Grange liaisons were reported successful, and the Board voted 10-0 to completely reorganize itself into an expanded form.

The "National Crisis" was the country's entry into World War I. A national push was on to boost farm production to meet war needs, and the Board was appointing itself the local booster. "Can the Kaiser. The Kaiser *Is* Canned!" the war posters of the day proclaimed. Housewives were being urged to can and preserve produce as never before.

By the end of 1916, the new bylaws were adopted and Grange representatives and community representatives became a permanent part of the restructured Board's Executive Committee. As Egbert Bush turned over the reins to Burris Snyder of Pittstown in 1918, he could look back on an unusually successful three years. The Board had changed from a group that often complained of lack of community interest to an organization that was in the middle of the activ-

ity. Even school children, previously involved in agricultural clubs, were now, by way of government boosting, members of the Junior Agricultural Army.

But there was a possible problem: farm people tended to respond strongly, as they were now, during a crisis or during a period when improving their prosperity was possible. When the crisis passed, when the prosperity push worked or failed, interest generally waned. So to achieve a real change in grassroots participation, the Board would have to transcend this tendency. The times had given it momentum and energy. Now it was to spend that energy freely in changing people's habits, and in discovering ways to work with them, to keep them changing continuously.

Each year, the county agent question was a major issue, and each year tightfisted freeholders and the conservative farmers who backed them would reject an agent. Instead of backing down, the Board maintained an overall initiative of trying anything useful to farming.

Along with Snyder, the new officers were: John Spencer Dilts of Three Bridges, vice-president; W.W. Case, who had served as secretary in years past, was again at that post; and W.A. Drinkwater of Whitehouse was treasurer.

The Smith-Hughes Bill, which the Board had supported three years earlier, had become reality, enabling Flemington High School to begin a vocational-agricultural program. To tie local children's groups closer to national aims, the first 4-H Clubs were formed in the county, and the state provided funds to make Sherman Tharp the temporary leader.

By April the Board had appointed a special committee to confer with the draft board on the exemption of skilled farm labor. And by September, Columbia University met with the Board to consider establishing an "agricultural branch" in Hunterdon! Strange that a New York university should come as far as Hunterdon to look for farmers with whom to work. Although nothing came of the proposal, the Board explored it enthusiastically.

At the same meeting Freeholder President John Johnson was invited to give his opinion in support of a $2,000 county agent appropriation. He said:

"If the people in general desired such an agent, one would be employed; but if they did not so desire, the freeholder board did not feel like taking such an action on their own volition." At the December meeting, Board members voted 14-5 to explicitly request such an appropriation by the freeholders. It was rejected.

Snyder and the other officers were reelected for 1919, but the freeholder rejection apparently had a depressing effect for the only minutes entry for the entire year is December 27, and concerns itself with another reelection. This time vice-president Dilts stepped down and the post went to John C. Haynes of Annandale.

Other things happened in 1919 that advanced the Board's causes, however. For one, David Agans began a three-year term in the State Assembly. Fred Totten of Ringoes organized the first dairy herd improvement group in the county.

Totten was an affable, hard-working farmer who completed his unfinished grade-school education by doing crop production sums in his head as he followed his one-horse plow. He continued his modest but extensive self-education his entire life. Conservative farmers who distrusted well-educated professors would listen to men like Totten because he knew the figures backwards and forwards and had taught them to himself.

During all its years, the Board had implicit partners in men like Totten, and the numberless conversations such men had with farm neighbors kept the new kind of farming evolving in Hunterdon on an even keel. It was easy enough for a farmer in these years to buy a tractor and catapult himself into 20th century farming. Many followed this path without much help from anyone other than a tractor salesman. But there were crucial tests when the tractor broke down and couldn't be fixed at the farm, or spun its wheels in wet spring fields that a horse could have walked through easily.

One of the staggering events of 1920 was a nationwide agricultural depression that lasted until 1924. Prices that had soared during the war for farmers, now plummeted to abnormally low levels. But purchases of items needed by farmers continued at inflated and costly highs.

It was also the year that women won the right to vote.

The census for 1920 showed the population of Hunterdon stagnant at 32,885. The county had actually dropped 600 persons since the 1910 census.

And a "Saloonless Nation" came into being. In other words, backdoor speakeasies and homemade stills were established all over the nation, including Hunterdon.

The decade of State Police raids on bootleg stills would show that it was mostly large-scale criminal elements that were doing the bootlegging. But it would also be a risky opportunity for a backwoods farmer hard-pressed for cash. Even a few gallons quietly produced behind the barn could bring in important cash in a pinch.

For the Agricultural Board 1920 was marked by an active push for new members — an all-out campaign brought the Board's roll to 300. It had fewer than 100 members before the push. Snyder and his officers had been reelected and by February they had held a membership drive meeting in Flemington and appointed delegates from each township to begin visiting and enlisting their neighbors.

On March 30 a special meeting was held and the decision made to print 1,000 membership blanks as well as a circular describing the Board's work. The drive that followed in April brought membership to 263, as reported at the May 15 meeting. The rest of the year was spent getting new and old members used to the notion that the Board wanted to see a lot of them.

A first move was to join the State Council of County Boards of Agriculture. Assemblyman Agans was offered a vote of thanks by the membership for "his splendid stand during the present session for the agricultural interests of the state."

On August 14, the farm of Frank Welsh near Lebanon became the site for the large quarterly meeting. The afternoon program included refreshments, inspections of the farm, and talks by state officials.

A final campaign for new members was conducted in November, and another large meeting held in December. Nominations were taken from the floor and the officers for 1921 were elected: president, Frank Welsh of Lebanon; vice-president, John C. Haynes of Annandale; secretary, Percy Bush of Stockton; and treasurer, John Tine of Stanton.

The Executive Committee was slowly evolving to its final form. At this time it consisted of the officers plus six men, each of the six holding a three-year term. The membership at large elected all of these, and delegates to the State Board and the State Council as well.

With that work done, members listened to institute-style speakers, including an address on "cooperative associations" that was to bear fruit the following year.

The new Executive Committee met the following day and immediately decided to set up a $5 a year membership fee — the equivalent today of perhaps $100! This would buy the farmer membership in his County Board, in the State Council of County Boards, and the American Farm Bureau.

The first "farm bureaus" had been county level groups that supervised the work of the new demonstration agents. By 1918 there were nine state-level federations of these county level groups, and in 1919 the American Farm Bureau Federation was formed with 12 states joining. The goal was to get every farm state to join. The movement would lobby for farmers' interests and be an informational watchdog in Washington and elsewhere. Its leadership would come from county level boards like Hunterdon's.

From a group that met four times a year with sometimes no more than the officers in attendance, the Hunterdon Board had changed into a 300-member organization with a great many irons in the fire. Never again would the Board's secretary-reporter note that there was a sad lack of interest in the group. The effort to create wide interest had paid off.

The next two years saw crystallization of the Board's new identity through repetition and refinement of the methods already used. Membership would eventually be brought to 1,000 farmers, and the vision of the Board as a coordinating agency among Hunterdon's farm organizations would become commonplace to all of the county's farmers, not just a few idealistic leaders.

The year 1921 was when the national agricultural depression hit bottom. And it was the year the Board of Agriculture had the money and leadership to do something about it. In the process it turned a good many friends into bitter enemies.

At the January 31 meeting, those attending learned that winter's talk of "farmers' cooperatives" was a preparatory move. John Hankinson of Woodsville, secretary of the State Council of Boards, was back to talk about the business methods used by cooperative associations. William Mount, president of the Mercer County Farmers Cooperative Association, described his group and how it worked. A half dozen Executive Committee members made short comments. And then "on motion it was decided by a rising vote that a Co-operative Association is wanted by the farmers of Hunterdon County."

But what were they cooperating about?

They were setting up a feed mill to compete with every small business feed dealer in the county to give farmers a better price on the feeds they needed to supplement the fodder raised on their fields. Farmers like Mount provided advice. So did A.L. Clark from the State Bureau of Markets in the state's Agriculture Department. It sounded easy, simple, and bound to succeed. It

hated and unpopular a person with changes to make can become.

In the eyes of many arch-conservatives, Clifford Snyder was a dubious revolutionary — he had gone to college. It was one thing to joke mildly about those college-educated fools who didn't know how to harness a horse properly, but it was quite another to have one in the middle of your quiet community talking about changing things.

Snyder didn't fit the cliché picture conservatives had of him. He was a graduate of M.I.T. and Cornell, a top flight farm college that had

In this photo taken before 1900, Frederick K. Porter, left, mans a team of horses cutting hay, while another man rakes with only one horse. The steel bridge in the background identifies the field — across the Raritan River from Tenneco Plastics in Raritan Township. Today it is part of the farm of Eugene Brokaw, Porter's grandson.

had to, because by July the Board, which never had more than a few dollars in its treasury, was set to loan the new cooperative $1,000.

Everyone who joined the cooperative to buy feed from it would have to pay $5 and make themselves liable for up to $50 more if that were necessary. Despite immediate success, the men who knew all the details kept their fingers crossed just the same. One of the nine directors was Burris Snyder's young son, Clifford, who had worked in previous years on the membership and reorganization committees. Now he assumed a bigger job and soon learned how

pioneered the county agent concept that had caught on with more than 90 percent of the farm communities in the nation. He wasn't some young inexperienced weakling who hardly knew real farming. Burris, his father, was a frugal Quaker who believed in simple virtues like pay-as-you-go, and he did not send his son to college. He told Clifford he could borrow an empty field and some of their equipment, for if he wanted to go to college he had better earn himself some money from the field to pay for it.

The adolescent soon became a man, with a well-tilled potato field, who was saving to go to college. He paid back the money his father loaned him, for as one source put it, if Burris loaned you a dollar, he expected it back, even if you were his son. Now, back from college, young Snyder was ready for bigger things, such as the feed mill project, and the rancor that went with it.

It came from the many small feed dealers around the county who bought small amounts of feed and sold it at high prices. They couldn't buy in large volumes and sell at lower prices, so the extra cost was passed on to the farmer. The Hunterdon County Cooperative was making them obsolete. And the young college farmer was one of those who put it together and was running them out of the feed business.

Clifford Snyder's wife, Melda, remembers his recalling those early years of the co-op and how, when he went into Pittstown on errands, people he had known and liked for years looked right through him as if he did not exist. He would nod in a patient and friendly manner, say a polite "Good Morning" or "Good Day," and go quietly about his business. To a young man with ideas of big changes, it was an invaluable lesson in how bitter good people can become over the confusions and hardships of changing times.

Eight others were on the Co-op Board of Directors and taking the same chaff, among them Frank Welsh, president for 1921, and Theodore Dilts, who was to join Snyder as an officer on the Board of Agriculture the next year. The Co-op was closely tied to the Board, which had staked its own reputation on it. Business was conducted out of a railroad boxcar with farmers coming to pick up their feed when the train came in with a shipment.

Within a few years the successful business would require major changes, but for 1921 it was a matter of getting it going, lending it money, even buying a $150 mimeograph machine for mutual Board and Co-op use. There was a great deal more than the Co-op project that year. In January the Board voted to send out 1,050 questionnaires purchased from the State Board Association to learn opinions on issues of the day. The opinion poll became a habit, for a memo of one of the yearly questionnaires is preserved in the minute books: rural police, 279 in favor, 228 opposed; daylight savings time, 13 in favor, 535 opposed; methods of national taxation, 40 general turnover, 25 limited turnover, 36 retail sales, 375 opposed to all three; consolidated rural schools, 161 in favor, 348 opposed; and immigration, 34 free, 152 prohibited, 342 restricted.

The Board's dedication to regular communication with members led to a newsletter being authorized in the spring. It was to be published off and on over the decades. Egbert Bush got it started. Also that spring, the Executive Committee constituted itself the Calf Club Leaders for the entire county, beginning a support of youth

William Lauderdale, one of the Executive Committee's strongest supporters over the years, talks with Walter Roland of Ringoes, probably about 4-H, his favorite subject.

A homemade water wheel at the Homestead Farm in Oldwick in the 1920s. John Emmett Rinehart, father of the present owner, John Alfred Rinehart, installed the device to produce electricity. Today, such energy-saving methods are again in vogue. (John Alfred Rinehart.)

clubs that became a permanent fixture of its activities. The Board also published the winner of a Farm Bureau essay contest in the local papers at the Board's expense.

In July, a permanent realtionship with the Flemington Fair Association was begun, with a committee named to see if the Board could put together an exhibit for the fair. Association with the Fair became closer over the years in recognition of the tremendous social role the organization played in the life of the county.

The two groups had started off on uneven terms in 1886 when the Fair Association offered to help the Grange start the County Board, provided it centered around reviving the fair's then failing prospects. The Grangers sent them off in a huff, but within a few years good relations had been restored. By 1921 the Fair Association was actually offering the Board $100 for expenses in putting up an exhibit.

Finally, there were the big membership meetings of the year. The summer field meeting was held at Burris Snyder's farm and the annual meeting at the Palace Theatre in Flemington. The latter opened with election of officers, at which time Clifford Snyder as president and Richard Schomp as secretary began their lifetime of leadership of the association. Vice-president was Alvah Bush and John Tine was re-elected treasurer. There were speakers from the Dairymen's League, the GLF (Grange-League Federation), now Agway, the Farm Bureau, and the other farm groups with which the Board was actively involved. Also a separate farm event was announced for the month: community motion picture films on farming in conjunction with Board of Agriculture talks.

The abortive resolutions were offered on the perennial county agent question and when the details were finally settled, the Board decided to send a questionnaire to each Board member, allowing 10 days for a response by postcard.

With the results 2-1 in favor of a county agent, Snyder, Frank Funck, and Schomp went to the freeholders. Freeholders John C. Haynes, Harry Philhower, and John J. Horn said yes, they would budget the funds, providing there were few objections at the public hearing on the budget. That was hardly likely. Every organization in the county interested in an agent was ready to support the idea at that hearing.

Thus, 1922 opened with the prospect of a county agent for Hunterdon at last, but the prospect faded quickly as the freeholders got cold feet. They called Board members five days after their agreement and said they'd have to readvertise the budget if the county agent issue was shot down at the public hearing. Not wishing to incur even such modest expense, they decided to do away with a county agent.

The Board of Freeholders set an unscheduled public hearing in three days when proponents could present their arguments. If the freeholders became convinced of farmer support, they might put the agent item in the budget. By the time three days had passed, the Board of Agriculture had contacted men from the Hunterdon Poultry Association, Sergeantsville Grange, Delaware

Township Committee, Hickory Grange, Flemington High School, Spring Mills Grange, Flemington Cow Testing Association, Oak Grove Grange, Hunterdon Holstein-Freisian Association, and Locktown Grange. In a meeting with the freeholders, the respresentatives didn't convince them that a majority favored an agent.

Freeholder Horn, whose wife was ill, wasn't present. Funck, in his account of the event, displayed a certain scepticism as to the truth of that claim. Such was the animosity that had built up over the years. Funck and others had suspicions they had witnessed a collapse of committment coupled with a weak and phony attempt to make it look fair. When he wrote about it in the Board newsletter, he was both furious and eloquent:

"We regret to report that the opposition was led by one of the members of the Executive Committee of the Board of Agriculture, Mr. Theodore Dilts, who reversed himself and joined his two neighbors in opposing the movement. We can forgive Ex-senator Foster [John R. Foster, who served one term in the state Senate beginning in 1898.]. He has always opposed a county agent. Martin A. Smith brought up the rear. He takes special delight in showing the dust on the back of any picture.

"Their talks were all on the same line: the County Agent was going to cost money, the money had to be raised by taxes, taxes were high and were going to be higher; everything was gloomy and the sun would never shine again.

"Freeholder Hayes read a tentative budget for 1922, placing special emphasis on the deficit of $85,000 from 1921, which had to be met this year, together with more figures; all of which made us very sad.

"We could not help picturing the natives of dear old Hunterdon in nakedness at this time next year, having been compelled to hock everything to pay our county debts."

The county agent proponents were then asked to consider whether they would like to withdraw their request. "We went away, we considered, we ate oyster stew," Funck reported acridly, for everyone already knew all the arguments by heart. The freeholders then went off to confer with Freeholder Horn at home ("We are pleased to report that Mrs. Horn is much better."). They came back and said they did not feel like having a county agent, by a 2 to 1 vote.

"It is hard to believe that the judgment of three opposing (non-unanimous) individuals as to the wishes of farmers of the county was sufficient to outweigh the judgment of 11 agricultural organizations," Funck wrote. "We are assured by one Freeholder that such was not the case. But it is equally hard to see the economy of again refusing the $2,000 (aid for an agent) from the State, which makes $8,000 in the past four years... Is it any wonder that they refer to Hunterdon County as the 'China of New Jersey'?" (China at that time was regarded as a very backward nation.)

The freeholders may not have had the vision of the Agricultural Board, but they knew their politics. The county agent question was put on the ballot later that year and roundly defeated. Farmers were just learning how to stop being conservative, and the agricultural depression that had started in 1920 had knocked all the wind out of their more liberal sails.

Although 1922 was cruel to the Board on its main issue, it was a good year for smaller, less visible ones. One was a new businessman who had come to spend his life in the county and devote his career to the community's welfare. D. H. Moreau would never sit on the Executive Committee, nor lead any of the other agricultural organizations, but he would eventually be regarded as an equal in his contributions over the decades. His business was the Hunterdon County *Democrat*.

There were seven newspapers in the county at the time and all were pretty much alike — one-man operations with the publisher serving as editor, selling ads and often doing much of the mechanical work as well on the printing press in the cellar. Income was limited and little time was spent collecting news. The majority of the paper consisted of syndicated stories sold to small town papers on a national basis. Local news was minimal, yet always eagerly read when printed.

Moreau, who decided to satisfy that eagerness, sensed Hunterdon was ready to throw its support to a full-fledged newspaper and set out to turn the *Democrat* into the county's leading newspaper. He combined his profit motive as a businessman with a sense of faith in the community that told him supporting its progressive leaders and encouraging their projects — or condemning them — was the way to build a large and profitable readership. Moreau was right, and his appearance proved crucial to the Agriculture Board.

County youth were being drawn further into the Board's scope of activities as well in 1922. The

Bearing Fruit

newsletter that blasted the freeholders also contained the happy news that the Flemington High School agricultural team was the grand champion of the state at the annual judging contests in Trenton. Henry Velehradsky had made the performance even more outstanding by having the highest individual scores in the state, 96 points out of possible 100. Two years earlier the school had won first place in cattle judging and third in swine judging. Clarence Alles, whose cattle won first place, was to go on to a successful career in farming and service to the community in a dozen different areas.

The 4-H Clubs scattered over the county also became more visible in 1922, with Charles Oliver from Rutgers assigned to work with the clubs on a part-time basis. The county's young men and women were learning the best kinds of agriculture and responding amazingly to any encouragement. The Board, in turn, intensified its efforts to encourage them.

The Board itself had grown so adept in the past several years that it was taking on a half-dozen jobs for farmers at the same time and handling each well. For example, the February meeting dealt with: setting up an arrangement with local businessmen to make plows available at special reduced rates to Board members; ordering its legislative committee to attend a state hearing on milk pricing; organizing a school corn contest; planning a picnic with the Pomona Grange; refunding dues to any members dissatisfied (a half dozen were recorded); and getting ready for a banquet.

The banquet was an experiment which evolved in later years as the annual Businessmen-Farmers Picnic — a kind of courteous thank-you to the business people of the community for their help and usefulness to the farmer. The affair had the usual elements of good food — served by the Flemington Baptist Church ladies — entertainment, and speakers. Much was also new. The entertainment consisted of a quartet from the Industrial School at Bordentown. Every banker and newspaper editor in the county was invited. A representative from the Federal Reserve Bank in New York gauged some of the agricultural strength of Hunterdon, and later reported his observations to his superiors a copy of which appeared in the Board's newsletter.

Snyder and the others realized that bankers and business expertise would be extremely important in the future. Quite commonly a county's businessmen and bankers know little or nothing of what farmers are doing, and farmers know little about how the resources of business and banking can help farming. The May 12 banquet, with its 153 tickets sold, was the beginning of this facet of Board work.

With an almost meticulous thoroughness, the Board helped promote the socializing of farmers and their neighbors by creating in August the Annual Auto Tour, which must have been at least as exciting as a trip to a World's Fair or Exposition. It started in Flemington and sped

Route 579 in East Amwell near Ringoes being graded about 1920. Pulled along by the tractor, the grader blade was continuously adjusted by the man at the rear. The machine gave the road a slight crown so that rain would run off. (H. Smith)

directly to Frenchtown and the Kerr Hatchery, then in its prime as producer of baby chicks by the railroad boxcar load. From there the entourage of 20 autos raced up to Mount Pleasant to see Sylvanus Apgar's herd of purebred Holsteins.

Charles Tharp at The Hickory was the next host in the high velocity review of Hunterdon farming. Tharp showed his giant Percheron horses, his Shorthorn cows, and the bee yard that the State Beekeepers association kept on his farm. The group went on to lunch at Adolph Gobel's farm, opposite the present North Hunterdon High School and is today site of the vast Exxon Research and Engineering Center. Gobel charged for refreshments and donated the proceeds to the county Red Cross. The High Bridge Band played spirited music, and various speakers were heard, among them Colonel H. Norman Schwartzkopf, head of the State Police, an organization that men like Agans and groups like the Grangers had worked for years to create.

Things turned back to business in October, when Dr. Frank App from the State Federation of Boards gave a detailed report of activities to the Executive Committee, including a recommendation that gave explicit form to the initiatives of the board: "That the county organize as a unit by getting the various county organizations to agree on a program which would adequately meet the needs of the county."

The Committee wasn't naive enough to believe that agreement was necessary, however. It simply set up a meeting with representatives from all other organizations, asking each to make up needs and goals for their groups. And that became the "program." In addition, the Board accepted recommendations on what it should be doing.

"Program For Agriculture In Hunterdon County — 1923," read Clifford Snyder's typed notes that he used at the annual meeting in December. The details of the program were not novel. What was novel was that everyone was going to know what everyone else was doing — and they were going to discuss it at regular meetings of the County Board of Agriculture. Snyder said:

"The poultry association may have a subject that interests them very much. The same question may or may not interest the Dairymen's League or the Holstein-Friesian Association. Suppose they find a subject of common interest? It is then highly desirable they pull together. It is the purpose of the Executive Committee to ask

A work team of men, women, children, and two horses lines up alongside a grain-binding machine in the early 1930s. They are members of the Louis Cerney family. The horse-drawn machine cut the grain and tied it in bundles, which were thrown on the ground, then transported by wagon to the thresher. (Harold Platt.)

the Grange and other farm organizations to meet with the County Board at their regular meetings and act as an advisory committee. We want them to bring their own particular problems, and also help in the discussion and working out of ours. We hope that these County Board meetings will serve as an agricultural clearing house for the whole county."

The dreams of many different men and women over the past decades had become a beginning reality — a dream of farmers working together as a unit to promote their mutual prosperity and improve the well being of the community. An apparent impossibility had been changed by the will of the farm people. And it happened at the right time. The period from 1923 to 1926 was right in the middle of the nation's roaring, wild bronco-busting 20s. During this period the Executive Committee's minutes literally grew into chapters. The work of the Board came to be done largely by specially appointed committees of two or more persons, which were assigned definite tasks and reported progress or completion at the monthly meetings, sometimes asking decisions from the Executive Committee needed to keep things going.

So many things were happening during the decade that it's unlikely anyone could look at it

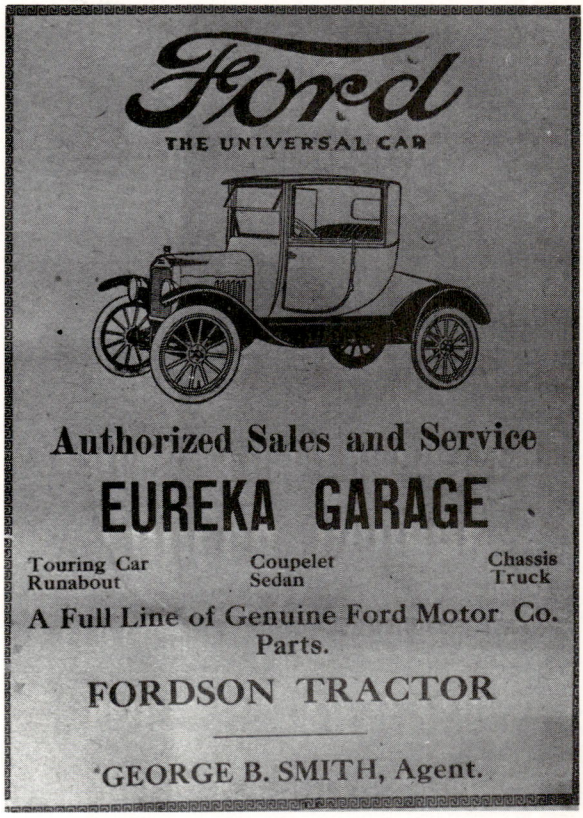

all and see the general trends that were shaping everyone's lives:

*During those years the county lost 59 square miles of its farmland, about 15 percent. The land was going to new roads, new buildings around the towns, and some was simply marginal land that was dropped out of farming because it wasn't profitable. Naturalist Vincent Abraitys of Sergeantsville estimates there are thousands of acres more woodland in Hunterdon County today than there was at the turn of the century — when every spare acre was farmed and only a small amount of land kept in woodlots.

*Wheat and corn land, the two major crops, dropped from 74 square miles to 49 planted, for reasons of profitability. At the same time, production per acre was growing as farmers learned the new techniques of using better seed and more fertilizer.

*Hunterdon gained nearly 2,000 new residents during the decade, a six percent increase, contrasted with the drop in population during the preceding decade.

*Milk production increased nearly 25 percent and egg production nearly doubled.

Essentially, Hunterdon was responding to nationwide changes and competitions. Field crops could be raised more cheaply in other parts of the country like the Midwest. As a result, they lost some popularity here, except where they could be fed to cows and chickens to increase production of milk and eggs, perishable products sold to the booming metropolitan areas of New York and Philadelphia. Distant areas could not compete here because they were not close enough.

It cost more money to farm, money that had to be risked, as always. To reduce the risk, farmers were gravitating towards serving the city markets. A farmer could listen to the institute experts speak in the 1880s and dream. In the 1920s, he went to a neighbor's farm where several test varieties of corn were being grown and compared them to his own standard brand. Then he could go to the Board's annual corn show and read off the acreage yields and look at the corn, and ask about whether it was grown on the same kind of soil as he had. Finally, he'd go see the seed dealer.

Frank Reading of Rosemont was the Grand Champion entry in the annual corn show in 1925 with his White Cap Yello Dent entry. Farmlands around Bloomsbury, Lambertville, and Pittstown had entries in the show. The shows and demonstrations were not narrowly focused. People could go to the fruit demonstration in a neighbor's orchard, or the chicken culling demonstration, or the vermin control demonstration. And anyone could speak to an Executive Committee member for a special demonstration that hadn't been thought of yet.

The demonstrations were useful. The "progressive" farmers were winning the contests and everyone was winning at home where it counts. Of course it did take a lot of time to make all those trips, and there was nobody around who had all the information on tap when the demonstration was over. There would be if there had been a county agent in Flemington. People could stop by his office and pick up a mimeographed circular on the best crops for local soils. Slowly, however, attitudes toward a county agent were changing. Even Theodore Dilts, on the Executive Committee, had changed his mind on the subject and now favored an agent. The Agricultural Board had not given up on an agent, and it was continuing yearly membership campaigns with vigor — so much vigor that it finally had to pay the membership campaign leader 75 cents an hour because there was so much work involved.

Arthur Danberry of Ringoes, who was to head the Board in the 1970s, remembers the care with which the Board always sought new members:

"The way membership was maintained by the County Board was by each township having a chairman back in those days, and he would call in a group he thought he could ask to do this volunteer work.

"We were indoctrinated on what the Board was doing for that year. We'd meet around the stove and enjoy a good talk in the evening, and then we'd go out and solicit membership.

"When you'd get toward the end of the year and hadn't made your quota, you'd begin to wonder whether you might need to put a paid solicitor on the road, but beating the bushes voluntarily hard enough, it always came in."

The potential member was thus approached by a well informed neighbor and treated as a respected equal who was being asked to do something constructive for himself and the county. Clifford Snyder himself took part in soliciting in his neighborhood over a long period of years, and said he considered it one of the most important things a Board officer could do to introduce the organization to a new farmer and maintain the Board's presence in the farm community. Ultimately such methods won out in the battle for a county agent. The special pleas to the freeholders were repeated every year, with the opponents appearing as well. During one of these hearings, probably the last, Snyder had been hit in the jaw by an infuriated farmer, but had restrained himself. Moreau humorously reported in the *Democrat* years later that the 1924 meeting was "looked forward to by this time by some citizens as boys looked forward to a circus. And this meeting proved to be almost that."

The Board had built up a membership of over 1,000, but the freeholders knew they hadn't convinced a majority at the grassroots level. The public vote in 1922 had shown many more people in the towns favoring an agent than in the rural areas. Every responsible farm organization in the county had joined in support of an agent. Maybe the freeholders were getting tired each year of being looked upon as a circus for the

Bearing Fruit

frivolous, who would watch sincere but uninformed opponents call the State Director of the Extension Service "a parasite and a sapsucker" and the editor-publisher of the *Democrat* "a young whippersnapper."

Something happened, for no apparent reason other than a decade of pressure: the freeholder's proposed county budget for 1927 had a $2,000 item in it for a county agent. People girded themselves for what was to be the last battle. The hearing was adjourned to the courthouse, for only its main courtroom was large enough to hold the crowd. The debate lasted hours and both farmers and extension experts spoke in favor of an agent. Angry opponents had their say as well.

"The long hearing came to an end," Moreau wrote, "without serious difficulties, and this largely the work of Freeholder Director J.D. Dilts, who was a sweet-tempered leader." He knew how to keep things in perspective.

Dilts was the lone freeholder voting against a county agent — possibly a matter of soothing political diplomacy to men who would not forget the matter quickly.

Seated in the back row of the room and quietly smoking his pipe during all the oratory was a young man named Edwin Armor Gauntt. Director H. J. Baker of the New Jersey Agricultural Extension Service had left him in the back while Baker went up front to take the gibes and the rough and tumble. Gauntt's turn would come next month, and it would last longer than three or four hours. He was to be Hunterdon's first county agent.

Chester Smith, left, of Ringoes gets a handshake from Extension Soil Specialist Herbert Cox for the prize-winning corn entry he and his brother, Horace, produced. The Smith brothers won numerous Board of Agriculture ribbons during the 20s and 30s. (Chester Smith.)

II
Faith And Cooperation

The period from 1927 to 1934 took farmers from the binge of the Roaring 20s to the depths of the Great Depression. When the Board sat down in 1927 with Extension Director Baker to select the new county agent it had fought 12 years to get, it must have had divine guidance of a sort, because it wound up with a man who had all the qualities needed to help farmers through a period that was going to be more chaotic than anyone had imagined.

Ed Gauntt, a galloping extrovert with a heart of gold, was so sure of himself that he told Director Baker he was nuts to offer him the job. Baker should be getting the best man in the state, Gauntt said, because it was going to be a challenge. Baker didn't want the best man in the state in terms of learning and technical excellence. He wanted a rough and tumble person like Gauntt, though all he told Gauntt was that "he had made up his mind." With this Gauntt stopped being the state's dairy specialist and became Hunterdon's new agent.

"I got in hot water right after I got here, because the first thing that happened was 'Doc' Dilts, the director of the Board of Freeholders, called me in and said, 'Well, we've got your secretary picked out for you.' "

"Now wait a minute, I'm picking my own secretary!"

"Who's paying for her?"

"You are."

"Well, then, we pick her!"

"No you don't!"

The discussion ended with Gauntt going to see Richard Schomp, who knew most of the farm

Edwin Armor Gauntt, Hunterdon's first county agent, as he appeared several years after his appointment in 1926. (New Jersey Department of Agriculture.)

community. Schomp told him the woman named as secretary wouldn't be any good, and to go back and fight. Gauntt later reported that Dilts didn't understand how or why he was losing the argument, but gave in with good grace. He wound up with a young German woman from Cherryville who hitchhiked into work every day.

"One of the people opposed to me picked her up one morning and brought her down to town and said, 'You'll be out of a job after the next election because they're going to throw that Gauntt out of there' and she jumped on him with both feet, and then came in and told me what she did. 'Now look,' I said, 'you let me do this fighting and mind your own business or you're going to get us all in trouble fighting with that fellow because he's quite a farmer!' " Another farmer was heard to remark loudly 'So that's the pup!' when Gauntt was pointed out to him on the street one day, and Gauntt didn't forget the man:

"He told me one time, for instance, if he ever caught me on his farm, he'd run me off with a shotgun. I said, Now look, you'll never catch me on your farm. I've got plenty of work to do. I've got 4-H clubs as well as county agent work, and I'm not looking for work. I'm not that ambitious. So just don't worry about your shotgun. I'll never be there till you send for me. Later on he sent for me. I visited his farm, and we wound up good friends! But there were a few of them that were really rough."

One of the people who annoyed Gauntt the most was a born haggler. No matter what Gauntt said or did, he always doubted it, always made predictions it would fail, and if it worked, wondered if it was a fluke. He apparently was the one man who ever made Gauntt lose his temper, for Gauntt went to Clifford Snyder one day and told him his griefs. He said he was going to confront the man with his complaints, whereupon Snyder advised: "Don't get involved in a spraying match with a skunk!" That put things back in perspective and whenever Gauntt thought of the man after that, he laughed.

"I felt I had a big break because the farmers wouldn't have bothered to support the county agent if there hadn't been opposition. The result of the opposition was I had men like Clifford Synder, Theodore Dilts, Dick Schomp and Breve Conover, and I could name 100 good farmers who were out working for the county agent."

Gauntt sensed he had been hired to make Hunterdon the top agricultural county in the state. "They were backwards in their farming. They didn't enter the farm shows, they didn't do anything because they didn't have anybody to do the work. The farmers were too busy to do it themselves. And I remember as soon as I got in there, I organized corn shows and we got down to Trenton and began to take the red and blue ribbons for corn shows each year. That way the county became known for its agriculture. The

Anne Sliker of rural Califon took this snapshot of her family's farm in the late 1920s. At left is the house her father, Samuel H. Sliker, built when they acquired the land at the turn of the century. At right are a poultry coop and barn, beside which are stacks of dried corn for winter fodder. The shed behind the barn, a "barrick," consisted of four posts and a roof that could be moved up and down for the storage of hay. The farm is on Sliker Road and the house and barn (now a residence) remain, as do four of the Sliker children.

In the 1920s Hunterdon orchardists were losing their apples, peaches, and pears. Consumers wanted blemish-free fruit, so farmers adopted sophisticated spraying rigs like the one shown.

other county agents were pushing their counties, and Hunterdon, with no agent, was just behind the eight ball."

"One fellow came to me, for example, and said, How do you like these peaches? And they were nice, big Alberta peaches, but they were covered with scab. I said, well, they're a nice size, but you've got some disease on them. He said, young man, I've been growing peaches before you were born and we've never seen a Alberta peach without those marks on them. That's what we call 'summerspot'. Call it what you please, I said, but it's a disease and ought to be sprayed. He never sprayed." But Gauntt had some ideas on how to get farmers thinking differently. No more lectures.

"The first year I took charge of the agricultural exhibit at Flemington Fair, I called upon Howard Sachs, county agent in Morris County and a fruit specialist who knew his fruit very well, to judge the fruit. He didn't give out a single blue ribbon for fruit. He said there wasn't an exhibit in the fair that was fit for a blue ribbon. I said, put a red one on it, then. Do whatever you want.

"Of course the farmers were mad as hell at me for getting that kind of judge! — who was so strict — and he put down on each ribbon why they were not awarded a blue one. We had one farmer up near Cokesbury, named Dick Wais, who had been in charge of the college farm in New Brunswick and knew his fruit and was a good grower."

Gauntt sent Wais in as a ringer the next year, sending his wife up to his orchard to pick up the fruit. She was astonished at how long it took to pick five apples of perfect size and appearance for that kind of contest. Wais' peaches and apples won all the blue ribbons that year. "From then on we had some real agricultural displays. They began to spray and take good care of their fruit."

Gauntt used similar methods on the vegetable entries, and got the same positive response. "Agriculture really boomed through the publicity, and the editors of the little country newspapers all really played the thing up, until Hunterdon got to be the number one agricultural county in the eyes of the state, instead of being one of the backward ones. For three or four years in a row we got the grand champion blue ribbon at the state corn show; they'd never had a corn show entry from Hunterdon before. It got quite a lot of publicity and I made the most of it."

The result was more than a feeling of euphoria at winning the corn show. It was good training in the advanced farming methods of the time that acted as a cushion when bad times came along. Compared to the other farm counties in the state, Hunterdon weathered the depression years rather well. The dollar volume for the different major crops and livestock run as follows between 1929 and 1939: dairy, state volume up 28 percent, Hunterdon up 34 percent; poultry and eggs, state dropped 24 percent, Hunterdon dropped 11 percent; wheat threshed, state down 34 percent, Hunterdon down 18 percent; and corn for grain, state down 35 percent, Hunterdon down 20 percent.

The figures are the kind that show up in a contest judging, where the winning contestant is far ahead of the other entries. Luck or good cropland or other factors sometimes makes one entrant jump far ahead of the others. But when you take 1,000 farms and average out their performance, the figures for one region will generally be close to those of another. Each region has its cream of the crop and bottom of the barrel, and they all average out. Because of this effect, Hunterdon's economic durability during the depression years was highly unusual. There were no special advantages the county enjoyed, nor were the actions of its leaders unusual or novel. The strategy had been explicit in a motto on the back of the program for the first Get-Together Banquet of 1922: "If you want prosperity, try hard work, faith, and cooperation."

Meanwhile, Ed Gauntt busied himself carrying out a Board strategy that had matured over a decade, at the same time the Board itself was applying its expertise to unexpected and difficult problems that the times brought.

One of the most emotional and tragic of these began December 21, 1926, weeks before the Board's final battle to win an agent. State police had surrounded a farmhouse near Jutland, shot out all the windows, threw in tear gas bombs, broke down the door, overpowered the people inside and arrested them. The occupants were an Irish farm family, Tim and James and Beatrice Meaney. Beatrice was found in a closet off the kitchen. She had been shot in the side, and died soon after.

The alleged crime that brought the troopers to the Meaney farm was neglect of their cattle, which were later examined and found in acceptable condition. The Meaneys had been un-

Meaney Homestead Scene of Fight With Constabulary Men; Gas Bombs Used.

Family Resisted S. P. C. A.

One woman was probably fatally wounded, two troopers slightly wounded and two others required hospital treatment as the result of a gun battle which started late Tuesday afternoon on the Meaney Homestead farm at Jutland and ended after daybreak when the troopers smoked out the besieged with tear gas.

The woman is Miss Beatrice Meaney, 28 years old. When the Democrat went to press last night she was in Somerset Hospital with small chances of living. Her two brothers, James and Timothy, were also hurt. The former also is in Somerset Hospital with a bullet wound in his leg. Timothy is not seriously hurt, his injuries being only those inflicted by the troopers after they entered the house.

The battle at Jutland started Tuesday afternoon when two agents for the Society for the Prevention of Cruelty to Animals, Harry Hanaway and Lester Duesenberry, visited the premises and found the animals on the place suffering for want of proper care. The law permits S. P. C. A. officers to make arrests without a warrant and when the officers encountered Timothy Meaney, described as a six-footer and husky, he resisted and ordered them to get off the place.

Hanaway and Duesenberry left and later returned with Trooper Larson of High Bridge.

First Shots Fired by Meaneys.

At this point the fun began. the officers found the doors of the farm buildings locked and the two Meaney brothers standing guard.

cooperative when troopers appeared with a warrant to inspect the cattle. They ordered them off the property. Police persisted, the Meaneys persisted, shotguns and clubs and revolvers were brandished, a trooper received a minor wound, and one of the Meaney men was shot in the leg. In this confusion, the Meaneys retreated to their home and police began preparations to arrest them.

The Meaneys were regarded by neighbors as mildly reclusive, but such behavior was not that unusual in the country, because farmers respected their neighbors' rights to live as they pleased. There was no local police protection to speak of in the county in 1926 and most farmers kept a shotgun handy at all times in order to protect their families if the need arose. If a visitor was not welcome, he was ordered to leave. Sometimes the appearance of a shotgun expedited the departure. It had been the standard method of protection for 200 years in a rural, isolated community where there was no police officer to call upon.

The paving of Flemington's Main Street did not deter the hustle and bustle of farm women shopping while their husbands picked up feed at the mill. This was Flemington about the time of the Depression. In view are the National Bank clock, left, and the flagpole in front of the Courthouse, right. Some doubted the wisdom of paving Main Street and worried about permanently covering the 19th-century wooden waterlines.

This had changed a few years earlier in a small way when the first state troopers began patrolling Hunterdon on horse, motorcycle and car. They worked out of Somerville, but there were only a few of them covering a huge rural area and they had no police radios. Their presence was important and valuable, but shotguns were still needed for protection.

Granges and other rural organizations were proud of the troopers' presence. They had lobbied long and hard to get them, and everyone saw the coverage they provided as vital, because mobile thieves living in urban areas had begun to make inroads in Hunterdon. Chicken thieves were particularly grievous, and two years before the Meaney incident the Agriculture Board had written a letter of thanks and commendation to the State Police for capturing several of them. But the Battle of Jutland, as the Meaney incident came to be called, cast a cold chill on the presence of the troopers. Although the Meaneys were not a typical farm family, the incident was too close for comfort, for it suggested that something similar could happen to any farm family.

In the jury trials that followed, one trooper was convicted of manslaughter, and two others of atrocious assault. Mishandling of the incident was a basis for the convictions. One trooper had fired his weapon into his auto many times in order to deliberately falsify the "resistance" put up by the Meaneys, reporting they had fired the shots.

Farm people had to be convinced that the Meaney incident would not be repeated, and that the troopers were friends and allies to be trusted. The Agriculture Board settled on two strategies, the first being to tell State Police Superintendent Colonel Schwartzkopf his men had to be trained more adequately in diplomacy. A general meeting was called in Wilburtha, and the Board sent its president and vice-president with instructions to "criticize quite severely some of the methods under which the State Police have been operating."

The Board's second strategy appears to have been a God-send. It was to expose the troopers to farmers in a comfortable atmosphere where they could discuss mutual problems and get to know each other in a relaxed manner. In July the board instructed its secretary to write Colonel Schwartzkopf and tell him it would be agreeable to us to have someone from his department present at the next meeting if he so desired. Schwartzkopf himself appeared and gave an interesting talk about the work of the State Police Department, the minutes recorded. He made it a habit in following years to attend the Board's monthly meetings. By the following spring, in April, 1928, State Police Captain Nichol was formally requesting that "police committees" be appointed in various areas of the county.

Committees were duly appointed for every grange in the county. It became a tradition for a grange to have a trooper in each year to speak and answer questions — a tradition that continued into the 1950s.

At the time, Board President Snyder was also sitting on the State Board of Agriculture, and beginning to be well-known throughout the region as a farm leader. The pressure that he and the county's state legislators and other leaders could bring to bear was considerable. Colonel Schwartzkopf, in turn, was already aware of the problem. In an unrelated incident, a trooper in a display for bravado had shot a man's hat off his head in a bar when the man dared him to do it. The man was unharmed, but when he later thought it over, he became frightened and outraged. Schwartzkopf had to watch his force constantly to eliminate such dangerous nonsense.

Colonel Schwartzkopf, in another move to correct the situation, hand-picked five men to set up a station in Flemington for more central and efficient police coverage. One was a quiet-spoken, keen-eyed ex-farm boy from Freehold, Raymond Bastedo. Trooper Bastedo was destined to become county detective in the 1930s. The local politicians were so impressed with him that they had state laws changed so he could go back to being a trooper if he lost his county job because of local politics. Bastedo refused to consider the job unless they made that promise. He continued as county detective until his retirement in the 1960s.

Trooper Bastedo had already patrolled Hunterdon County out of the Somerville Station and never had much trouble understanding farmers.

Hunterdon County Democrat

VOL. XCIX.   FLEMINGTON, NEW JERSEY. THURSDAY, OCTOBER 25, 1923.   NUMBER 15

SUGGESTS A REWARD FOR CHICKEN THIEVES

W. E. PEDRICK ASKS FREEHOLDERS TO PUT UP $1,000 FOR THEIR APPREHENSION.

Wholesale robbery of poultry roosts thruout the county that have continued during the year still go unchecked and in order to bring about apprehension of those responsible, one prominent poultryman, William E. Pedrick, has addressed a letter to the Freeholders in which he requests the Board to offer a reward of $1000 for the apprehension of chicken thieves in the community. This letter was read at the regular meeting of the Board last Thursday.

After discussion of the question Clerk Dineen was directed by the Freeholders to reply to Mr. Pedrick to the effect that the Board hesitates to offer a reward because it is felt the $1000 would not hasten the capture of the real robbers, it being more probable the money might be paid to some petty thief having no connection with the recent big hauls made by the thieves.

Until recently there has been a lull in the activities of chicken thieves after they had made several very large hauls in the summer months. Last week a roost near town was visited and 175 fowls and 23 turkeys taken. Mr. Pedrick's letter undoubtedly was prompted by this report.

The Boro of Flemington will receive $1000 from the 1923 Motor Vehicle Fund for maintenance of connecting links in the county road system within the corporate limits. Frenchtown will get $500 and High Bridge the same amount. Flemington gets the larger allotment because there is about twice the mileage of county roads in this borough than in the others.

Director Horn and Clerk Dineen were authorized to sign a contract with Snook & Sons of Neshanic, for the construction of a new county line bridge at Pottersville. Contract for this work was awarded at a joint meeting of the Hunterdon and Somerset Boards held at Somerville on Sept. 11th.

A letter dated October 9 received from J. H. Dilts of Whitehouse, requesting the Board of Freeholders or the State Highway Commission to furnish an off and on light to be placed in the center of the road where the Whitehouse-Flemington road meets Route No. 9. The Clerk was directed to reply and also request the State Highway Commission to advise their position in the matter.

County Treasurer Robinson was authorized to borrow $6,000 from the Hunterdon County National Bank on a note payable December 27, 1923, this to be used to pay current bills now due and borrowed in anticipation of taxes. Current bill totalling $6,430.42 were ordered paid. All the members were present.

One day while patrolling in Somerset County he stopped a suspicious man with a truckload of chickens. The man said he had purchased them in Hunterdon but had no receipt. Bastedo demanded to be taken to the farm where he'd bought the chickens.

Knocking on a farmhouse door, Bastedo asked the woman who answered if she had a coopful of 30 broilers. She said she did and asked what business it was of his? He told her to look in the chicken coop. She did and they were gone. Then he explained he'd found the wandering hens in the back of a truck in Bound Brook and had brought them back for her.

The farm to which Bastedo returned the chickens was the Meaney farm in Jutland. After that the Meaneys knew one state trooper they could trust. A few years later, when the family dog was ailing, she called Bastedo to ask him to put the animal out of its misery.

More than the special meetings and the rhetoric, this chance event symbolized the harmony the Executive Committee wanted, and achieved, in police-farmer relations. The accomplishment was outstanding.

Police-community relations are as touchy today as they were then, and there appeared to be three elements to the success: 1. Make sure your people understand that you are going to go all out for them, and not merely "smooth things over" and hope they'll be forgotten; 2. Don't just criticize police; make specific demands for improvement and change, and negotiate with them; and, 3. Expose people to police officers in a setting where people are "on their own ground" and thus can feel comfortable and uninhibited in speaking to them. This sets a pattern for relations later on when tension might otherwise be high.

The Board might have publicly condemned state police in an outraged way and contributed to creating a dangerous situation. Or it might have pretended to consult with police and assure members that "measures were taken for correcting the problem" when nothing real was done. Both tactics are frequently followed to everyone's loss. But the Agriculture Board was nonpartisan and had developed the theory that political problems are solved at the grassroots level, not behind closed doors. They found in Schwartzkopf and his men the same belief. The end result was a half century of high quality coverage of rural municipalities by state police, who continued this work until communities established their own police forces in the 1970s.

Dory Dilts of Three Bridges proudly displays a sign warning chicken thieves that his poultry are tattooed with the owner's identifying number.

One strategy for leadership success gives integrity an equal role with political popularity, and when he looked back over the decades he'd worked on the Board and off it with men like Snyder, Harold Everitt of rural Flemington commented: "I always liked Clifford. I liked him because you always knew right where he stood. You didn't have to wonder." Since you didn't have to wonder, half of one's energy wasn't tied up in wondering. So you did your share of the job with strong optimism, and found out that unusual successes were not uncommon in this kind of atmosphere. That may have been what got the Board to have the feed cooperative it had fathered taken over by the multistate GLF, or Grange-League Federation, in 1928.

Since its start, the small Cooperative had been a shoe-string success — undercapitalized and running ragged with day-to-day operating problems as a result. Eloise Schomp of Stanton, a bookkeeper for the Hunterdon County Farmers Co-op, recalled its problems: until its merger with GLF, "It was all car-door business and on-sight draft. That means if you got a boxcar load of grass seed in, you had to pay for it before the car doors could be opened. The car door wasn't opened until you gave the money to the bank, and then you would take your sight-draft to the freight station, and they would unlock the door for you. It was ordered through the individual farmers and they would come there and pick up their order and it would go all over the county that way."

That always meant a problem of getting the money together quickly. The Co-op was low on funds and by the time it had been going a year, its manager couldn't handle it well enough. Mrs. Schomp continued: "It was on the rocks, and they were going to give it one more try. So they asked my husband to see if he could bring it out of the red, because the farmers had so much money in it and they would have lost all they had in it, of course, if it had gone."

Richard Schomp wasn't married at the time. He met his future wife during the take-over, courted her when she wound up working in County Agent Gauntt's office, and did so with such discretion that Gauntt thought Schomp wanted to see him about business. Schomp pulled the Co-op back together, but it was still pretty rocky, and he and the others decided to try having GLF take it over and establish a real feed mill in Flemington.

GLF sent a woman executive to investigate the proposal, which would guarantee the firm instant customers if it set up a mill. Like a suitor bent on offering his best prospects, Co-op officials and executive committeemen from the Board prayed devoutly that she would not talk to any of the Board's more outspoken farmer critics. The Executive Committee could handle that kind of rough stuff, but an outsider might conclude the atmosphere was too unstable to take the risk. GLF was impressed and everyone breathed a sigh of relief. Schomp was taken on as manager, and he remained there until 1948, going into a non-manager post earlier when the feed business he built up grew so extensive that he didn't want the job any more.

That actually turned out to be a mistake, because Schomp was so meticulous, accurate and outspoken that the man GLF put there to run the mill couldn't handle being second-guessed so frequently and accurately. A committee of local farmers was overseeing the Hunterdon GLF operation. They called in Snyder and a GLF executive and went into a huddle. They retired Schomp with a decent settlement and made him an honorary member of the store committee, where his expertise would continue to be a benefit.

Today, GLF is known as Agway. Its growth and changed role exemplifies very well how the agricultural economy has changed over the years. Agway is now big agri-business, serving much of the northeast. It is listed in the Fortune 500 of leading corporations in the nation. It still buys farmers grain and sells cattle and chicken feed. However, in addition, it supplies fertilizer, owning its own blending plant and providing direct farm spreading service. It provides gasoline and heating oil, products of its own refineries in the southwest. Its farm supply and home and garden stores carry a wide variety of products, and it has even organized a helicopter service to plant rye grass for winter cover on cornfields.

One fundamental change has occurred, however. Few farmers, if any, feel the loyalty to the Co-op that they felt to their own local organization. If they can buy more cheaply elsewhere, they do, but without question the efficiencies of the large Co-op have helped to hold down prices and improve services rendered by Agway, as well as its competitors.

It is interesting to note that Clifford Snyder, who served on the board of the Co-op from its earliest days, continued through its years as GLF

Faith and Cooperation

and, up to the time of his death in 1967, was on the board of Agway.

Another important project for 1928 was helping the Hunterdon Poultry Association organize an egg laying contest with the Board giving $100 in prize money. The contest building, erected several miles south of Flemington, had 50 pens, which made it possible for the county's large contingent of chicken breeders to have their flocks officially tested by the state for superior qualities of productivity. During the year, Sergeantsville, Pittstown and Oldwick were the locations of three of the Board's regional meetings — held locally so members living far from Flemington could attend. Attendance at the Pittstown meeting was 165.

At the year-end annual meeting, by a prophetic irony, Dr. Samuel Graflin of New York gave a talk titled "The End of The Rainbow." The end came in the fall of 1929 when investors abruptly lost confidence in a stock market that had been pushed to unregulated excesses for years. By the end of that year the nation's stock corporations had lost 40 billion dollars of value. Five thousand banks were to close in the country, and seven million wage earners were to find themselves without jobs.

New hen coops for the Hunterdon Egg Laying Contest face onto the Flemington-Sergeantsville Road, where some men work on grading the lot, among them James Weisel, fifth from right, and Charles Cane, second. In the ditch is County Agent Ed Gauntt. (Poultryman's Association.)

Faith and Cooperation

It must have felt good to be a farmer, since they could still remember their parents' frugality. Living without money became commonplace again. A Little York women, who grew up during the depression, put it this way: "We were awfully poor when we were kids, but we never knew it because everyone else in the neighborhood was poor, too. There was always enough food, and we had a wonderful time."

Not only was there good food in abundance as always in the country, but parents and adults were not quite as moody and anguished in the farm community as the less independent city folks. Some who had mortgages lost their farms and the years of work and hope they had invested. But most farm families had a decent chance to keep going and weather the bad years. Young men ready to marry and begin a farm career of their own could bring their brides home to the old family farmhouse and work in partnership with their parents. Sons, daughters, and relatives who had left the farm for the city could move back to the farm. There they could continue their search for work without building up anxious debts if work took a long time to find.

Asked about the depression years, many a retired farmer will claim not to remember too many foreclosed farms, and usually will recall with pleasure how well farm families coped. "When the banks closed in 1932, we had our milk check or we wouldn't have had any money," Alvah Haver of Clinton Township commented on those years. A Granger, he sat on the Executive Committee from 1934 to 1962. "It didn't affect us very bad because we didn't have very much in stocks. And we'd just cashed our milk checks so we were all right for a few days, but the banks were closed tight. I wonder what would happen nowadays if everybody should go to the banks and want their money?"

The onset of the depression that impressed Haver so strongly was responded to by the Agriculture Board's Executive Committee in a fundamental way: it created a "Committee on Committees." It was just what it sounded like — a group that could have the names of good men ready instantly when the executive officers decided another new committee was needed. The Executive Committee was forced to double its size and its activities in order to keep track of all the rapid changes going on in the collapsing economy surrounding it. Richard Schomp, Dory Dilts, and William Lauderdale of Mount Airy were on this committee.

The committee doubtless kept secretary Schomp busy, but then he was the man who knew what everyone was doing, so he had to be on it. Dilts eventually became so good in state level political activity, he became a legislator in 1937. He did remain a farmer true to heart, for as Haver said of Dilts: "I wouldn't call him a politician; he was too honest to be called a politician!" Lauderdale also was a candidate for state assembly at one time, but never held a post higher than that of township clerk. But he was so astute that he became known as a power behind the throne, and often a pretty alert and humorous one.

One friend remembered well the time Lauderdale attended a political gala wearing a button favoring the opposition candidate. Asked by his party's man why he wore the button, Lauderdale smiled in his disarming way and said he was going to vote for the other man because he was a better man. And that was that.

The three had their work cut out for them: most of it would come from outside the county. The Board had its alliances with the State Board, the State League of Boards, the State Farm Bureau, and the national farm bureau. Then there was the Grange with its state and national levels. And the dairymen with their groups, and the poultrymen with theirs. All were formulating plans to meet the depression. Last but not least were the nonfarmers, the legislators who were going to pass laws to keep the milk and eggs and food flowing from the rural areas.

These groups couldn't coordinate effectively unless everyone communicated constantly. The meeting of February 12, 1930, that followed the collapse of the stock market was when the committee on committees got going, and business was concerned with reports from the other sectors. Dilts was reimbursed $10 for two trips to Trenton. Hunterdon's delegates to the State Board of Agriculture reported. County Agent Gauntt reminded the Board of a meeting the following week with the Morris County board. Assemblyman Rittenhouse reported on the legislature. And Dilts reported on the state Dairy Advisory Committee. Dilts was also vice president of the New Jersey State Taxpayers Association, and quite a busy farmer.

There was "considerable discussion" of non-local issues. And there would be more but not much would be done beyond that. The state and the country were busy getting used to being poor, and it was more a matter of keeping the faith at that point, than of getting anything done. Thus, State Secretary of Agriculture William Duryea came by in July and reported that the committee Dilts was sitting on was log-jammed because the big milk companies disagreed with the grading and other standards being considered in reorganizing the state's milk industry.

While the rest of the state might be lagging that year, farmers in Hunterdon were creating the Flemington Auction Market for eggs, the first of its kind east of the Mississippi. It became a success that brought substantially better prices for Hunterdon eggs, so much so that it helped tide many families over the depression. The Agriculture Board and many prominent farm leaders had supported the project in the face of lack of rank-and-file interest. Finally, Gauntt had tipped the scales by declaring in the newspapers that Hunterdon poultrymen were too apathetic and lazy to support the project. The instant and profitable success that followed gave county residents something to feel good about and something for the rest of the nation to copy. The auction grew so fast that within a few years it was auctioning dairy cattle and other animals and helping dairymen, too, in a lesser but important way.

A more human-sized issue for the Board was the putting up of $25 to send Lambertville High

In one of the first Flemington Fair 4-H Cattle Shows, eight of the finest are paraded in front of the grandstand by adults in 1931.

School student David Johnson to Kansas City to the national convention of the Future Farmers of America. Johnson came home the Future Farmer of America for 1930, and brought a $1,000 prize with him. He attended Lambertville High School although he lived across the river in Pennsylvania, so Hunterdon had to share honors with Bucks County. But he was a grandson of former Board president Egbert Bush.

The Board also managed to gain a part-time 4-H agent, Brandon Wright, and thereby free County Agent Gauntt for more work with the farmers. John Glass had spent part of a year as an assistant-in-training with Gauntt, before going on to an outstanding career as a 4-H agent in Gloucester County. Other than that, Gauntt had been handling 4-H in Hunterdon.

At the end of 1930 there was the annual county corn show, and a Rutgers expert said it was one of the best he had ever seen in the entire state. That was quite a change from Gauntt's deliberate annoying of unmotivated farmers three years earlier, and probably meant more to the farmers than Assemblyman Rittenhouse's request for suggestions to the Legislative Commission on Agricultural Relief.

There was no relief as yet, and dairymen in particular found prices steadily sliding to almost unbelievable lows. No one had money to buy milk. And 1931 turned out to be the same kind of year for farmers.

The Board showed its regard for Colonel Schwartzkopf's responsiveness to rural problems by passing a resolution supporting his reappointment.

Meanwhile, the time had come to hire a cost accountant to help Hunterdon farmers become expert in handling larger amounts of money. Also, John Tine, Board treasurer since 1921, moved from the county and John Hudnett was appointed to the job, one he would hold for 30 years. The annual auto tour was kept up and included a visit to State Dairy Field Day at Washington's Crossing. In other business, GLF was loaned $1,000 by the Board to help keep the local mill going.

"We know that times have been hard, but we believe things would have been worse, had it not been for some of the things this organization did," read the membership drive letter for 1931. Schomp, Dilts and Lauderdale worked on the drive, with help from a State Farm Bureau expert.

A pamphlet listing 20 accomplishments pointed to the county agent helping the poultry organization with the Egg Laying Contest and the Auction Market, but it could only tell dairymen that Dilts was on the State Dairy Committee, and that the Board had joined the successful push to get higher import tariffs on milk, butter and eggs.

Minutes for 1931 indicate that the Board was concerned about its leadership and wanted to try some changes. At the first meeting of 1932, the changes came quickly with the eight-member Executive Committee being formally dissolved. A 15-member committee was created to get better representation from around the county. Other farm organizations that had been sending representatives to the meetings were now given a voting membership in the Executive Committee. The February 4 meeting that followed was devoted exclusively to dairying and held in the Flemington High School auditorium. Speakers from the Extension Service and the Dairymen's League were heard, and discussions ended with Stephen Neogescu of Jutland proposing the following resolution:

"Whereas the dairy industry is suffering as a result of demoralized markets, and

"Whereas the conditions thus created are being seriously felt by all industry, and

"Whereas the correction of present conditions will need the united thinking of everyone along constructive lines, therefore be it

"Resolved that a committee be appointed by the chairman as an emergency metropolitan milk committee to act with other committees of similar character, should they be formed, in order to unite the thinking and acting of dairymen in the New York territory behind any constructive program for the betterment of the dairy industry."

Negoescu himself would go on to be founder and president of a Farmers Union local that year. The Farmers Union was a national group pushing for more membership and agitating for milk strikes and "direct methods" of solving the milk price problem. But the problem was not going to be attacked by the federal and state governments after a nightmarish two years of ineffective attempts. In May the state created an emergency Milk Control Board which could fix minimum prices to be paid farmers for milk sold in New Jersey. It was just in time. Two months earlier, as recorded in the Board's minutes,

"Alvah Haver reported his visit to New York and told of bottled milk being sold for four cents."

Farmers had no control over what they could get paid for milk, and some were selling for anything they could get. Now the minimum price law would keep prices at some break-even level, and the consumer would thereby be protected from severe milk shortages caused by business failures of dairies. The New Jersey law, passed in May of 1932, was followed by a control law in

New York in 1933, and Pennsylvania in 1934. All the markets Hunterdon sold to were protected.

The New Jersey law worked well, probably because of the preceding years of study and research people like Dilts put in on the State Dairy Committee. Another reason for success was that Hunterdon's role as a major dairy county led to effective representation on the control board. David Agans of Three Bridges had spent 1927 and 1928 working part-time for the state Agriculture Department's Division of Markets in milk marketing. With the control board now in existence, Lauderdale served on the three-man group from 1936 to 1938 as the only dairyman; the other two men were the secretary of agriculture and the head of the state's Department of Health. Chester Schomp of Whitehouse Station served in 1938 and 1939, and in 1941 Arthur F. Foran of Flemington began a long term as director that ran to 1949. Schomp also returned to the board in 1949 as a deputy director.

Other than the Milk Control Board that got started in 1932, the Agriculture Board did not take on large projects. It was discovered that the oil companies were overcharging farmers 1.5 cents a gallon for gas and vigorous action resulted in the overcharge being reduced to 1 cent a gallon. Lauderdale was appointed to a state committee to study taxation and became its chairman. But it was an election year and everyone was really paying attention to that, since nearly everyone was desperate. The county selected Franklin D. Roosevelt and the New Deal.

For Hunterdon farmers a major part of the New Deal would be the Agricultural Adjustment Act (AAA) that went into effect on May 12, 1933. It provided for price control of commodities like corn in an ingenious fashion — farmers who agreed to reduce their corn acreage a certain percentage were paid by the government a support price for the corn they did produce. This fixed a bottom below which corn prices could not go for these farmers. The mandatory acreage reduction got rid of the compulsive overproduction that farmers were normally committed to for survival. With overproduction gone, corn would tend to sell at a decent price, and the government thus wouldn't even have to do "supporting."

But the first full year of the new program would be 1934. And although the Executive Committee's intense participation in state and national projects to help farmers' interests continued unabated, there was a sidelight to the AAA program of restriction — almost no one in Hunterdon participated in it for several years.

Faith and Cooperation

County Agent Gauntt resigned his job in May 1934 for greener pastures as a state dairy specialist. By 1936 he was back in the county in a different role the man who was "selling" the AAA restriction program to farmers all over the state. Many impoverished farmers stood to benefit greatly from the program's price supports, yet no one was signing up. Local leaders hated government "relief" programs, which struck them as a form of government paternalism not far from welfare. "In Hunterdon, Clifford Snyder was among those objecting to the AAA program," Gauntt said. "Farmers just didn't like the idea of being subsidized and they showed it. Clifford, for a long time, did not take the payments that he was entitled to. Neither would he sign up for acreage reduction.

"My job was to try to get him to sign up. I finally shamed him into it. I said, look, Cliff, you're one of the big farmers in this county and you ought to show a little initiative. After I got Cliff and Dory Dilts and some of those leading farmers in, the rest of them came along in pretty good shape. But the job was first to get the leaders in. Bill Lauderdale was another hard nut to crack!"

Arthur Danberry of Ringoes tending to his flock of Barred Rock pullets in 1927.

It was an unpleasant irony. The whole federal program had been set up by grassroots farm leaders, some from the Grange and the Farm Bureau. The technique of reducing acreage to normalize prices was one that farmers in the nation had tried unsuccessfully to organize for decades without government intervention. Now men who preferred to run their farms without government aid and take the risks and losses quite cheerfully were unhappily signing up for "help" they disliked because they didn't want their less prosperous colleagues in farming to imitate their reticence and go under as a result.

Everyone was a little uneasy about the over-governing involved in the New Deal, and Gauntt quit his job as AAA promoter when he found the federal-level bureaucrats were treating him like a schoolboy sent on meaningless errands. One time he was taken to task because he reported some measuring tapes used to measure farm fields as "lost" because the many people handling them had lost a couple. His superiors demanded that he falsely report the tapes as "broken."

The different style of the county Executive Committee with its minimal rules and constant insistence upon actual results had appealed to the agent more. He could endure the hardships and tough jobs involved, recalling it had been the happiest time of his life. Gauntt could not work for bureaucrats who would sacrifice results in favor of trivia. He went to work for the state GLF organization, saving Hunterdon farmers a huge loss a few years later. A wealthy farmer who had gone bankrupt owed the local GLF a huge amount in back bills. One of the most skilled and powerful lawyers of the day in Hunterdon represented the farmer and told Gauntt as GLF representative to forget the bill — he'd offer him a few cents on the dollar on the obligation. Gauntt looked him in the eye and told him it wasn't his money to play around with — it belonged to the farmers. And he got the money.

For men who believed in minimal government, there was still the matter of constantly adjusting to a society that had chosen massive government regulation instead. In the past the Board's major role was to re-moralize the farm community and get it out of its own, dangerous lethargy. Now the big problem would be acting as a go-between to help farmers deal with "government" and "bureaucracy."

Readington Township's School Board Secretary for 25 years was a farmer from Three Bridges, William Davis. Davis' personal success was an example of how a great many rural leaders adapted to the new law of bureaucracy. He was asked to be board secretary and refused because he had never finished elementary school. But board members insisted that the job didn't take schooling, it took good judgment, and would he like to try?

Davis had a friend in Trenton who was a school principal, so he visited the man, and gave himself a lightning course in budget writing, the most important part of the job. He became school board secretary and did a fine job. One day he got curious about that state's regulation of education. He had been getting notes for years that his budgets were not perfectly written according to the minutiae of state law, and threats that state aid would be withdrawn as punishment. He had always forgotten about the letters, and nothing had ever happened, but eventually he became curious. So he talked to the county superintendent of schools, another local man, and asked him what it was like down there in Trenton.

Go and see for yourself, the county superintendent told him. So Davis got into his car and drove down to Trenton. He went to the office of the State Commissioner of Education: "The whole room was full of clerks and one thing and another. Everybody stopped work. I suppose they wondered who the thunder I was. I finally saw the man all right. And I smelt rum on his breath! Well, that was enough for me, because I had always been strict temperance, no fooling around. So I came back, and I told the board of education, I said, we'll run this business to suit ourselves; you don't want to pay any attention to that outfit down there; they're beneath us!"

Davis might have been intimidated by his "lack" of schooling, but he was not. He lived in a community of rural people who saw his ability and told him to trust himself. When "that outfit down there" became confusing, he went to take a look for himself, and reached his own judgment of what he saw. And if the state had persisted in bothering him, the resulting publicity would have pictured a man with liquor on his breath against a hard working farmer who gave his time for nothing to help his community have good schools.

Faith and Cooperation

The Executive Committee leadership had assumed the right attitude in handling the new government: don't withdraw like the old-timers who didn't want a county agent. Attack, and get the decent deal you deserve out of the confusion. The "committee on committes" worked like that. Instead of being a vehicle to proliferate useless committees, it was a kind of strike force needed in fast-changing times.

Mrs. Samuel Weber as a contestant in the Chicken Calling Contest at the Poultrymen's Picnic.

Prominent among those farmers who served the Hunterdon Board of Agriculture in the 20s and 30s were, left to right, William Lauderdale, Wallace Suydam, Richard Schomp, Clifford Snyder, and Dwight Babbitt, the second county agent. The photo was taken aboard a Hudson River excursion boat in 1938. (Thomas D. Mulhern.)

III
Changing Times

Independence against bureaucracy — that was the style of leadership. It was almost intangible, and it was vital now. With the New Deal having arrived, and the fantastically effective county agent Gauntt gone in 1934, what could the Agriculture Board do that would best express that style?

The Executive Committee replaced Gauntt with a man who was his total opposite in personality. Quiet, methodical, meticulous, Dwight Babbitt was hired for the job. Typically, it was the loyal Gauntt who found Babbitt and "stole" him from his job as Cumberland County agent, getting bawled out by Congressman Elmer Wene from Cumberland. "He called me all sorts of names for pushing Babbitt into Hunterdon, but I did Babbitt a favor, and I did Hunterdon a favor, because Babbitt was an excellent agent!" Gauntt recalled.

Babbitt was especially excellent in handling 100 different things at the same time, complete with paperwork. As his successor, William McIntyre, remembered him: "The thing that was needed at the time was a good coordinator. Babbitt could do that very well. I remember he always carried a little pad in his pocket, and he was always writing notes. He had these as a file system that just came out perfectly — he always called so-and-so, always had this-and-that set up. It was his way of doing things."

Ed Gauntt came back to see Babbitt after he had been installed in 1934 and taught this meticulous man one more thing he needed to know — that he wasn't there to do someone else's

Changing Times

work, but to coordinate. He found Babbitt as he was leaving the office with an auger to take soil samples at some farms. Gauntt exploded, explaining to the new agent that Hunterdon farmers weren't like those in Cumberland. They didn't want to see their agent perform trivial chores they could do themselves.

"I said, look, I haven't taken soil samples in at least two years. You're going to go out and ruin all the work I've done here. The farmers here bring the samples in. You haven't got time to go out and take them."

Babbitt did not believe Gauntt at first. He reluctantly put the auger away. Four years later he told Gauntt: "I've never seen a county where the farmers are so appreciative of what you do for them!"

Instead of doing soil tests, Babbitt had been overworking himself with the more important organizational jobs. He was becoming a "key man" when anything had to be done, and the farmers really did want it that way. As he wrote in his first annual report: "About the usual number of poultry troubles were reported to the agent and about 300 autopsies performed. Poultrymen have come to realize the agent's time is so taken that it is impossible sometimes to make a visit on short notice, and they are bringing their birds to the office for examination."

The 38-page single-spaced report was a marvel of conciseness and a history of how Hunterdon farm leaders were accomplishing things that year. It showed:

   *A highly coordinated series of educational activities and demonstrations, publicized so interested farmers could participate easily;

   *Recommendations on local problems, such as planting corn three weeks later in the south county to avoid severe Japanese beetle damage, plus the bolstering of that advice with the report of a south county farmer who tried late planting the previous year and found it a complete success;

Fred Totten of Ringoes climbs the courthouse steps on a routine visit to see County Agent Dwight Babbitt, who provided Hunterdon farmers with both personal advice and printed material on a myriad of agricultural topics.

*Successful diplomacy. Babbitt reported that vegetable growers wanted to start a cannery, "but this has not been looked upon by the local agent as a solution to their problem." Instead he attempted to get some of them to try the Hightstown Auction "as an outlet that may prove a little better than the New York market or the local chain store buyers;"

*Rutgers used Hunterdon farmers to help others. A Poultry Economic Management Club was set up with extension help and the 14 members studied modern cost-of-production record keeping. The records of success these men immediately experienced were then loaned to the Extension Service to help convince others of the value of the program. And three of the men agreed to become leaders in lecturing on the program to other poultrymen;

*The county now needed a detailed analysis

The Account Book of Calvin Danberry
June, 1931

June 1 — Ringoes Lumber Co., 5 bags feed, 2 bags lime, $13.15
  2 — Loversol, fish, 50¢
  2 — VanHorn, bread, 2 loaves, 20¢
  2 — Haircut and shave, 70¢
  2 — Mutual Store, meat, 97¢
  3 — Sol Berkowitz, 73 lbs. old hens @ 23¢, $16.79 received
  3 — Sol Berkowitz, 20 broilers, 55 lbs. @ 30¢, $16.50
  4 — VanHorn, 2 loaves bread, 20¢
  4 — Flemington Auction Market, 2 egg cases, 30¢
  4 — Mutual Store, groceries, $2.22
  6 — VanHorn, 2 loaves bread, 20¢
  6 — Hafner, potatoes and oranges, 53¢
  7 — Church collection, 10¢
  8 — Amwell Community Club, 8 old hens, 23¢, $9.20 received
  8 — Ringoes Lumber, 5 bags feed, $11.75
  8 — Grange mortgage burned, 50¢
  8 — Hiram Bellis, 2 gallons of gas, 25¢
  8 — Hafner and VanHorn, potatoes and bread, $1.35
  10 — Flemington Auction Market, 45 dozen eggs, $8.50
  12 — Joseph Crosdale, shoeing team (horses), $3
  13 — Hafner, vegetables, 55¢
  13 — Ed Venable, meat, 97¢
  17 — Judiah Bielsdorf, use of corn planter, $5.25
  19 — Al Pittenger, making tongue for wagon, $2
  19 — Cows examined, $3
  20 — Nevius, one pair of stockings, $1
  27 — Ringoes Lumber, 100 lbs. fishmeal, $3
  30 — Arthur L. Danberry, wages, $35
End of month, income $539.67, paid out $243.83.

The income does not necessarily signify a good month, since a farmer's expenses and income often came at different times of the year. What is shown in this record of a large, working farm that supported two families, is the flow of money. A decade before it might have been half as much and a decade later it was probably double.

of educational and other programs for the coming year in order to produce even greater effectiveness;

*Three Executive Committee members, plus poultry leader Charles Cane and *Democrat* Publisher D. H. Moreau attended an economics institute at New Brunswick, where they heard and grilled national authorities on the subject. In turn, three local meetings on the subject were held in Flemington, and turned in a higher attendance than anywhere else in the state; and,

*Twenty-three farmers were started on modern record-keeping with Extension-prepared farm account books.

Government programs, providing limited loans to farmers for specific purposes such as better seed purchase and for emergencies, had come out of the 1933 New Deal. Babbitt saw to it that farmers could apply for these aids easily. In some cases they had to go to the federal or state agency to apply, and here, Babbitt reported, the interested farmers were discussing the terms with him to make sure there was no confusion.

By now there was a profusion of special committees, groups, agencies, programs, and enough of a labyrinth to send an interested man on endless trips to the wrong agency with applications for the wrong program. In the middle of this hurricane of new government was the county Board Executive Committee, whose members would talk face to face with any farmer in the county and go to bat for him. More likely, a farmer would first seek Babbitt, who would quietly pick up his phone and unobtrusively find out what the devil was wrong and just as unobtrusively see to it that it was straightened out.

It was an old lesson learned anew: There were numberless insect species that wanted to destroy farm crops and a myriad of diseases that wanted to plague their animals. Farmers had learned over the years they could never eliminate these pests entirely, but that using just the right amount of counter-attack and just the right method, they could neutralize them. They got so they knew 100 different tricks at least, and they all did their bit.

Now these lessons were applied to the difficulties of living in an economically depressed society run by a government creating new programs guaranteed to have "bugs" in them, too. Sometimes the county's farmers would fail in this task. But sometimes it doesn't rain, either, and crops may fail.

As Babbitt started his first full year of work in Hunterdon in 1935, Fred Totten was beginning to work with a new federal soil conservation program that would lead to an overhaul and correction of the county's worst erosion problems. It was as new as the bulldozers that were used to reshape Totten's steep, hillside farm near Ringoes. A friend of Totten told the federal program agents he had a problem and would be a likely cooperator. Totten, with his lifelong love of learning, took the bait.

A system of terraces was built to catch the rainwater as it ran downhill. The terraces were designed to meter out the water slowly so soil wasn't carried with it. The earth-shaping job was done, the first rains came, and the terraces caught the water as they were supposed to. "Well, it didn't seep out," Totten reported. "It stayed and I had a beautiful set of frog ponds all along that side hill."

Soon experts returned with an old man who walked along quietly poking his cane into the terraces and then solemnly announced that the soil had just enough impermeable clay in it to seal it against seepage forever. Step one was a failure. "They redesigned the terraces," Totten said, "And my neighbors said I would starve to death before they got through with it. I wasn't sure they weren't right."

After the work was done, Totten found they had made the strips of cropland between the terraces so narrow he couldn't get his farm machinery on them! "I broke up my side rake, I broke up my hay loader, and I had trouble with my grain binder." So, the government did it again, removing some of the terraces to make the strips wider for farming.

"They spent about $40,000 on my farm," Totten said. "At that time, if they'd given me the money I'd have moved out of the doggoned place. It was experimental work entirely. I was a guinea pig." But he learned it wasn't only farmers who can be obstinate. "The fellow who was soil conservationist at the time went by the book, and nothing but the book," Totten recalled. "It didn't make any difference what our opinion was, for the book was right. As the years went on, he and I had a lot of terrific arguments. I told him this whole thing is based on education, educating people to the benefits. Then you'll be able to do something for them. If a fellow's got trouble with a gully in his side hill or a wet place that should be drained, go in and show him how he can fix it and repair it. You'll make a 'believer' out of him. He'll come along and sign up without any trouble. But I said you go in and show him this 'book' and tell him he's got to sign up and promise to do all these things for five years, and he'll run you off the property!"

Totten failed to get anyone in government to listen to him, but he stayed in the program and became a local leader over the years. By his estimate, the government got around to his idea of how to treat farmers by 1960, putting him several decades ahead of his time. Back in 1934, it was a matter of being a guinea pig. Totten accepted the role, reported to the Executive Committee on his problems, and somehow the unresponsive and unwieldy government agencies were brought into line.

The aggravation of dealing with the agencies was worth it dozens of times over. Four years later, in 1938, Dr. E. E. Evaul of the Soil Conservation Service could report that 190 farmers in Hunterdon representing 15,000 acres were cooperating in the program. "Square and rectangular fields have been combined and in their place one finds strips or bands of crops laid out across the slopes and curving with the contour of the land," Evaul noted in a *Democrat* article. "Hunterdon enjoys the distinction of being the first county in New Jersey in which such soil saving practices . . . . were practically demonstrated."

Eventually a federal soil conservation district was established, with its business supervised by a local governing committee of farmers. William Lauderdale, Dory Dilts, William Wagner of Flemington and Arch Gulick Jr. formed the committee that worked with Totten and helped make the programs a reality. Probably nine counties out of ten would have sensed the difficulties in dealing with inexperienced government agents and rejected the whole thing as an impossible aggravation. They would thereby miss out for years on having 15,000 acres of farmland upgraded in quality and productivity.

The year 1936 brought the usual work for the Executive Committee. But there was something new and unusual, a new kind of person whose appearance in Hunterdon was being reported on: "There has been a marked increase during the past year in the purchase of farms by new people, principally urbanites. While many of those have purchased farms for homes, a majority have plans for making the farm self-supporting, and a great number of these have called on the county agent for farm management plans," Babbitt's report for the year read. The urbanites had wound up mostly with the lowest quality farmland ("not well adapted for agriculture," the report noted) and so Babbitt recommended a lot of reforestation and anti-erosion measures to build up the soil.

Some of these new farm owners became farmers, but most were white collar workers and professionals with the idea of hiring a man to operate and manage the farm for them. One, Dr. Alex B. Timm, who settled in the Ringoes area, used to welcome weekend guests to his "farm" by offering them either a glass of champagne or a glass of milk. He explained that considering his efficiency as a greenhorn farmer, they both cost the same to produce. He reported his experiences in the 1937 Agricultural Issue of the *Democrat:*

"When my mother, who is 80 years old, came to visit me, her remark in response to all my enthusiams was, 'I know, but I didn't raise my boy to be a farmer. I raised him to be a doctor.' She, in her infinite wisdom, knew they were both full-time jobs. I knew it very soon thereafter. I learned what every so-called 'city farmer' has to learn very soon, that farming is a very serious business. That in order to make a success of it, one has to know what's going on all the time. Another thing I learned very soon was that a farmer has to know chemistry, bacteriology, physiology, dietetics, obstetrics, geneology, surgery. In other words, in very short order I learned to take off my hat to any good farmer — because he's a master of every trade from roofing to doctoring."

While praising farmers, Dr. Timm also praised his own kind: "We are helping you all by buying old farms and restoring them to productivity, thereby increasing all your land valuations. We want to enter into your civic movements. We've joined your Granges, not because you asked us, but because we felt that it is a great American institution and we love it now as much as you do. We want you to help us, if you will, when you see us making mistakes. Please give us a hand, and with all of us joining our forces we can make Hunterdon the best in the land."

That promise was kept dozens of times over in the years that followed. The city farmers were welcomed and aided by farmers and wound up offering valuable support to local programs in response. In modern times, names like Phillip Hofmann and J. Seward Johnson, both executives from the worldwide Johnson & Johnson Company, are well known. In the late 30s, they included a New York advertising man, Bill Millard, who experimented with imported plants to see if they could be grown here; Ralph Hitz, who raised pigs for his chain of hotels; Harry Keuls, the inventor of glass brick, who experimented with raising tulip bulbs. Also among the new people was Lloyd Wescott, who had resettled in Hunterdon as a farmer after living an urban life for a while.

tricity could have milking machines for their cows, and coolers for the milk, lights for the chickens to keep them laying eggs longer, refrigerators and other time-savers for the hard working farm woman.

A committee of John Hudnett, Alvah Haver and Babbitt, found that the federal Rural Electrification Administration's programs couldn't help Hunterdon at all. They finally got the electric company to reduce its charge for new lines from $1,300 a mile to $1,100 when at least ten miles were to be installed. The Three Bridges area became the beneficiary of such a farmer-paid project and plans were made for a similar effort in the south county after that. Farms close to towns and powerline routes had had the benefits of electricity for some time and everyone wanted them.

J. Seward Johnson, operator of Cedar Lane Farms in Tewksbury, shows off this herd to two young future farmers. Johnson, a director of Johnson & Johnson, also served on the board of the Hunterdon Medical Center and headed its 1963 fund drive.

Auctioneer Herbert Van Pelt auctions Martin Ulrich's horse equipment at a sale near Milford. William Kinney says the sale took place in the early 1930s and recognizes some of his neighbors of those years: Paul Crouse of Little York, Charles Manning of High Bridge, Mr. and Mrs. Albert Hageman of West Portal, Harold Strouse, Russell Kinney, and Bill Irwin.

All of these men would be of value to the Board of Agriculture. They were preceding a great wave of city immigration to the rural areas and their knowledge of city ways was needed. For the moment, they were being welcomed by farmers and farm leaders alike, and being treated and judged as equals.

Another project begun in 1936 was the Board's push to get electric lines to all farms in the county. It was a productivity issue. Those with elec-

Another successful project of 1936 was set up by a committee of Lauderdale, Norman Fulper of Ringoes, Tom Barry of Lambertville, and Wallace Suydam of Quakertown. They contracted with the Campbell Soup Company to produce canning quality tomatoes. Truck farming had always been a minor industry in the county with the local soils suitable for quality production. Twenty-one farmers contracted to produce 139 acres of "canhouse" tomatoes for $19 a ton, U.S. No. 1 Grade, and $10 a ton for No. 2s.

Production was a success and 74 percent of the crop was U.S. No. 1 with the soup company being quoted as saying the overall quality was very high. The most interesting part of the project was that most of the farmers had no experience whatever in raising and picking tomatoes! But they soon learned, following Babbitt's meticulous recommendations carefully.

Another major item for 1936 was B. F. Ramsburg coming to the county as full-time 4-H Club Agent. Part-timers had supervised the clubs in the past. Ramsburg himself had served in the county from 1924 to 1927, and now he was back again until 1960, when he went to the State 4-H office for two years before retiring in 1962. The tremendous interest farm families had always shown in their children would now be focused, with Ramsburg attending the Executive Committee meetings, and working in harness with anyone who needed help.

Ramsburg, who hailed from West Virginia, reported he found Hunterdon people easy to work with because they had the same independent attitude as the hill farmers he had known as a child. Hunterdon's 4-Hers did so well over the years with Ramsburg that at one point the Mount Airy 4-H Dairy Club records on costs of raising heifers were picked up by the State Extension Service and used as a basis for its recommendations to farmers in dairying. They could point to the records and say, "Here's what happened when the kids followed our advice."

Ramsburg found Board Secretary Richard Schomp a hardworking cohort where 4-H was concerned, and was impressed with the Executive Committee's understanding: "They gave the

Willette Case receives the New Jersey Junior Breeders Fund banner for 1937 from State Agriculture Secretary William Duryee at the Flemington Fair. On the farm, arbitrary sex discrimination was, and is, unknown. Willette also won a milking contest at the Fair.

club program every possible support. One time when I gave my report I said I was sorry to hear they were strapped for money, because I was going to ask for some. Clifford Snyder stopped me and said they weren't so hard up that they couldn't support the 4-H Program."

The program was strong in the county because of unusual cooperativeness, Ramsburg found. One new 4-H Club leader was astonished at the cooperation, since she was a recent arrival in the area. Ramsburg explained to her that in Hunterdon everyone helped everyone else, and without much fuss. The 4-H helped the Granges, the Granges helped the 4-H, thus multiplying the effectiveness of both groups. He saw this reflected in the strategies of the Board: "Hunterdon's Board was unique in that it had representatives of every agricultural organization in the county. If a new group was started, even though it might be considered as being opposed to the county Board, they would still invite them to send a representative. They listened to them if they had anything to say. And practically every one of them sent representatives. It made for very good relationships and also reached a lot of people who probably would not have been reached."

The Board's favoring of 4-H was common-

The time is the late 1930s and the banqueters are either the Poultrymen's Association or the County Board of Agriculture, but it's not possible to tell since virtually the same men would be seated at the head table. Guest of honor was William Allen, State Secretary of Agriculture, and on the Quakertown School stage is a five-piece country and western musical group.

sense wisdom applied in a commonsense way, and the fruits it bore over the decades might best be seen in a conversation that took place in judges chambers in Hunterdon County Court in the 1960s. Judge Philip Gebhardt was talking to ex-Trooper Raymond Bastedo, then a county detective for over 20 years.

"How many kids did you say you had in that 4-H club of yours?" Gebhardt asked Bastedo, who was leader of the 4-H Pegasus Horse Club.

"There's 60. And the whole county has about 1,600," Bastedo replied.

"1,600. And not one of them has ever shown up in juvenile court. Listen, forget about the detective work and take care of that club of yours!"

Every government agency, every special social group, vows openly to "reach all the people." In Hunterdon it was actually happening. The first Businessmen-Farmers Picnic was held in 1936 as a method of cultivating good relations with the community's businessmen and bankers and plumbers and carpenters and all the nonfarmers whose work supported the farm community. It was a form of "thanks" offered to these groups, a way of saying "we don't see each other much because we're both so busy, but once a year we want to show our appreciation." The picnic was not even mentioned in the minutes for the year, but it was such a success everyone wanted it repeated the following year, and it carries on to this day.

The year 1937 was a year of celebration. The *Democrat* put out a special issue celebrating the 25th anniversary of the creation of the Extension

Changing Times

Service. At its annual meeting on December 15, a large crowd sat down at the Quakertown School and listened to radio station WOR present a special program on the subject. Entertainment consisted of speakers on the county's progress in different areas of farming. President Synder presented a comfortable easy chair to Board vice-president Dilts in honor of his years of work, and the Grange amateur competition for the kids provided the dessert. A tap dancing team of Shirley Dilts and Violet Barth took the prize for Riverside Grange.

During the year there had been numerous Board initiatives. Perhaps the most important was the systematic effort to get farmers to sign up for the federal crop restriction programs. Gauntt had persuaded the leaders to "come along" and the program was a success: participation went from 252 farmers in 1936 to 1,130 in 1937. Gauntt used the grassroots approach. Supervisors for every area of the county were selected and given special schooling in the program. They talked with farmers, then helped them fight through the red tape and enroll. The following year Dilts was named to a state-level committee overseeing that program in all the counties.

In 1938 the Board made world history by establishing the first artificial breeding co-operative for dairy cattle in the country. Offering artificial breeding to a dairyman is like saying: "How would you like your cow's sires to be the best bulls in the country?" This was possible because semen taken from bulls can be diluted and used to inseminate thousands of cows.

Professor Enos J. Perry, Rutgers University extension dairy specialist, had brought the news of the technique to the Board. It sounded like the craziest sort of science fiction. He said, years later, he went to Hunterdon because he thought they had the only farm leaders in the state who wouldn't laugh him out the door. Within months of Perry's first visit, the Board had put together a regional organization including nearby counties, and gave $500 to get an expert sent over from Denmark to insure success.

In due course the first artifically bred calf was born at Richard Schomp's farm near Stanton. Sceptics were satisfied that it did not have two heads or other strange features, and the program began expanding exponentially in the state, all over the country, and all over the world. Its effects are still being felt today through continuing increases in productivity and quality in cattle. The technique had been developed in

The first artifically-bred calf being paraded for one of her many photographs, which appeared in newspapers throughout the nation. The date is February 15, 1939, and the farm is that of Richard S. Schomp of Stanton.

Denmark, which was cut off from the free world during World War II. Because Hunterdon dairymen had picked it up so rapidly, the technique was available during the war as another aide to the Allies' need for increased farm production.

1938 was a year in which the successful canhouse tomato contracts had grown to 500 acres. The executive committee had Robert Crane of Quakertown busy checking developments. Crane had come to Hunterdon in the mid-1930s after graduating from Cornell's agricultural college. He'd wound up buying a farm near Synder and working for him a few years to learn the ropes of real farming. Now he and his wife, Almena, were active in community affairs. She would wind up serving on a committee the Board appointed in April of 1938: "The following committee was appointed to assist the board in selecting a home demonstration agent for Hunterdon: Mrs. Ulmont P. Pastorino, Mrs. Craig Skillman, Mrs. Luella Allegar, Mrs. Cora McCrea and Miss Sarah Strong."

Sarah Skillman had written to the Executive Committee in 1937 as the county Parent-Teachers Association secretary. The PTA wanted a home agent. The Board wrote her asking how strong the sentiment was, and she appeared at its next meeting, along with Extension Director Baker, who said it would cost $3,200. The freeholders had provided the funds and a selection committee was needed. Miss Geneva Wolfe was hired for the post in July and the Board sent $12 to Quakertown School for the use of its auditorium to hold a reception for her.

The selection committee became the Women's Advisory Committee to oversee Miss Wolfe's work. Mrs. McCrea, of Milford, became chairman and immediately enlarged the group to get better community representation. Added were Miss Jennie Haver of Clinton, Miss Melda Chambre of Flemington, Mrs. Charles Hamp of Lambertville, and Mrs. Vernon Wortman of Pottersville.

"Because the Extension Service is for the people, we believe that any or all programs should be determined by the people. This starts with the needs or interests in the community. The individual committee members know their communities and act as spokesmen for the people whenever possible," Mrs. McCrea noted in her report to the Board. Her group would meet monthly. By May of the following year, Mrs. McCrea had also been appointed a member of the executive committee of the State Federation of County Home Economics Committees.

Some of the early members of the Women's Advisory Committee of the Hunterdon County Board of Agriculture were, from left to right: Mrs. Cora McCrea, president; Mrs. Luella Allegar, secretary; the Home Demonstration Agent Mrs. Geneva Wolfe Higgins; Mrs. Charles Hamp; Mrs. D. H. Moreau, a visitor; Miss Sarah Strong; and Mrs. Craig Skillman.

Changing Times

The home agent and her advisors worked busily. There was a program for homemakers that grew quickly into the complete information service for women that the program remains today. The title, "Home Demonstration Agent," was changed in 1946 to simply "Home Agent." In 1965 the assignment became known as the county "Home Economist," and in 1971, the "Extension Home Economist," a position currently held by Mrs. Nancy Crutchfield.

Meanwhile, 17 4-H Homemaking Clubs that had lapsed because there was no home agent were reorganized and new clubs were begun. In August of 1939, the women's advisory group was studying the possibility of dental clinics to reach school children neglected by their parents through lack of funds. That kind of initiative showed the group to be not merely a subcommittee of the Board, but an independent group that could take on important jobs in the years to come.

There was another event of significance in 1939. The Agriculture Board went on record against the Princeton Survey of State and Municipal Government, which recommended that hundreds of municipalities throughout the rural areas of the state be erased and lumped into larger units. In its opposing resolution to government leaders, the Board noted that most municipalities were being run by unpaid elected and volunteer officials at no cost to anybody. Because the municipal communities were small, the municipal employes knew all their problems, the Board noted, whereas larger units would involve paid employes who were more distant from the community and could not begin to operate as knowledgeably.

Past experiments by the state in adopting Princeton Survey recommendations had led to increased costs with no increase in efficiency whatever, and it characterized the survey as: "False in its assumption of economy, unfair in its assignment of local representation and opposed to the true Democratic principle of Home Rule."

Hunterdon was still a rural community with 80 percent of its population living on farms. But state planners had ideas this was going to change fast and had decided the state ought to take over rural leadership and erase its present forms. The planners had quite clearly not bothered to talk to the Board about it, and the end result was that the Executive Committee was forewarned of a great change coming, and especially warned that it would not necessarily be the kind of democratic change in which the people involved were consulted.

The Reverend Edward Dunbar of Flemington, who sat on the Executive Committee in those years as a representative of the community's churches, saw other signs of change. "There was no involvement in zoning at that time, but I think they saw those little salt boxes going up around Bound Brook near Somerville, cheap things, and I think that worried some of the people here greatly," he recalled.

The keen and somewhat anxious awareness of the Executive Committee would be a base in the coming decade for a massive response by the county's "grassroots" residents to these impersonal changes.

Governor Harold G. Hoffman sizes up the 16-foot corn stalks produced by Frank Curtis of Rosemont. They earned him a prize at the 1938 Flemington Fair.

⟶

Bob Crane of Pittstown looks on as junk dealer Joe Finkle of Lambertville and one of his men cut up farm machinery that was no longer useful to serve in the war effort. The wooden beams on the old horse-drawn implements had been used to convert them to tractor use. Now the high-quality steel was being converted again.

IV War and Peace

Nick Butkewicz, Russian-born farmer of Rosemont, put $75 of the $88.88 he received as an agricultural conservation payment into defense bonds. He had served in the Russian artillery in the Russo-Japanese War in 1904. Hunterdon farmers like Butkewicz contributed to the U.S. Department of Agriculture's "Food for Freedom" campaign during World War II. The photo was taken in May, 1942. (U.S.D.A. Photo by Forsythe.)

War and Peace

The year was 1940 and Europe was rapidly falling under the sway of the Nazi dictator Adolph Hitler. American officials were earnestly promising that the country would not get involved in the continent's troubles. No one knew what to believe.

The Board's work for 1940 was the expected round of events, meetings, recommendations, actions, reports, appointments. But County Agent Babbitt's report for the year appeared concentrated and narrower: "The Extension Program dealt primarily with the problems confronting poultrymen and dairymen, since these are the leading types of agriculture."

After 68 pages of single-spaced typewritten data, he reiterated that existing problems would have to be attacked more systematically in the future, adding: "Like all previous programs, the limited facilities available do not make it possible to devote much time to these numerous problems as they require. In each year's program it is the case of weighing the problems and handling them according to their relative importance in the county's agriculture."

Babbitt sounds like he was complaining about being overworked and hinting he wanted to cut back. It was hardly likely in a man who worked all day, then spent his evenings at lengthy organization meetings. Everyone at his level of local leadership was overworked. The agent was actually telling anyone who cared to read between the lines that he had been making plans and projections for Hunterdon's role in World War II, and that the planning showed a lot of items would be neglected to make a big push for dairy and poultry production.

Nowhere was the possibility of war mentioned. It was not necessary in 1940. Poland had fallen, and in April Norway and Denmark were taken, then Finland. In May and June the Low Countries fell, tanks roared over the Maginot Line into France, and the Battle of Britain was under way. Hundreds of the county's farmers were recent immigrants from these lands, still thousands of others were first generation Americans whose relatives in Europe were now incommunicado. For Americans of German and Italian descent the situation was equally unpleasant. Charles Lindbergh, whom county residents had seen a few years earlier at the kidnap-murder trial in Flemington, was heard speaking for isolationism and for leaving Europe to the victors.

Gazi Nemeth of Kingwood Township, head of Farmers Union Local 3, had tried to organize a peace meeting in May as Europe was falling. By the fall, the country was actively aiding Britain, had passed a $37 billion defense budget, and begun a "peace-time" draft. Roosevelt won a landslide electoral vote and a small majority of the popular vote to earn an unprecedented third term. Perhaps what helped was his emphatic declaration that American boys would not be sent into any foreign wars. It probably impressed realistic farmers as a hopeful fantasy more than anything else. Political experts estimated the country elected Roosevelt because "It isn't good to change horses in midstream."

In Hunterdon, the Businessmen-Farmers Picnic for 1940 was at Lloyd Wescott's farm north of Clinton, where the artificial breeding cooperative was located. Historian Hubert Schmidt was beginning his career during these years by working on his *Rural Hunterdon* history for the Board, attending Executive Committee meetings to give reports and short talks. What impressed him, Schmidt said, was the quiet efficiency and speed of the group as it worked through its lengthy monthly meeting agendas. Everyone had apparently primed themselves on every item coming up, he said. Discussion was allowed, but no wandering. Concise statements were made, decisions were set, and it was on to the next item with a deceptive smoothness.

Board members had two decades of highly successful experience in organizing a coherent farm community in an often emotionally turbulent atmosphere. They were well prepared to guide Hunterdon's farm community through the difficult years to come.

There was not much to do during 1941 beyond conducting business as usual, while everyone listened to the latest radio news and wondered. One item was continuing to further prepare farmers for modern business. The Farm Account Books that had been passed out in previous years were supplemented with the hiring of a bookkeeper who would visit the county part-time to train farmers in handling the growing complexity of their books. Robert Crane reported 39 farmers were participating. The Internal Revenue Service was brought in to hold an Income Tax School. As a member of the state dairy council, Dory Dilts reported work on revising milk controls, and Richard Stevenson of Califon was selected to work on a state committee overseeing the work.

On December 7, the nation was plunged into war with the attack on Pearl Harbor. The Board met the next day to begin a long series of coordinating moves as part of the national food-for-defense effort. Dr. Ralph Henderson from the State Agriculture Department asked for a volunteer township to be used in a Bangs disease control program for cattle. He had appeared earlier in the year to lay the groundwork and his request was approved. Robert Crane reported on labor, which was the county's major problem during the war, and the Board ratified a State Farm Bureau motion to coordinate labor shortage problems on a statewide level. Crane also suggested doubling participation in the successful bookkeeping project.

effort. The Executive Committee appointed a special committee to investigate a program for boys and girls too old for 4-H and too young to join the Board of Agriculture.

Harold Everitt of Flemington was named chairman of the local War Board set up by the U.S. Department of Agriculture. Scrap iron campaigns were organized. The Draft Board was asked to give deferments to farm workers when possible. Intensive labor investigations yielded some extra help, but not enough. Barney Slamp, at the Board's request, organized by map all of the county's milk collections so they could be done without wasting precious gas and tires. He noted the same thing was being done for the egg auction. Senator Wesley Lance was at work lowering the driving age for farm youths so they

Hunterdon's War Loan Committee on the steps of the Courthouse in Flemington in 1945. Most of the complex rationing and emergency help provisions the federal government made for farmers were administered locally by appointed or elected farmers. Back row, left to right: John Dalrymple of Sidney, Clayton Stains of the Flemington Auction Market, R.S. Sorby, Eugene Sharer of Lebanon, County Agent Dwight Babbitt, and William Rittenhouse. Front row: John Volkmar of Whitehouse, Walter Bartles of Stanton, Alvah Haver of Clinton Township, Robert Hodulik of Oak Grove, Walter Hunt of Ringoes, and William Kinnamon of the Hunterdon County National Bank. (Hunterdon County *Democrat*.)

At the next meeting, in January 1942, the Board ordered questionnaires sent to farmers on individual labor problems. It decided to ask school boards to eliminate Easter vacation and cut the school year back so young people would be available for things like fall tomato harvesting. 4-H Agent Ramsburg reported that the children had organized a 4-H Victory Corps, and had come up with 35 different projects to aid the war

could drive to town to pick up supplies or drop off eggs.

The Artificial Breeders Cooperative repaid with interest the $500 the Board had loaned the group four years earlier. The Board invested $2,000 in Defense Bonds. Three conscientious objectors began work in the county as cow testers.

The main item of the war was improved production with a twist thrown in to make it almost impossible: new machinery and increased fertilizing were both ruled out because of shortages, yet these were the two major ingredients of productivity increases. Nonetheless, Hunterdon farmers accomplished the following between 1940 and 1945:

*Milk production was up seven percent, the smallest increase. Increases were retarded by labor shortages, shortages of new materials for barns, and an increase in crops that could be used directly as foods instead of being fed to cows.

*Egg production increased 50 percent though numbers of hens went up only 25 percent. This reflected the ease of increasing hen flocks and in converting unused buildings for poultry use.

*Wheat production was up 25 percent, though the acreage increase was only 17 percent, an outstanding accomplishment considering fertilizer shortages.

*Corn production for grain was down 50 percent. With feed for cows short, large amounts of corn were being turned into silage for the cows.

*20 square miles no longer classed as farmland was brought back into use.

*Horses and mules still used in farming dropped 35 percent as the faster and more productive tractors took over.

Tomato production was increased, too, with the result a severe labor shortage in pickers: 300 were needed in 1943. Every imaginable source of labor was investigated. Interned Japanese, inmates of the county's boys' and girls' reformatories, women enlisted in the Women's Land Army, and 19 families from the hills of Kentucky were considered. A small group of stranded British sailors was almost obtained. School emergencies were declared so school children could work on farms during spring planting. Most of these sources did not work out, though the Kentucky farmers who were married worked out well, and over the war period there were a great many women and children at work in the fields.

Young farmers were in an uncomfortable position — their town and school friends were going off to war, and their pictures were appearing in the county's papers as they were reported dead or missing in action. There was little they could do except keep farming and do the best job of it. Tragically, Robert Crane, who was one of these younger men, died of heart failure following an asthmatic attack in 1942. Farmers who were used to working long hours seven days a week were working harder than ever. Sometimes it was too much of a strain.

Farmers had to deal with at least a half dozen government agencies, or more. There were waiting lists of farmers who wanted scarce machinery and committees to approve their need, rationing and special programs. Both government and farmers were scraping the bottom of the barrel in terms of resources and the Executive Committee handled the tremendous organization work load with a proven tactic: it increased the special representatives on the committee from 17 to 28 during the period.

State senators, assemblymen, freeholders, bankers and heads of special war offices were added. A tremendous amount of time and energy was saved in not having to make telephone follow-ups or write letters and wait for replies. Unproductive effort could be dispensed with simply by having everyone who might be needed at the same place at the same time — the regular monthly meeting.

In the midst of this tremendous effort, the Board found it had become so efficient it still had time to develop important community projects. So it became the first county board in New Jersey to offer Blue Cross medical insurance to farmers and nonfarmers alike at reduced group rates. That job was accomplished almost single-handedly by Ann Stevenson, whose husband Richard was on the executive committee: "Somewhere about March of 1943 I was appointed to the Associated Women of the County Board of Agriculture. I was discussing with a friend, Mrs. Henry Barlow, what I felt I might contribute, and she brought to my attention an article on the Blue Cross which the Missouri and Minnesota Farm Bureaus had established for their members. I took the article to the next meeting and after explaining it, I found I had suddenly been appointed chairman of the Blue Cross Committee."

Mrs. Stevenson contacted the state Blue Cross, learned a 1,000-member organization like the Board would require 100 sign-ups, and took the idea to the county Board. It was at a time when accidents from new high-powered farm machinery were becoming more and more serious, and when hospital expenses were beginning to get beyond the means of the average farm family. The Board approved the project.

"To spread the good news of hospitalization available to farmers, I spoke to every PTA and every Grange that would invite me, and if I encountered a friend or acquaintance on the street, I would talk Blue Cross to him or her," said Mrs. Stevenson. "There was some opposition from the Blue Cross at the time. They had a very dim view of farmers and felt they spent their winter months creating large families rather than doing barn chores. And I had been told during this period when I was talking all over the county I would never get 100 farmers to sign up, that the farmers were too sceptical."

The pessimists were right. As the deadline neared, the sign-ups were nowhere near 100. "But the thought of returning all that money to the farmers who had subscribed and explaining to them we had failed was such an appalling idea, that I put on extra pressure," she said. "We got our 100 members, and it has never been necessary since to drum up trade for the Blue Cross. People have sought us out to subscribe."

It cost subscribers $9 per month for a single person and $24 for a family that first year. Nonmembers of the Board of Agriculture could join the Board with special limited memberships for $2.50 so they could become eligible for the program. By 1956, when Blue Shield was added to available coverage, there were 900 individuals or families belonging. Once more, the Board — which no longer had an entirely masculine identity — acted just in time. In 1944, three weeks of hospitalization for one Blue Cross user cost $145. Blanche Hoffman of Flemington, who administered the program for many years, estimated it would have been years, possibly into the 1950s, before the Board got around to Blue Cross if Mrs. Stevenson had not acted.

The changes in medicine and hospitalization were so complex that the issue of health care was going to be raised even further. In the 1930s, Crane had remarked to the Executive Committee on the shortage of doctors in the county. He had taken on the job of trying to do something about it. That was a problem still unsolved in the mid-40s. County doctors could not be expected to handle severe machinery accidents. William McIntyre, who became Babbitt's assistant in 1944, remembers the problems well: "Folks had had about enough of having to go to Belvidere or to Doylestown or to Morristown or to Trenton. That was where you went to the hospital if you needed a doctor for surgery or something serious. If you had an accident, by the time you got there, maybe you didn't need to get there anymore in the first place. Some pretty awful accidents occurred, and there was no place for these people to go — the local physician, that was it. It was a pretty chancy thing."

Mrs. Rose Angell was county welfare director at the time and even more aware of this problem because out-of-town hospitals often didn't want her welfare cases. The Reverend Dunbar of Flemington recalled Mrs. Angell as a quiet, mild person who was keenly aware of the developing public service problems in the county. In 1946, Mrs. Angell noted the problem in her annual report to the freeholders. The report was accepted and filed without positive comment. So this quiet woman had a talk with one of the brashest people the county had seen since County Agent Gauntt.

Louise Bonnie Leicester of Pittstown was a new resident to the county, a public relations woman who had "taken up the New York World's Fair and popularized it after it looked like a lost cause," one news story of the time claimed. She was so brash she even nettled the quiet spoken Dunbar, and taught him some new lessons in patience and humor: "I know sometimes I disagreed with her. She would try to argue me down, and many times she was right. But she was always talking about 'weasel words' — and 'weasel words' was anything she disagreed with!"

So an Angell and somewhat of a devil put their heads together and wound up not at the freeholder's office, but sitting in the county agent's office before the Executive Committee. All they asked for was a hospital. Of the highest quality. "I'll never forget," McIntyre recounted. "Clifford Snyder was sitting next to Lloyd Wescott and Lloyd said to Mrs. Leicester, 'You know very well that the only people who would support this sort of thing would be people who have more than the average amount of money. And people like that are not going to use a little country hospital that we could afford here. Forget it, this is foolishness. The kind of hospital we might have wouldn't be worth having — anybody who has enough money is going to go to the city hospitals where he can get really good medical care!' Mr. Wescott felt it was foolishness. That it shouldn't be done. And Clifford Snyder said to Lloyd, 'I'm going to put you on a committee to study this thing, and I think you better kill it.'"

War and Peace

A farmer might say the same thing of an ailing animal that couldn't be doctored. You have to be practical. But Wescott remembers an additional part of the dialogue between Snyder and himself: "I said I really don't think we can make this work. And Clifford said, 'I know. But it is too important to let it go.'"

It was a difficult moment. Both men were realists and knew it would be debilitating and demoralizing to the community to lead it into a gigantic project that required dedication and energy from all members, and then have the whole thing flounder. They'd learned from practical experience that this kind of failure cost more than biding one's time and waiting for better opportunities while making the best of what little you had. And yet they hated to let it go. It was the same as Anne Stevenson's feeling about giving the Blue Cross deposits back to the farm families who had invested their faith in the idea. Except for Mrs. Stevenson it was only a matter of making an exhausting last-ditch effort out of desperation during the last lap. This was going to be that way from the start.

Secretary Schomp struck a neutral but positive note when he sat down to summarize the lengthy discussion in his minutes: "There was considerable discussion on the question of a hospital. Most of those present felt the need for more information before a definite decision was reached. It was moved and carried that a committee be appointed to secure information and facts about a hospital and report at some future meeting. The committee is: Lloyd Wescott, Waldo McNutt, Charles Cane, Richard Schomp, William Lauderdale, Herbert VanPelt, Mrs. Leicester, Mrs. Stevenson, and Mrs. Crane."

They met in a spare courtroom over the jail, but were politely ousted when the inmates complained their meetings ran late into the night and their voices made sleep difficult. As the investigation began, Mrs. Leicester decided the best sources were needed and went after a man she had a nodding acquaintance with: Dr. E.L.H. Corwin, an eminent public health expert and an officer of the New York Academy of Medicine. Corwin's secretary refused Mrs. Leicester an appointment, explaining he was booked for so many months in advance it was pointless. Mrs. Leicester told her that she knew there were always last-minute cancellations, and if she didn't mind, she would sit in the waiting room and wait for such an opening. After three days, Corwin's secretary relented.

Corwin fell to Mrs. Leicester's persuasive pressures as well. He had never done anything remotely like a survey of a rural community's hospital needs. But, after talks with Mrs. Leicester and the rest of the committee, he agreed. The hospital committee had spent 1946 in meetings with state health department officials about possible federal funding, and also in adding more people to the committee, and getting its basic research done. Thus, the year 1947 was occupied

The goal these youngsters set in raising money for the Hunterdon Medical Center is the equivalent of about $2,000 today. They achieved their goal. (Hunterdon County *Democrat*.)

with Corwin's survey work and exploratory meetings with the New York University-Bellevue Medical Center.

Corwin advised the committee that an affiliation with a large teaching hospital would be crucial in creating a rural hospital that could provide superior care. There would be access to the resources of the larger hospital. New York University was just beginning such an affiliative program. By 1949, the rural hospital committee had secured such an affiliation with NYU and by special agreement had an even closer relationship than the other hospitals involved in its program.

The rural hospital design finally reached also was to make the county's general practitioners staff members of the hospital, working in coordination with the full-time specialists at the hospital. Thus, the different medical people responsible for a sick person's care would actively work together in handling the case.

"No record of a previous experimental organization of this kind has been found in the annals of American medicine," Dr. Raymond Trussell, director for the new hospital, wrote years later. The concept of "home rule" was an old one in Hunterdon, and it included things like the idea of having a hospital specialist talking to and working with the doctor who had been caring for the patient for years and knew them well.

Corwin's survey was completed in 1947, and his cogent facts confirmed the subjective estimates of the county's leaders — that the medical services available to county residents were quite inadequate compared to the care urban people were receiving. Corwin found the County Medical Society's general practitioners uneasy and pessimistic about the burdens and problems they would face if a hospital were set up. He also found them unanimously willing to go on record that they would cooperate to resolve those problems in any way possible. Corwin himself stated he was lukewarm to the project in terms of its usefulness unless it undertook to become a county center for community health services that went far beyond a conventional hospital. And it had to have a big hospital affiliation, he believed.

In 1948, his complete report was opened to the public at special meetings. And reaction was dour — $1.2 million would be required for a federal grant of $600,000. That was $114 required from every family in the county. One man who went to the hospital meeting at the Grandview Grange Hall in Flemington commented that he "couldn't see $3,500 in the whole crowd" let alone the kind of money that was going to be needed. It turned out that a fund-raising professional was going to charge 15 percent or $180,000

Groundbreaking for the Hunterdon Medical Center, 1951. (Hunterdon County *Democrat*.)

War and Peace

just to attempt to raise the money, success or not.

The hospital committee had no affiliation with a large hospital at the time, had local doctors who were pessimists about getting good cooperation, and had a general public that was shaking its head about the money. So it decided to go ahead. It would disband itself and create a non-Board of Agriculture group that could encompass the whole community. And they would raise the money. The familiar Board membership campaigning techniques would be used — contact each person individually, explain the situation thoroughly and clearly, and make the request.

Alvah Haver of Clinton Township recalled his surprise at his participation in the fund raising: "I wasn't for or against a hopsital to start with, but after I thought about it a little, I was for it with both feet. So in February of 1949, I was asked to sit down with another fund-raising lady and prophesize how much Clinton Township would produce, how much would they contribute?

"I laughed at it, and said it's ridiculous, but we sat down and classified the people — poor, medium, and good. And we didn't know how much money they had any more than they knew how much I had, but we guessed. We spent a day at it. We came up with $60,000. Believe it or not, when the results were in, Clinton Township had $65,000! I thought that was the best guesswork I ever did."

There were a lot of surprises everywhere during the fund campaign. Families that were considered poor were pledging and fulfilling contributions that no one considered possible. People from every municipality in the county participated in the fund-raising. McIntyre estimated it was the whole grassroots leadership concept, and County Agent Babbitt in particular, that was important in helping the committee through each step. He'd spent his entire career in Hunterdon getting the right people together and discovering when you did it dissolved pessimism.

"It's part of the whole job of being an extension agent to get people to help themselves to the kind of information they need," McIntyre said. "So then it really doesn't come from you, it comes from them. And then, you know, it's kind of their baby and — 'don't you touch my baby!' And this is what Babbitt did, and this is the way the committee operated."

It worked and by the time Governor Alfred Driscoll kicked off the fund campaign in May 1949, the notion that Hunterdon needed and wanted a top quality hospital belonged to the people of the county. Farmers without any money donated cows, heifers and hay that were sold for the fund. Two small boys pledged they would raise $200 by shining shoes in front of their dad's barbershop. They made good on the pledge. There were a thousand volunteer fund raisers, 10,000 families were contacted, and by the end of two months, $754,000 had been pledged.

For the leaders, perhaps, it was misery, for horrendously difficult problems kept cropping up, and now they absolutely had to be solved. Somehow they were solved, and the dramatic details of how it was accomplished are recorded in Dr. Trussell's book, *The Hunterdon Medical Center*.

On July 3, 1953, the medical center was officially opened. History had been made that attracted attention from medical professionals all over the nation. In the decades that followed, the growth of the hospital to meet the county's burgeoning needs led to additional dramatic accomplishments. When the Medical Center publicly aired problems arising in administration and staff relationships in the past few years, the public relations officer for the hospital became accustomed to receiving phone calls and correspondence from administrative specialists all over the country. They were listening to the disputes from thousands of miles away, and hoping for solu-

War and Peace

Rain, mud, construction materials and unfinished work at the Medical Center, but it was time to inspect the building to see if it measured up. It did. (Hunterdon County *Democrat*.)

An early photo of the Hunterdon Medical Center Board. Standing, left to right: Waldo McNutt, Herbert Stem, Wesley Lance, James Weisel, George Bushfield, Bonnie Leicester, J. Seward Johnson, Frank Dalrymple, and Rev. Edward Dunbar. Seated: William Lamont, Lloyd Wescott, State Senator Samuel Bodine, and Joseph Moskowitz. (Hunterdon County *Democrat*.)

tions that might give them ideas for their own problems.

"Twenty Years of Community Medicine, A Hunterdon Medical Center Symposium," published in 1974, records some of the details of the hospital's continuing growth. The Board of Agriculture's role in helping the community create its own hospital had turned out to be its major accomplishment over many decades of accomplishments, major and minor. What made the accomplishment even more significant was that it was essentially a visionary intuition that farm-

ing was "on the way out" in Hunterdon County, and that the people who were going to live in the subdivision homes on the former farm fields would need something done for them now, in 1946, so they and the remaining farmers could have the best medical care.

The whole role of agriculture in Hunterdon was about to change drastically, and Executive Committee members were responding in ways to make the change harmonious for everyone. There were several major forces at work:

*Post-war prosperity was bringing millions out from the cities to live in new country-suburban homes.

*Taxes were climbing swiftly on farm lands to pay for the education of the new suburbanites' children.

*An acceleration of farm technology made the amazing advances of the previous decades seem inconsequential. That began turning modern farm families into near millionaires in land and equipment investment, and near paupers in the return they were able to earn on that capital investment.

The Board's major work in the post-war years involved helping farmers to adjust, but the new residents were never forgotten in terms of their needs. The hospital project had taken care of medicine. In a less dramatic way, farmers and farm wives tackled the equally important question of education as they helped to create the 11-municipality North Hunterdon Regional High School district in 1947, and the other elementary and high school regionalization projects that followed all over the county. Similarly, farmers who had served on the one-room school boards and township governing committees in their younger years found themselves and their grown children sitting on the new planning boards, zoning boards and boards of adjustment.

Since they knew the land with a closeness born of lifelong experience, since they had leaders who could intuitively sense the needs of future decades, their contributions were often crucial. The effective modern planning and development controls that exist today were created by the foundation they laid. But there was work to be done back on the farm as well. Two questions might be put to a mythical average Hunterdon farmer of 1946:

Q: "Do you want to keep farming, considering that nowadays you're going to have to change more of your methods in one year than your father had to change in ten years?

A: "Hell, yes, I want to keep farming till I retire. I'll change enough to make that goal. There's as good money in it as there is in going into some new job I don't know anything about."

Q: "Do you want the leadership to help make it possible for your sons and daughters to be farm people?"

A: "Most of our sons and daughters these days don't want to farm. They want to go to college or into business. I think that's great if they do. But the ones who want to stay in farming, I want them to have the best chance possible. I don't want any backsliding from our leaders just because some say 'farming is on the way out.' Can that. They better keep on the ball. There will always be farming until people get tired of eating. And I want to see it here in Hunterdon, whether it gets urbanized or not."

Though the questions are imaginary, the events that followed World War II in Hunterdon suggest questions like these were being considered by every farmer in the county. It's unlikely they were discussed openly with any thoroughness. Things were happening so fast; it was the developments of the moment that were getting the attention. But in the decade following the war, the average age of a Hunterdon farmer increased 10 years to about 55. This meant that few youngsters were going into farming. Only the existing farmers were staying on, and getting older each year.

War and Peace

Workers at Clifford Snyder's farm in Pittstown conserve scarce burlap bags during the war by using a silage blower to put feed into a second-story bin. The process also reduced the labor involved in moving heavy cattle and poultry feeds.

Shortly after the war, the Delaware Valley Farmers Cooperative that poultryman Oscar Grossman had founded to help Frenchtown area farmers and the older GLF (now Agway) used large delivery trucks. Feed, no longer a solid, was now treated as a liquid and was pumped through a hose at the back of the truck into a farmer's storage bins. This replaced the farmer having to tote a ton or so feed in 100-pound burlap bags.

V
Population Shifts

Since its reorganization in 1915, the Board has followed an aggressive campaign to create a stable farm community, and from the enormous labors that thousands of organized farm people put into this goal, had been visibly rewarded in dozens of ways. Now there was a new world coming along and its first rule was that farming would be of ever-diminishing importance. The Board would have to discover the new rules of the game and the farmer's place in it. Leaders would have to communicate optimism to their fellow farmers and instill confidence so they would follow wise judgments.

What were the wise judgments? They were not so easily seen, since nothing before of the magnitude of change going on had ever happened. Men had plowed with horses as they had for thousands of years, and wound up driving around on tractors with a skill and ease that seemed as if they had been doing it for hundreds of years. They had simply adapted to every change that came along, and the changes had occurred on every level.

This labor-saving setup at the Whitehall Farm in Pittstown utilizes a high-powered vacuum to draw up the chopped silage and shoot it into the silo with little hand labor. The time is 1949, the beginning of an era when farmers learned to use complex, expensive, and delicate new machinery.

For the Board officers who began their leadership in the early 1920s and 30s, the new times of the post-war 50s were the last chapter of their careers as they turned the offices over to men they'd worked with many long years, but who were a few years younger and could continue with the work. In 1948, Theodore (Dory) Dilts of Three Bridges died in office and young Lloyd Wescott, who had come to the county in the 30s, took up the reins. Wescott was a logical vice-president to replace Snyder if needed. He had that same rare ability to be obstinate in his opinions and fair to the individuals or group that disagreed with him. The two men argued and disagreed violently over the years on a number of issues, and yet remained loyal friends. Perhaps they knew they could trust each other completely, because each was his own man.

Snyder continued as president until 1953, when he retired. He remained active in Board work until his death in 1967. When the new Extension Center building for farm agencies opened in 1963, just north of the Medical Center, Snyder was on the building committee. That same year he was interviewed by a GLF (Agway) man for the history the co-operative was writing of itself. Snyder had served on the board there from 1932. As such he had become a director of one of the largest farm co-ops in the eastern U.S. He had helped make decisions that affected the future and prosperity of farming in a huge area, including New Jersey.

Snyder told the interviewer his new job had begun with him feeling "very much like a cat in a strange garrett" and that he had listened a great deal more than he had talked. The interviewer reminded Snyder that his early beginning had been followed by an active phase where he quite definitely did speak out at length, and in great detail.

After discussing the past, the two men then spent most of the rest of the interview discussing GLF in its present and future, rather than its past, and Synder had quite a few things to say. "I still have faith that we can learn how to market better. I just don't think that we have learned it at the present time," he said. Yet he knew those new problems would soon have to be solved by new men, so he retired from the Board presidency to spend more time on other projects connected with agriculture.

When Snyder and his colleagues on the Executive Committee retired, a new style in leadership emerged — the Board would no longer be run and organized by men who'd make it a second career. The young men growing up in the 40s and 50s had not plowed 20 acres of potatoes to pay their way through college. They had grown up in a highly cosmopolitan farm atmosphere that suggested their future might not be in Hunterdon County. They might move to Pennsylvania or other states as dozens did, or take up a career in the agricultural colleges, or the nationwide farm groups like the artificial breeding groups that Hunterdon had started, or in other special farm-related businesses.

The Board could not take the period of 1920 to 1950 and start it all over again. Times had changed, and so the Board of Agriculture adapted itself accordingly. Hunterdon had available:

Agricultural Conservation Program employees, left to right, Marie Dalrymple, Louise Bell, and Dorothy Flaherty use a surveyor's planimeter to measure the precise acreage of fields from an aerial photo. The ACP program was to avoid surpluses of feed grains and other products through farmers agreeing to restrict plantings to a precalculated amount.

Population Shifts

*A lot of older and mature men who planned to continue farming until retirement.

*A few younger men who planned to farm here, but who had to consider moving out of farming or the county if the economics did not hold up. One young farmer of the 1950s worked for 12 years without taking a day off. Finally he quit farming, saying his children were growing up and he'd never even taken them

The Agricultural Conservation Program of the 1930s became the present-day Agricultural Stabilization and Conservation Service, whose major concern was verifying that farmers who participated in its programs restricted their crops as promised. Justin McAghon checks an aerial photo against the farmland.

on an outing to the seashore.

*A tremendously effective and complex Board when it came to overseeing dozens of different developments in farming simultaneously.

*A record of openness to the "nonfarm" community in inviting anyone interested in any part of agriculture to join actively in leadership.

*A fair sized group of new immigrants after the World War II who came to invest in intensive poultry farming for the decade or so it would be profitable.

*Growing participation by women. They had always tended to be given equal opportunities in the past, and were accepted in their expanded roles with respect and cooperation.

*A lot of retired farm men and women with some energy to give to community life and its problems.

*A decreasing role for farming in the economic life of the county that needed to be carefully watched due to the rule of political history that minority groups often tend to be neglected.

These were the forces at work. There was no coherent, simpler farm society looming in the future, either. The development was towards further diversity of background, and personal needs, and futures. The Board recognized this new situation in the simplest way — by evolving into a system where the top posts are short-term ones. Thus, when Snyder retired in 1953, William Phillips of Milford took up the post, not for 30 years, but for eight. The men and women who followed would do likewise. Wescott, who might have been seen as a man to follow Snyder as president of the Board, decided to devote his time to the equally important Medical Center board.

Phillips remembers with humor how he expected to hold the office of president for a year or two and then Wescott would get his "turn." But Wescott always managed to put him off another year, and continued serving on the Executive Committee and participating in its often mammoth labors, yet remained his own man and evaded becoming a second Snyder. Similarly, the new style of many leaders evolved in an unspoken way. It probably would have been rejected with much fuss and controversy if it had been announced as boldly as the new Board of 1920 had announced its plans. To a man like Clifford Snyder, that would be a waste of time, as he told the GLF interviewer in a different context:

"Don't present a question to the personnel or to the membership that you have too much doubt about; you'd be wasting your time. And I'm not sure but what it would have an adverse effect on the membership. Present worthwhile questions, questions that have an interest, questions that any right-thinking man would say 'yes' to."

Men like Snyder might be expected to be dogmatic after 30 years but that kind of policy would have led to a rigid and wasteful posture. Instead he chose to be a man who did not know all the answers in black and white, but knew it was essential to keep people unified and working together. He was a visible symbol of that kind of man or woman, and many others echoed that style in their own life's work in farming in Hunterdon. Such harmony gave the Board the strength to persevere during times that would make many groups go under.

The minutes of the Board in the postwar period running to 1955 were twice as long as the minutes before the war, and the Board's activities had likewise grown. A typical meeting was that of November 5, 1947, held in the grand jury room of the courthouse:

*Bill paid, $117.

*Miss Susan B. Fox from the County Library reports that the county Board-sponsored film of Hunterdon's rural library system is 'a globe trotter for UNESCO and was now in Paris and soon due in Mexico City.'

*Mrs. Crane reports on programs the Women's Advisory Committee is active in.

*Mrs. Leaming of Whitehouse Station writes to thank the board for furnishing luncheons at the 4-H Leader Training meetings.

*4-H Agent Ramsburg reports on current contests, meetings, and state and national awards. Gets two loans approved for 4-Hers to purchase animals to raise.

*McIntyre reports on annual rat eradication campaign, the Poultry Breeders Club, the Older 4-H Youth dinner.

*Mrs. Stevenson reports on her Blue Cross work for the Board.

*Henry Barlow of Lebanon reports on the American Farm Bureau's recommendations to Congress on production control, having sat on the Bureau committee that formulated those policies.

*Andrew Cray reports on the annual membership drive, membership being the core of the group's strength.

*Rev. Edward Dunbar reports that the rural ministers group in the state will have a special Farmers Week program, including a talk by Board President Snyder.

*Waldo McNutt from the Farmers Union says his group and the Farm Bureau are cooperating more effectively than ever before. He also notes Flemington High School has the heaviest enrollment of veterans taking farming courses — 37.

*County Agent Babbit reports on Seed and Feed Dealers Conference he attended, prospects for late planted wheat, and Grange plans for next year's Fair.

*Snyder reports he has appointed Stanley Douglass to Hunterdon's seat on the State Dairy Council to replace Board vice-president Theodore Dilts, who died.

*Douglass reports on his first meeting with the Dairy Council.

*Arthur Danberry reports on a recent United Milk Producers meeting in the county.

*Two-man auditing committee reappointed.

*Babbitt asks approval of 1948 Extension Budget of $13,480, and $15 a month raise for the two secretaries.

*Board of Freeholders and all the county's townships are invited to Board-scheduled meeting to consider county-wide fox, fire, and snow removal problems. (The Agriculture Board, working with the various local fire companies, developed a plan to help the companies respond to alarms. The county map was divided into numbered grids and each farm given a number. Thus, in case of a fire, the farmer knew which company to call and the company knew where to locate the property.)

*A man from the State Forestry Department will be at the next meeting to discuss a proposed forestry bill.

*Hunterdon State Senator Sam Bodine to be invited to discuss a new school bill that affects rural counties. (North Hunterdon Regional Board was in the process of formation at this time, with the county Board and farmers showing a keen interest in making the program work.)

*President Synder was named to attend the annual national Farm Bureau convention as Hunterdon's delegate.

*McNutt suggests news stories to be gotten out on a cooperative hunting plan in the county. Babbitt assigned to take care of it.

*Babbitt gets leave from December 1 to 4 to attend National County Agent's Association meeting.

That was the meeting itself. Most of the real

Barns filled with dry hay were fire hazards. Executive Committee member Charles Burd lost his barn during World War II and praised firemen for protecting his other buildings from the same fate. A series of meetings between county fire companies and the Board of Agriculture resulted in the "Fire Block System," with a code number for every half square mile of the county.

work was being done outside the meetings by the following committees: Legislative, Farm Bookkeeping, Dairy, Poultry, Fire Prevention, Vocational Agriculture, Tomato, Soil Conservation, Blue Cross, 4-H Membership, and Women's Advisory Committees.

In the 20s, Executive Committee officers did much or most of the committee work. But the Board had offered help to so many agencies and groups that the favors were being returned. In 1947, there were about 50 people serving on committees, and many of them were from these other groups and agencies. There were in fact more "outsiders" on the Executive Committee than there were representatives for the Board of Agriculture. Many of them, like Lloyd Wescott representing the Artificial Breeding Association, were regarded as key members of the Executive Committee. This complemented the trend building up for a diversified and changing leadership — that there were also "nonmembers" helping to run the organization. Even a paid secretary-business-specialist doing a crucial job might wind up a Board officer, as occurred with Blanche Hoffman. She served as Executive Committee treasurer from 1963 to 1972, before going on to become Flemington Fair manager. Thus, as the number of farmers in Hunterdon began to diminish, the number of available leaders remained the same or even increased.

One of the problems with large, diverse group leadership, however, is getting all the members to attend meetings. For decades Secretary Schomp had kept an attendance tally sheet for each year that went into the minutes. Those who had gotten lax could check on their record, and correct it, or consider passing the job to someone with more time.

So the problem was small while the number of people on the Executive Committee remained small, and now it required something new to maintain high attendance. Thus, in 1956 Arthur Danberry offered a resolution that Executive Committee members who did not make 50 percent of the meetings be automatically dropped. The resolution passed and prevented the problem of the person torn between different responsibilities neglecting the Board.

As the Board moved through the 1950s, it found its responsibilities as severe as they had ever been. The big focus was to protect the small farmer in an atmosphere that did not favor him. Progressive methods had always been the ideal. Now they were an urgent matter of survival. As the capital farmers invested grew larger and larger, the risks of failure became more dangerous. The old-fashioned diversified farm could take numerous losses and survive because there was always one crop that came through. This protection had been abandoned in favor of specialization which could be used to raise large amounts of cash. If a specialized crop or other project failed, there was no money, yet there were debts from the intensive capital investment in the special project.

A new kind of diversity was growing — diversity of skills and executive abilities in handling the new specialization. Could a man invest $100,000 in an entirely new kind of farming operation and then make it work perfectly from the start? If he could, his skills had to range from high caliber financing and bookkeeping all the way to the most detailed kind of crop or animal knowledge.

Dr. Timm's compliment to farmers as Renaissance Men 15 years earlier had largely been an exaggeration — you could always remain dumb and do exactly what the extension expert told you, and you had a good chance. But now to be a successful farmer you went beyond even that, if you had the diversity of skills needed. "He ought to have his head checked out" became more and more an anxious comment about a fellow farmer who was going all the way with new recommendations that had not really been thoroughly tested. The man was on the road to the poorhouse or else he was about to prove that he had even better skills and judgment than his neighbors. In which case he was soon imitated.

The result was that the Board became more and more demanding of its Extension Service experts. Since these men also tended to be self-sacrificing perfectionists, relations were largely excellent. There was always an occasional individual who took a condescending and pessimistic attitude towards the ability of a farmer to innovate. Now even one such man out of a dozen was unacceptable, and Snyder reportedly put more than one such pessimist "through the ropes."

The national evolution of farming during the post-war decade created situations that were the

Charles Thompson, extension service leader, delivers a lecture on dairying at the Stanton Grange Hall in 1951. He showed that Hunterdon dairymen were doing their best with "balanced" dairying, but that the big question mark needed to be erased by better prices for milk if farmers were to show a profit.

Population Shifts

The quickened pace of scientific development during World War II led to modern computers that could process business records faster than ever before. By 1953 the Board of Agriculture was learning about the use of computers in farming, how to be more cost-efficient in animal feeding and milk production, for example.

Board's most frustrating problems. Regulation of surplus crops was poor on a national level and led to a farm economy where violent price swings occurred from year to year. Price depressions lasted for years and often left farmers making from a bushel of wheat no more than their greatgrandfathers made in the 1800s.

"The big farmers never really had any trouble because they had the capital to hold out and stay in business while everyone else was getting wiped out," poultryman Oscar Grossman of Frenchtown said of those first years of modern farming. Grossman had created the Delaware Valley Farmers Cooperative in Frenchtown before the war to help supply small farmers who were too far from Flemington with a feed mill. But not even a feed mill could carry a farmer on its books for several years with bills unpaid because there was another market depression going on. Only some of Hunterdon's small farms could survive, and then only by being more innovative and efficient than even a large farm.

The improvements in productivity in all phases of farming continued. The number of Hunterdon's farms and farmers was steadily declining, but production was increasing so rapidly that milk, eggs, and grain figures for the county as a whole continued to set new highs.

Most lay persons today are aware of the importance of computers in efficient business operation and in performing super-feats of calculation to improve economy. They are so efficient they are being sold for $2,000 today, and rapidly becoming accessible to the "small" businessman. But in agriculture, the small farmer began intensive use of computers nearly three decades ago. The minutes of the 1953 Executive Committee mention a report by Assistant Agent McIntyre on the possible use of IBM computer systems in a group plan for keeping complex farm production records. These systems were first adopted by the Dairy Herd Improvement Association so that every cow a farmer owned could be studied and sometimes even fed individually.

Though farms were declining in number with retirements, the Board of Agriculture membership was not, for many retired farmers considered it well worth their while to retain their membership. The era, with all its difficulties, still had a comfortable glow of Indian Summer when the Grangers met for their sociables or the Board had its annual picnic. The average farmer was in his 50s and getting older.

The 1953 meeting at the now regionalized Flemington-Raritan School was the first with Snyder retired and President Phillips in charge. Several interesting items were reported as usual:

*The resolutions committee was active in garbage feeding regulation and insurance legislation studies. The county's representative for the federal commodity control program reported farmers had signed up for $210,000 worth of voluntary participation, but had been cut back to $58,000 because of federal cutbacks.

*Forty percent of Hunterdon's cows were being bred artificially to some of the most superior sires available. The annual Corn Exhibit was by the 4-Hers and they were experimenting with hybrid seeds. Soil tests were being asked for at the rate of 1,132 during the year in order to fertilize more intelligently.

*There were "100 Bushel" corn clubs, for that was the new per acre goal for crop farmers. Several club members reported the amazing productivity record of 138 bushels per acre. Any farmer who claimed 138 bushels before the war would have been quietly estimated to be a liar.

It must have been bitter for an older farmer to sit at the 1953 dinner meeting and think about how he was retiring soon because he couldn't keep the pace anymore. It must have been delightful, too, when he realized he had his equity intact for retirement and that he had changed and kept up for the past decade as well as any younger man. It was almost as if a large portion of the farm community had decided to retire together. There were 2,204 farm families in 1954 as Phillips began his second year as Board president, and 1,481 farm families left in the county five years later. Most of the losses were retirements. Some were simple business failures. Some were younger men moving to states where the ever-rising school education taxes were only five percent or ten percent of what they had become in Hunterdon.

National production and price controls during the 1950s were so disturbed and unreliable that by the middle of the decade some local farm leaders were bluntly stating that farming in Hunterdon would be dead by 1960 if improvements were not made. They were not, although Hunterdon residents did their best, some of them serving at different times on special "emergency" committees set up by the federal government to "find out what to do." Then a response to the situation began to develop — not on the national level, but on the state level with the Farm Bureau.

For decades the county Board had gotten its members to pay state Farm Bureau dues so the organization could function as a lobbyist and watchdog for all farmers in the state. For decades, too, the Hunterdon Board had exhorted its national and state representatives on tax issues affecting farmers. With the situation for farmers desperate in the 1950s, the Farm Bureau's Tax and Planning Committee began a study of state tax needs in 1957 with this argument: Get a break for the farmer, his farmland isn't creating students or requiring local government police protection or other services. Why are you soaking him?

But what would be fair in the way of a break? The urban populace was not going to approve a plan unless it seemed fair. The Farm Bureau answered: Tax the farmer according to the farm value of his land. If good farmland is going for $300 an acre in Hunterdon in recent sales, then tax him $300 an acre for his good farmland. But don't tax him $920 an acre because somebody just paid that to build a house. Tax him $920 an acre when the time comes that he sells out for housing. Otherwise leave him alone.

The Tax Committee found that only in California was something like this being done, and then only for land that was in special zones where only farming was permitted. "Little hope for such classification was held out in New Jersey; in fact a great many farmers themselves objected to it," the Tax Committee reported on this zoning method. They decided to talk to Hunterdon's Senator Wesley Lance on changing the tax legislation, since Lance was somewhat of an expert. He had served on the state's first Constitutional Convention in 1947 and would serve on a second one to come.

Lance thought they would need an amendment to the state constitution, and told them how to get that done. "He didn't seem too enthusiastic about its possibilities," the Tax Committee noted. Yet he made a suggestion to the group that later saved them — an extensive education campaign to acquaint the people with tax facts. But the commitee concluded its year-long series of investigatory meetings without any solution beyond the comment: "But simply because a desired objective may be quite difficult to obtain, that fact in itself is no reason not to make every possible effort to obtain it."

It sounded like Snyder and Wescott talking

about a new hospital in 1943 and agreeing that although it could not be afforded, it had to be tried anyhow. In the effort that evolved out of the Farm Bureau's study, farmers all over the state cooperated.

Different kinds of plans were explored until finally one called Farmland Assessment emerged. It required a constitutional amendment, which called for a 60 percent majority vote in both houses of the state government, and then a majority vote by the citizens of the state. The vote did not come until 1964. By that time the state was losing farmland at the rate of about 140 square miles a year. Meanwhile, farmers had taken the advice "Educate the people on tax facts" to heart, and most of the people going to the polls that year had heard one or more explanations of how farmland does not require additional tax-supported services.

The Farmland Assessment Act was voted into law by a landslide, with urban residents more in favor of it than rural areas! Possibly some less informed farmers feared their land value would be affected, and thereby their only retirement equity. Another possible reason was the fear by nonfarm rural residents that they would pay more since farmers were paying less. Neither fear was real, but some voters may have thought so.

The long-term result of the law was that the loss of farmland was slowed by 90 percent. Even though it still continued to disappear at a steady rate, it was no longer a massive collapse.

Hunterdon issued its first resolution of support for the Farmland Assessment project in 1959 when the Executive Committee resolved "that the New Jersey Farm Bureau be asked to bend all efforts towards obtaining an assessment policy whereby farmland can be assessed according to agricultural productivity rather than a real estate value."

That same year County Agent Babbitt took early retirement for health reasons. He had "worn out rather than rusted out," as farmers used to say of people who worked themselves hard. William McIntyre, his assistant since the war, became the new county agent.

Board member Snyder reported that year for the building committee that the freeholders expected to start building the new Extension Center in two years. The Board aided the effort of county government and taxpayers by contributing $5,000 towards the purchase of the site.

Clifford Synder, second from left, who retired as Board president in 1952, receives the keys to the new extension center in 1963 from Freeholder Linton Alles. Snyder had served as chairman of the building committee. At left is State Secretary of Agriculture Phillip Alampi, and at right is Leland G. Merrill, former dean of Rutgers University College of Agriculture.

A new kind of problem had begun to emerge. Babbitt had reported after the war that there were "a lot of new, inexperienced farmers," who were now being rapidly replaced by "a lot of new, inexperienced rural residents." They were moving into the new subdivision homes being built and they found them expensive. They were expensive because the planning and zoning the county had helped create made them expensive. What was worse, sewage percolation over most of the county was poor to awful for homebuilding. Large lots of two acres and even five acres were commonplace building requirements. The new residents thus paid dearly for their homes and they expected to find themselves in a kind of paradise.

They were reasonably happy until one day in the spring when some dairyman began unloading his winter's collection of manure on the fields prior to plowing, and all of a sudden there was an awful, unbelievable smell. To be sure, the subtle aromas of urban areas, the dissolved acids, the deadly monoxides and carcinogenic mixtures are really awful, but they don't smell awful to a person who has breathed them all his life. Cow manure, which is harmless, smells awful. Chicken and pig manure sometimes smells so bad a new resident will get into the car and leave the area until it goes away.

The odors left by spring manure spreading, spring chicken coop cleaning, and the like usually dissipated quickly and were gone completely when the plow turned the manure under where it could become a rich fertilizer. But the situation made new residents angry at their neighboring farmers, and inclined to complain to their township committeemen that 'something must be done.' The committeemen might understand and sympathize, yet find little to say that would satisfy the complainer.

At the same time, the situation got worse from another direction. Farmers were building larger and larger dairy barns and poultry houses. More and more farms were getting involved in such high intensity operations that odors sometimes were indeed a problem. "Spent the usual day with Mr. Krueger from Extension on ventilation problems in dairy and poultry houses," McIntyre's assistant county agent, Calvin Wettstein, reported to the Board at the year-end meeting in 1959.

Wettstein, meanwhile, was setting up a barn meeting at the William Teets farm near Lebanon to educate farmers on the new IBM computer programs, so they could intensify their dairy operations still more. Thus, farmers were beginning to be caught in a new double-bind — produce more effectively to stay in business, thereby be a more visible "nuisance" to your new subdivision neighbor down the road. The problem was rarely one of unfriendly neighbors, but of people brought up in an urban culture and unable to understand the problems and conditions of a semi-rural community.

Readington Township was first in the county to discover the new problem, and here's how Earl Hartpence of Stanton saw it: "I found out in the 1950s that the people who own land, if they were going to have any say at all, we're going to have to get on the advisory council to the planning board. So they appointed me. But most of the people you get on these boards are the new people who come out from the city. They want to get onto it. And then they don't know any of the answers. They never lived here in the first place; most of them come out of a city apartment, but they think they know all the answers. And they think the landowners shouldn't have anything to say about it. They think they have the right to run right over top of you."

That's how a farmer feels when he suddenly learns the township committee is quietly considering a new law controlling "nuisances" that will make it several times harder to farm. Farmers like Hartpence all over the county began realizing their influence had waned too much, and this intensified their willingness to serve in local government. They sought compromises to satisfy every reasonable person, but the complexity of the situation made it difficult. Quite often, too, the new residents were sympathetic to farmers as they sat on regulating boards, but were led by local homeowner sentiment to go hard on them. Hartpence himself had a last laugh.

"I was up at the Stanton Store a few years back, and this young woman who was there was saying — 'We're getting too many people out here. We shouldn't allow any more to come in.

"'How long have you been here!' I asked.

"'Oh, quite a good while.'

" 'Well, how long?'

" 'Three or four years. How long have you been here?'

" 'My wife was born in the house we're living in. And we moved back there in 1929, and we didn't want to see you come here, either!

" 'Oh, she was mad. You're just a newcomer, I said, but you want to tell the rest of us what to do!"

Thus, during the 1960s there was a state of fluctuating tension in most of the county's township governments as they struggled and fought to adopt planning and zoning codes that were equitable, or tried to update earlier codes that were inadequate. Often it was a classic "newcomer-oldtimer" issue, or so it seemed.

Delaware Township residents still have memories of how Mrs. Edna Horn was the major pusher for a planning board, how she opposed some of the township fathers with iron determination, how they finally created a board — and gave it a $75 a year budget!

Rumors as to "what was really going on" were prolific and unprintable. But after the new planning board and Mrs. Horn had been around for a few years, people began to notice it was doing a respectable job in planning and zoning. Not only that, Mrs. Horn was working with the farmers and long-time residents.

New and old residents alike were undertaking the complex job of literally creating a new society when the population of an area is rapidly doubled and tripled. They were serious about cooperating, for numerous townships in the state had done their "urbanization" 10, 20, or 30 years earlier, and the reports of their performance were available. Due to careless planning and nonseriousness, population growth had led to untold problems and miseries, many of which were not being corrected because of the terrific expense.

In the 1960s, most of the change and innovation in the county was choreographed by local and county government, not the Board of Agriculture. The Board made no attempt to usurp an initiative it should not have. Instead, many Board members served in local government, as they had for decades, and made themselves felt as best they could. For the Board, it was a subtle shift from being a central agency in community life to being an accessory organization that tended to the farm community. But it tried to make contributions to the county as a whole.

At the 1960 annual meeting State Secretary of Agriculture Phillip Alampi, who spoke on changing times in agriculture and marketing in New Jersey, said in order to survive "we must conform to these changing times." Conformity can be passive resignation at defeat, or something better. By this time, however, there were more reasons for farmers to feel defeated.

The men and women who had stayed on to round off their life's work in the 1950s were now mostly gone. Membership in the Board of Agriculture began dropping, a reflection of their loss. Younger men and women of middle years were in the driver's seat. They had worked with the older leaders and farmers and remembered them with a sense of affection and loss. Though they had many friends among the "new" urban residents, the new people could not easily share the values of this older farm community for they knew little of it. The numbers of active, full-time farm families were no longer in the thousands, but in the hundreds. The clear and active memories that seemed like yesterday — the 20s, 30s, and 40s — were no longer unbroken.

Ruth Ent of Sergeantsville, who spent her work years as extension secretary, remembers telling the young people of her family's first home electric plant and automobile. "They say, gee whiz, you sound ancient. Well, I am. I can remember these things." Continuity had broken in most minds. Now there were the "old days," separated from "the present time," to be recalled only in reminiscence.

In 1960, there was no future for farming in Hunterdon whatever, but the passage of the Farmland Act in 1964 restored life to that possibility. Investors began to own most of the farmland, big and little, dentists with a childhood love of the country or moguls who might purchase large tracts to speculate on a possible jetport in Readington Township. Without farmland assessment, the investors would have sat on their land and let it go back to early forest. With it, they became very interested in farming. They saved money on taxes that way. And that saving made them less anxious to sell the land quickly to make a killing before taxes ate it up. They could

As leadership of the Board of Agriculture's Executive Committee passed to the next generation, the new leaders took time to honor those who had worked on behalf of Hunterdon farmers over the decades. Here, Mrs. Ellsworth Higgins receives a citation for distinguished service from 1964 Board President Henry Fisher Jr. of Sergeantsville. At left is Vice President William Goddard of Jutland and, at right, County Agent William McIntyre.

Eugene Frazee points across the fields on his farm near Clinton, with his son John and grandson Tom. The occasion of the photo was Frazee's winning of a state dairy award for his many years in the industry.

rent to a crop farmer. Some, as Hartpence had learned in Readington, even began to dislike the rapid destruction of farmland they saw going on, and wanted to preserve the open lands.

This was the trend after 1964. It became evident because everyone in the rural communities was watch-dogging the special assessment for abuses and to see how effective it was. What the watchers saw as they looked at the overall picture was that at the very point of its shift to a subsidiary industry for Hunterdon, farm productivity reached levels that had never before been approached. Farmers, who had begun with 400 square miles in 1900, now cultivated 238 square miles and broke most of the exiting county records for total volume of output in crops, poultry, and dairy.

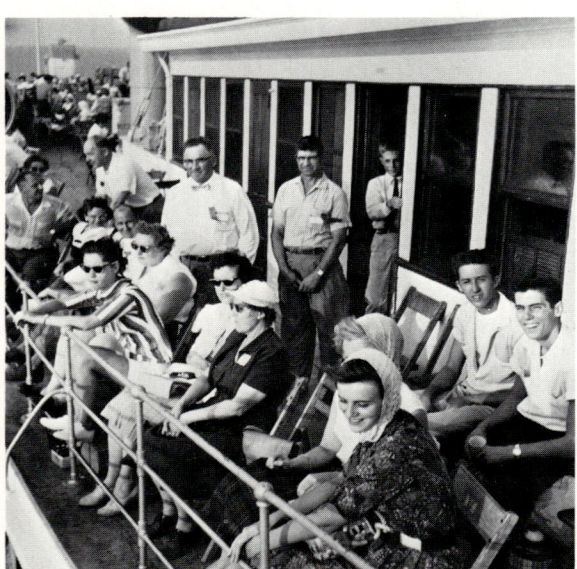

Well-dressed and attractive youngsters and farm wives in the foreground of this 1950s Board of Agriculture excursion photo suggests that the young people were preparing for a life different from farming. Standing in the doorway next to the white-shirted youth is Philip Mowery, Board president from 1961 to 1963. Behind him, leaning over to talk to a farmer at the rail is County Agent William McIntyre.

In the decade of the 1960s, farms would drop to 180 square miles and even then productivity would still be near historical highs. For an industry and a way of life supposedly old-fashioned, obsolete, "on the way out," that was a surprising and peculiar accomplishment. The answer appears to be that county farming and the Board of Agriculture were changing instead of dying. Those who wanted to stay in farming might not see the future in it, but they stayed another year and another and another.

Farmers retired, sold their farms to investors and moved into town. Then their farm neighbors were asked by the new owner to farm that land. The Extension Service, which the Executive Committee had cultivated, coddled, and badgered to fit Hunterdon farming, fit it as well as it ever had during the 1960s. Long-time Board officers like Fred Totten and the new ones continued to oversee the service's activities. Passage of the farmland law was a victory for morale as well as farming. It told farmers that as a minority group they had the skills to wield enough political influence to help their industry survive. The new people in the community liked the Fair and the 4-H, thus every effort was made to continue them.

The Board refused to give in to the new blitz of modern regulation that could make farming impossible. One resolution sent to the state tax division in 1961 was almost humorous in the bureaucratic absurdities it charged. In a resolution condemning the division's form sent to all property owners in the state demanding detailed and confidential information, the Board noted that: 1. It violated federal laws protecting individual privacy; 2. It was incomprehensible; 3. It was unnecessary; 4. It created hardships, especially for farmers; 5. It created additional administrative burdens; and 6. It would tend to curtail farm suppliers inventories. "THEREFORE be it resolved that we ask this form be cancelled and no further complications of this nature be placed before farmers, business and professional people in the state." It was not far from the letters sent to King George at the time of the Boston Tea Party. Indeed, the only armed insurrection the federal government ever had to fight over its tax laws had come from Pennsylvania farmers not too long after the Revolution.

While farmland assessment brought property tax relief and helped to keep farmers on their land, it became apparent that federal estate tax also adversely affected the agricultural community. Giving the farmer annual property tax relief was of little consequence if at the time of his death his family had to liquidate the farm in order to pay the estate tax bill. Many farms were forced out of business when the head of the household died, for estate taxes were so large that little funds were left over to continue the operation.

Farms have always represented a substantial investment in land, equipment, and buildings, with income low in relation to the size of investment. A farmer's financial situation is apt to be highly non-liquid, and his estate may be without the cash to pay a tax based on the inflated market value of the farm. When Clifford Snyder died, his wife, Melda, was so shaken by the estate tax that she promptly enlisted the help of the County Board and the State Farm Bureau to see what could be done to correct the problem. Other com-

Senior County Agent Calvin Wettstein in 1959 when he was assistant agent specializing in dairying. Wettstein served in the Marines during World War II and again during the Korean conflict. He and his wife live in Clinton Township.

munity and state leaders joined the campaign as the problem became acute with the growing size of farm estates.

John Hunter of the Rutgers Extension Service approached New Jersey's legislators in Washington early in 1968 with a plan similar to the Farmland Assessment Act. However, the U.S. Treasury Department called it discretionary and said that favorable treatment of farm evaluation for estate purposes was "unwise." But, as the years passed, the power of petition came into play and Hunterdon farmers, with their counterparts throughout the nation, worked for tax reform that would enable them to preserve rural land and keep their farms in the family.

The Tax Reform Act of 1976 permits the executor of a farm estate to evaluate the estate on the basis of value for agricultural use rather than on current market value. Further relief came with the increase in time permitted to pay estate taxes, from 10 to 15 years. Exemptions have also increased in recent years. As with the other problems confronting the farm community, cooperation at the grassroots level had once again influenced regulatory policy. As one Hunterdon farmer put it: "Even a small organization like our County Board could have an effect on federal legislation. Estate tax reform alone has kept many farms in the family."

Big issues, like the Farmland Act and estate tax reform, had demanded the Executive Committee's energies for years, but no one was forgetting that farming could be destroyed as easily by dozens of little issues. And the little issues never stopped coming. Thus, Secretary Totten noted in the March 1968 minutes that Bruce Drenning from the County Planning Board had been present. The planning board was to receive considerable aid from farm agencies like the Soil Conservation Service in preparing modern master plans that required accurate data on soil all over the county.

"County Planner Bruce Drenning spoke to us on the future of agriculture in this county, does it have a future? and if so, how can we as a County Board of Agriculture help in future county planning. This is a *real cry for HELP* which this board will be very shortsighted to disregard, for the time for action is NOW, while we still may be able to safeguard our industry in this area."

During the late 60s, Totten's minutes ran 2,000 words on the average, with an added two to five thousand words amended by reports from the County Agent, 4-H Agent, and Home Economist. As usual, thoroughness was the rule, and it was leading the Board and its agencies into the new times of Hunterdon with deceptive smoothness.

Any homeowner or gardener who visited the new Extension Service offices found more often than not they got to talk to Agent McIntyre or

Professor Roy DeBoer, Rutgers Department of Landscape Architecture, second from right, addressed the 1965 Businessmen-Farmers Picnic on the topic of land zoning. To DeBoer's right is John Middleton, Board president from 1967 to 1969. On the far left is County Agent William McIntyre and, at right, Henry Fisher of Delaware Township, then a member of his local zoning board.

Among the guests at the 1965 Businessmen-Farmers Picnic was George Parker of Flemington, at right. The affair was held at John Middleton's Kingwood Nursery.

Assistant Agent Wettstein without an appointment. Their questions were answered on the spot, and when this wasn't possible, special investigations were undertaken and carried through. In five or 10 minutes they might be on the way home with the answers for their termite problem, or the blight, or the solution to a poorly drained garden plot. Residents were impressed by the efficiency, speed, and above all the relaxed and courteous tempo.

They never knew that if their agent did not get them out of the office in 10 minutes flat he would be late for a dairy demonstration meeting, or a trip to a poultryman's farm to find out how to cure his much worse odor problem, or any of the hundreds of other farm activities the office handled. In modern urban life this kind of business contact is too often a rarity and finding that farmers work this way created a strong impression.

The policy that farm groups ought always to take or make time for the needs of the nonfarm community had been established through practice when the first new farmers and residents began showing up in the 1930s from the cities. The practice had been established carefully, and now it had become an integral part of the adjustment to the new urban community.

The Board maintained 4-H for many of the newcomers' children, who had a wonderful and wholesome time learning about animal and plant care, and leadership. The new people were invited to the Board's annual Businessmen-Farmers Picnic, with its "old fashioned" good food and good speakers. The Board treated anyone with requests or problems as if they had a special "in" with the farm community, so far as concern and assistance were involved. It helped to create the impression that farmers bear their troubles with dignity, only ask help when it's needed, and always offer help when they can.

Ultimately these habits of farm living prevented the formation of a strong anti-farmer sentiment among the population that would lead to confused and punitive regulations. For by the time the 1960s were drawing to a close, that kind of possibility had become a recurring one, due mostly to the growing complexity of the county's economic life. The courteous and positive approach has been kept up as new problems came along during the 1970s and the Board gradually found itself in the present-day urban community.

The major concern of the Board today lies both inside and outside the county. As the number of farmers within the state has shrunk, they have grown closer, and the liaisons the Board maintains with farm groups all over the state are presently a vital part of its work. New developments

Population Shifts

are passed back and forth as quickly as they would be among next-door neighbors, and the same efficiency occurs with cooperative projects that cross county lines.

Lloyd Wescott and William Losch of Lambertville became Hunterdon's representatives on the 21-member Blueprint Commission appointed by Agriculture Secretary Alampi in 1971. The commission was to come up with a blueprint for the future of farming in New Jersey. It projected the farmer to be a prosperous member of the business community who was also a wholesome benefactor who kept open land viable at a time when rapid development had caused air and water pollution problems that far exceeded the smell of fresh manure spread over a field.

The commission produced the well-known recommendation that land over the state be legally designated farmland by local government, and its development rights be voided. In turn, the state would pay the landowner the current market value of these rights in dollars. Land worth $1,000 as farmland is often worth $5,000 or $10,000 for "development land." The plan provided that the purchase would be made from a fund which assessed a three-quarter mill tax on *all* real estate transactions in the state.

The commission also produced a lesser-known series of recommendations for the systematic renovation of the agricultural economy to make it possible for such "permanent farmland" to be farmed economically.

To date, however, the program has failed. A pilot project of purchasing such development rights in a small area in South Jersey showed such poor results that it qualified as a failure. But it also was successful so far as learning the real reactions people would have in trying to work out such a program. The problems are difficult because they involve government taking away the rights of private landowners in a way completely different from the local zoning that everyone is used to. Unless the dollar value of lost development rights is assessed and paid for adequately, farmers and investors can only see the program as an attempt to rob them of equity that many spent their entire lives building.

A modern farmer with several hundred thousand dollars in farm buildings and equipment faces the situation that the resale value of that investment is zero. Equipment and buildings today become obsolete and worthless in as little as two or three years. The only stable value a farmers has is his land. Yet farm leaders estimate the blueprint program to be a vital one, since without stabilization of farmland it will slowly and continuously be taken out of farmland forever, and put into high value urban uses. Other approaches in local planning and zoning that preserve farmland are being pursued, but face exactly the same problems.

Yet, Hunterdon farmers and those over the state believe there is a value to farmland preservation that is completely unrelated to the value of the food grown there, and exceeds it greatly. They no longer see themselves as economically obsolete people being pushed into a deserved extinction, but rather as a segment of the economic community that has a growing importance in the future economic prosperity of the state. They point to polluting plants and industries and subdivision plots with their hundreds of school children, and say: "See that? Wouldn't it be nice if we had a few farms next door to that to even out the blow?"

Checking over computer printouts on the kitchen table are Assistant County Agent Roger Locandro, now at Rutgers University, and dairyman Richard Gulick of Flemington. Gulick's milk records are collated and analyzed by computer.

Population Shifts

Yes, it would be nice. Someday the voters of the state who voted in favor of the farmland assessment law may find themselves with a new proposal to approve, one drafted by the same kind of tenacious individuals.

In modern Hunterdon, "farming" is now a dozen different possibilities. The full-time farms are few, most of them large dairy and crop farming operations. Orchards, truck farming, poultry farming and other types exist as well. The loss of farms is presently moderate, with a little more than a square mile lost in the 1976-77 statistical year. The number of part-time farm operations in the county where one or more members of the family work off the farm number in the dozens.

Dozens of times more numerous than these are the "urban" farmers:

*The woman who keeps a three-acre truck garden to raise food for family and for a small restaurant business;

*The part-timer who has a dozen goats because he or she finds the work relieves the tension of office work;

*The family that bought a 10-acre home lot so they could have horses for the kids;

*The white collar family who lives in the old farmhouse and rents the fields to a neighbor for crops; and

*The family in Raritan Township who left a city existence to become full-time farmers, to the astonishment and admiration of the neighboring farmers.

The role of this new kind of farmer is perhaps as important as the larger family farms, for their numbers are much greater, and so they spread the news of farming further in the modern community. A similar job is done by the man or woman who has no land at all, but a dream about it, and are farmers at heart. If they see farming prosper in its modern place, they may join the Board of Agriculture, if they're not there already. And then they'll invite one of their "nonfarmer" neighbors to the next Businessmen-Farmers picnic.

Book illustrator Kurt Wiese of Kingwood Township penned this sketch of a typical firemen's picnic of the 1950s for the Hunterdon County *Democrat*.

In a 1942 photograph, Mrs. George Pearce of Whitehouse Station packs eggs for market. To prevent spoilage eggs must be properly cooled and packed — large end up. (U.S.D.A. Photo by Forsythe.)

VI

Poultry Grade AA

The goose that laid the golden egg must have been a distant cousin of the Hunterdon County hen. They both brought riches to their owners, although the Hunterdon hen was treated quite a bit better.

Chickens began their career in Hunterdon with their relatives, ducks, geese, turkeys and guinea fowl. They put meat and eggs on the farmer's table and cash in his pocketbook. There were not too many eggs, but chickens were a worthwhile part of the general farm of the past century. They were good scavengers and could be boarded in the barn, or in a small shed called a coop. During the winter they might receive a small ration of grain and even enjoy table scraps. Much of the year they could be seen in the barnyards and fields scratching for bugs and spilled grain.

There were 35,510 chickens in Hunterdon County reported in the 1840 census. Most of the several thousand farms of the period had 50 to 100. Before refrigeration they were a boon because one chicken was just enough for a meal, and you didn't have to store leftovers. A skilled farm wife or any of the family could kill one and prepare it for the stove in half an hour's time, which made them useful for unexpected company as well.

The farm wife might sell or barter eggs and meat to neighbors or the general store, the profits becoming what she called her "pin" money. In bad years when the crops failed, chickens were a source of income that was small but important.

Chickens only laid eggs in the spring and summer. That was when the farm wife would find a hen that wanted to "brood" and put her over a clutch of a couple dozen eggs, often in a little A-frame coop. Several weeks later there would be baby chicks, next year's chicken replacements, providing raccoons, weasels, fox, opposums, owls or hawks did not get the chicks or the adults first. Hens had a way of disappearing if they roamed too far, or if the coop wasn't sealed tightly. A raccoon develops tremendous strength and intelligence if it knows there are chickens on the other side of some loose boards. A weasel can squeeze through a hole or a crack the size of a pack of cigarettes. It took reasonable care to raise chickens. Thus, for the first 100 years and more of their stay in Hunterdon, chickens led a fairly static existence, an important part of the general farm, but almost never the major cash producer.

After the Civil War, Hunterdon's farm values dropped over a 50-year period, because of the railroad and the cheaper produce it brought from new lands in the west. This was a boon for the hen. It stimulated chicken production, so that by 1880, there were 155,000 hens, quadruple the prewar number. "The eastern farmer, to be successful, must confine himself to the production of such articles as cannot be raised in the west or that will not bear transportation for long distances," H.F. Bodine reported to the Board of Agriculture in 1886.

Eggs did not spoil as rapidly as milk. Before refrigeration, it was easy to take them in a wagon to a general store and from there to a train station and from there to the city and to another store, and, finally, to a city person's home. Eggs were great, highly nutritional food and very popular among the teeming masses of the city.

But how could you produce lots of eggs for sale with a bunch of good-natured hens that liked to scratch and cluck, and only laid a few dozen eggs in the spring? Or hid their nest so well that when you found it, the chicks in there were ready to hatch? Or hid their nest so you didn't find it, but a raccoon did?

The first step was the kerosene incubator that showed up in Hunterdon in 1880 when egg interest had already begun to rise. You collected your eggs from the best layers, put them into the incubator, and in a few weeks you had a fine flock of chicks. All indoors. You could do hundreds of eggs this way; it took less space and dozens of hours less labor than selecting brooders and having special coops for them. It worked so well your neighbor might buy her chicks from you rather than bother to brood them herself. So you had a new income source. Kerosene didn't cost much in 1880; once you paid for the incubator, you were set.

That meant the rehabilitated hen didn't spend weeks sitting on her brood when she ate little food and laid no eggs. Hens that tended to brood were put in special coops with hard floors to discourage this tendency. And their eggs were not used to breed chicks, so that trait was "bred out."

Poultry farmers next fixed up their old coop, or tore it down and built a fine new hen coop with milled lumber. Water tight and vermin proof, and in the winter the chickens' body heat would keep them warm enough, since they were sheltered from the wind. Installed in such an agricultural palace, the modern hen tended to lay eggs more and more into the fall and winter. But still not many. Then in 1889 some clever farmers began lengthening the day on the hens. When they lay a great deal during the warm months, the day is long, so they put a kerosene lantern into the coop at dusk and come back at 10 in the evening to put it out. The hens thought it was summer and laid more eggs. It wasn't until 1937 that agricultural scientists discovered that the pituitary gland is stimulated by light and that the lantern users had the gland fooled. And it stimulated the hen to lay lots of eggs just as it did in the summer. These eggs were sold in the winter market, when they were scarce and brought much better prices.

Some farmers wanted to raise birds for meat, and the incubator was perfect for them, since they could hatch large clutches whenever there were eggs, and then raise them the few months needed to call them "spring chickens." The term used to mean "hatched in the spring" but now they could show up any time. If the market was good for poultry, spring chickens could be held longer to grow into more mature, heavier "roasters." The old egg-laying hens were sold for stewing or other long cooking processes, such as chicken soup.

Poultrymen quality-inspected the modern hen. By feeling the bones on each side of the egg vent, a poultryman could tell if a hen was laying eggs or not. If she wasn't, then she was "culled" out and became stew meat. Egg producers were beginning to discover a new advantage in the modernization program over the farmer who raised the heavy broiler hens to egg laying age for egg income and then sold that special breed of hen for meat while still young.

The New York market found that the nearby fresh white eggs being shipped in by the new eggs-only producer were superior in quality to the somewhat aged brown eggs at general stores. The brown eggs came from the meat-bred hens. But breeders had found the slimmer white egg producing Leghorn hens to be the best if you concentrated on egg production. The new people who followed Bodine's advice were using

Thus farmers were getting a special monetary reward if they modernized their production methods. This is what Bodine noticed in 1886: "Considerable attention is being paid by farmers and others to raising poultry for the early market; most of them in the old-fashioned way of setting the hens, while not a few are using artificial means, incubators, building warm roosts, and taking better care of their fowls in cold winter weather; some farmers feeding three times a day the year round for the purpose of gathering in the golden eggs, thinking it pays better than raising chickens (for meat)."

In the ten years after introduction of the incubator in 1880, Hunterdon's flocks increased 50 percent. Farmers near the big urban centers all up and down the East Coast were all doing the same thing, and trading all the up-to-date know-how through their new agricultural colleges and their experts.

The production near cities was growing steadi-

It would be two decades or more before the neat, clean, perfected poultry operation in this 1908 photo would be commonplace — automatic waterers, covered feed troughs, well-sealed coops to keep out predators, and fences to prevent wandering. The scene is near Quakertown and shows the outdoor summer growing of pullets as replacements for the hens kept indoors. (Stryker Collection.)

these. It is interesting to note, however, that the preference for white eggs over brown is local. The Boston market prefers brown eggs, for example.

ly and slowly. But although she had been modernized, the Hunterdon hen was still being treated in a rather sedate way. Then, in 1892, Joseph D. Wilson of Stockton blew the lid off these limitations and sent millions of farmers all over the nation lying awake nights, dreaming golden eggs.

Wilson was 25 years old at the time, newly married, working for his dad, and not liking it. "He was paying me $75 a year and I don't think he thought I was worth it," he commented years later.

Young Wilson tried raising some chickens on the side while working for his father, but that failed completely. One day, working on his father's farm in Rosemont, the idea came to him. Twelve months later, he had quadrupled his income, been investigated by the federal government for possible fraud, been written up in newspapers all over the country as a rather strange bird, and was on his way to a long and prosperous life and fortune. When he died in 1961 at the comfortable age of 92, he had witnessed the entire history of modern poultry raising in Hunterdon.

Wilson, the kind of genius who discovers the obvious that had stared millions of others in the face without result, remembered that newly hatched chicks don't need food the first few days of their life. Remnants of the yolk sac inside their bodies supply them with nutrients. This means you can send them through the mail. This means you don't have to have those brooding hens, as you do if you buy fertile eggs through the mail. And it means you don't have to spend a whole day driving down to the neighbor who has chicks. They can be dropped off at your home by the mail wagon, the new rural free delivery. Or you send your son to the post office a mile away in the wagon, and he's back with the chicks in an hour. You can buy the best quality chicks, too. You don't have to take what's nearby if you don't like them.

"Young chicks for sale, just hatched, distance no objection, 8 cents each," ran the advertisement in the *American Poultry Advocate*. Soon afterwards, Wilson cut up an old packing case, lined it with feathers and sent his first shipment of 50 chicks to A. J. Runyon of East Orange. "Runyon was the first to answer and he remained a customer until he died," Wilson noted. Runyon lived on Evergreen Place in East Orange, and his simple faith must have impressed Wilson, for he named his new hatchery Pine Tree Hatcheries.

The next shipment was 500 chicks to Illinois and it was the one that put Wilson on the map. The Chicago papers of the time reported the event, and everyone wondered whether it was some new kind of zany fraud. Wilson found a government postal inspector at his door. The man was so impressed when he saw the whole operation, he stayed to dinner. He had come to inspect fraud and there was none.

There were thousands of small hatcheries like Wilson's all over the country. They were selling hatchable eggs by mail, but not those lovable chicks. Yet, for several years none of them touched Wilson's idea. He was that far ahead of everyone else. His first year's receipts of $350 doubled and trebled and quadrupled and quintupled as several years went by.

Eventually others caught on, one of the first being Wilson's cousin, Richard Kerr, who shortly thereafter founded Kerr Chickeries in Frenchtown. The inventiveness of his cousin must have seemed fateful to Kerr, for by 1923 his firm was mailing out chicks by the railroad boxcar load.

Wilson himself was no slouch. His first homemade incubator held 400 eggs, and the last one he built held 100,000 eggs. Even his father bought some chicks from him and his early fan mail typically read: "Chicks arrived lively as crickets and clamoring for a square meal . . . too cute for anything!" Even President Grover Cleveland had to do something after he got out of office. He bought that new dream of the bucolic chicken farm in the country, and wound up a customer of Wilson's.

Hatcheryman-breeder Max De-Jonge of Ringoes records a hen's tag number on a trap nest chart to indicate she has laid an egg. Through the year he knows her daily production and her monthly average. Thus, the best laying hens are used to hatch chicks to maintain the "breeding line" of quality egg producers.

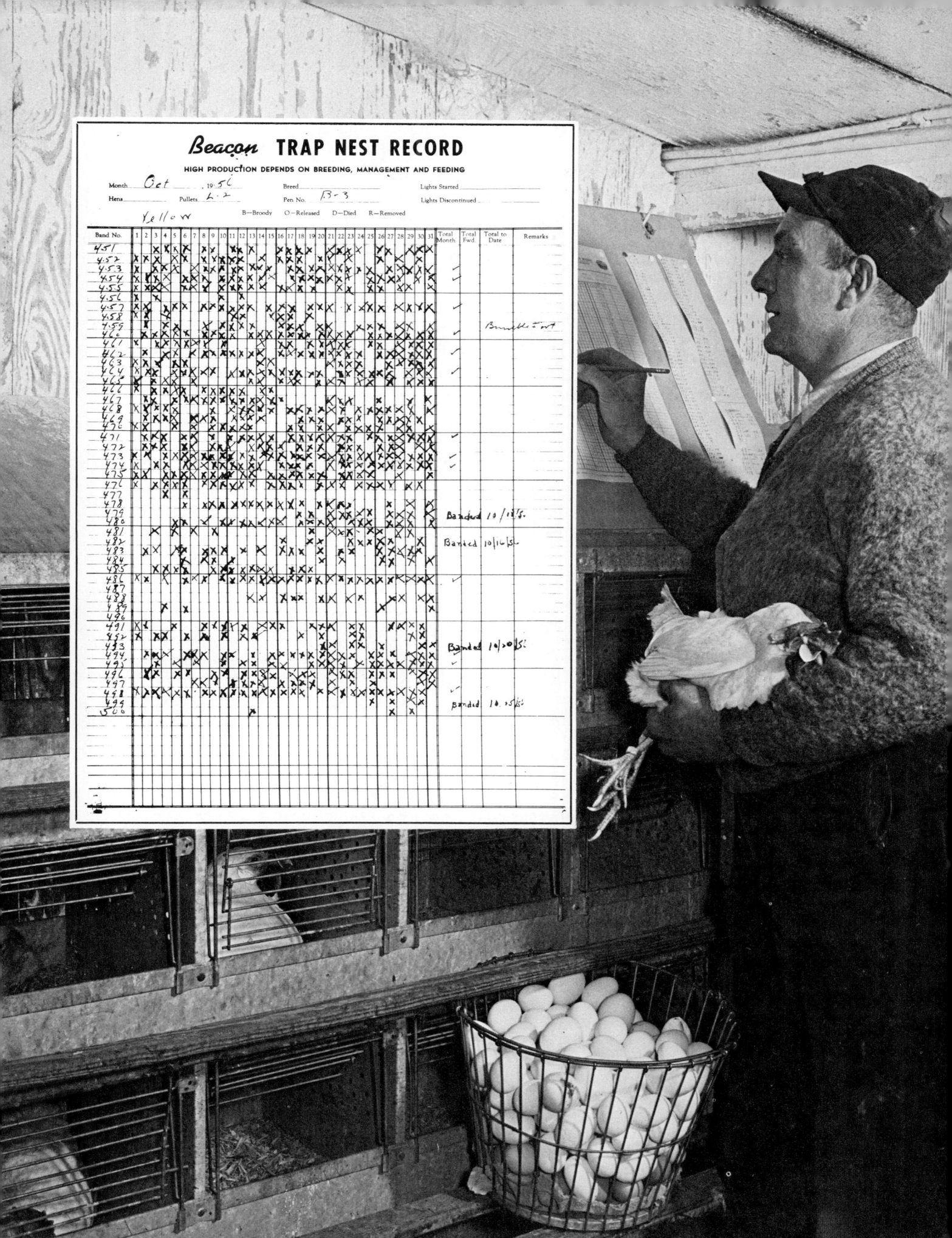

After the first four years or so, the others caught on, and Wilson was right in the middle of a business explosion that he had created. When he stepped out of it in 1945, the area around Stockton had a half dozen large hatcheries, and there were more in other parts of Hunterdon. The county produced more baby chicks than any other county in the state for a number of years, and was always in the forefront.

Wilson retired for the more sedate career of realtor, and he got an amusing shock when one day he told someone how, yes, he had been the first man in the United States to ship baby chicks by mail. They thought he was a crackpot, again! He managed to produce proof, and had the last laugh. He had started his career at a time when the modern working hen was the new reality, and there were thousands like him trying for new ways to sweeten that reality.

Breeding of hens now became the rule rather than the exception. Some hens are healthier than others. Select their eggs to hatch new chicks. Some hens laid more eggs than others. Select their eggs. Some hens tended to lay eggs year round. Select them. Some hens laid larger eggs. Take those.

It was impossible to tell which hen laid which egg in an open coop with nests in the corner, so the nests were given little latticed doors that quietly closed when the hen entered to lay an egg. The hatcheryman-breeder would then come through the coop several times a day, recording the kind of egg a hen laid, and releasing her to go and eat more mash for the next egg. Each hen carried a numbered tag to make identification easy.

For two decades, the Board of Agriculture had been pushing education. Farmers had given up evenings to walk or ride to the Grange halls and town halls and churches and hear talks like "Can A Profitable Living Be Made Raising Poultry?" Often, they had not been inspired. Now, in 1902, it was 20 years after the incubator and 10 years after Wilson, and the Board report for the year showed the inspiration was growing:

"The production of turkeys seems to be on the decrease, mainly because their roaming habits are incompatible with our present system of intensive farming and not from any fall in prices. The hen is now receiving more attention than ever before, and more careful attention and scientific feeding is resulting in a large increase in the egg product. H.S.O. Van Doren of Flemington has developed a flock of hens that yield an average of more than 200 eggs each year. Many others are doing nearly as well, and many farms today contain four and five well-populated henhouses."

Van Doren's figures were probably exaggerated, unless he also counted "peewees" — tiny thumbnail sized eggs that the earlier chicken laid a lot of at times. But the figures showed that the working hen was being taken very seriously.

Two other novelties showed up in Hunterdon's reports at the turn of the century:

"1904 . . . during November all hens went on strike, and owners of flocks numbering hundreds failed in many instances to get any eggs whatever and the same conditions prevailed up to December 15 . . . such a failure in egg production is not usual.

"1908: . . . poultry about as last year, although the high price of feed without an increase in the price of eggs tends to greatly lessen the profits of the business and a tendency is manifest to reduce many large flocks of fowls as much as 50 percent."

E. J. Rozzo of Quakertown increased his poultry production by putting out more chicks in the spring of 1942 in answer to the nation's appeal for greater food production. The coal-fed brooder stove with a thermostatic control sends out a blanket of hot air to keep the chicks comfortable. The sheet metal fence keeps them from wandering away from the heat. Once their fine fuzz turns to feathers, they will be let out to scratch for bugs on the range and grow up in the summer sunshine.

The 1904 strike was probably caused by some kind of disease making its rounds. Sometimes mild infections throw hens into a "moult" and they don't lay eggs again until they grow new feathers. And sometimes the whole flock may die from an infection. When you put lots of hens together in a small place you made it very easy for disease factors and parasites.

The 1908 report on rising feed prices versus poor egg prices was a permanent feature of mass producing eggs. For two years following the report, farmers increased their flocks again, because there was a turn-around and egg prices rose. This kind of rapid fluctuation would continue forever.

Whatever the problems, though, the kerosene incubator, and that fellow in Stockton with his mail-order chicks had shaken Hunterdon poultrymen quite a bit. There was money to be made. Or lost. Yet, going to a lecture institute to hear an expert on poultry every couple years and going home muttering complacently how "he's talking through a cocked hat" wasn't enough to put things on the winning side any longer. More was needed.

And so, in 1912, the first few visionary poultrymen of the county got together and organized the Hunterdon County Poultryman's Association. Rutgers' Extension Service began the same year. Fred Matthews of Lambertville got the use of the city hall, and invited Harry Lewis from the new Extension's Poultry Division. A small group of poultrymen talked things over, and agreed to found the organization.

They had disease to cope with. They had production to cope with. They had rapidly fluctuating markets to cope with. They might make a booming return on all that money and elbow grease they had invested in chicken coops and feeders. Or they might not do so well at all if the hens went on strike or they didn't follow the market forecasts closely. The organization, therefore, was another terminal in effectively disseminating new information to poultrymen. Of all the terminals, it was the most important, since local disease and other problems could be discussed. It was not the 20th century, after all. A few years earlier, a farmer might stand in the chicken shed in mid-winter and listen to the wind whistle through the loose boards and have

Poultry Grade AA

dreams. The dreams might include modest plans for repairing the building, or even of going all the way and building a coop to house 1,000 hens. There would be thoughts of better feed. Possibly, also, set up a deal with a hatcheryman-poultryman to sell fertile eggs at a premium price. Maybe Hunterdon could support a poultry club that would tour supermodern farms.

It was all beginning to happen. The modern egg industry in Hunterdon emerged between 1900 and 1930. The Board of Agriculture's Program for Agriculture in 1923 listed poultry as follows: 1) One poultry club. Continued; 2) Four culling demonstrations — caponizing and killing; 3) Poultry tour and field day; 4) Monthly meetings of poultry association; and 5) Monthly column in County Board News.

At the beginning of these first 30 years of the century, Hunterdon farmers had a quarter of a million hens. At the end of it they had a half million. Starting off, hens were still stick-in-the-muds from their recent past as brooders and averaged only 80 eggs a year. By 1930, they were producing a respectable 100 eggs a year.

Some of the farmer-businessmen were outstandingly large. Kerr shipped 3.5 million baby chicks out of Frenchtown in 1923 alone. Yet it was not a business for big operators. There were only two egg producers whose flocks went over several thousand hens. Hunterdon's average poultry farm had 100 to 400 laying hens. The census of 1929 found 2,230 farms had only 15 that did not have chickens. The humble hen had helped pull farmers through the declining values of the last century, and now she was sustaining them through the vast political and technological waves of modern times.

Among the major contributions to poultry farming was "sexing," a method whereby the sex of a chick can be determined soon after birth. Researchers first discovered that by crossing Rhode Island Reds with Barred Plymouth Rocks the baby cockerels early developed a light spot on their heads. Further experiments led to other hybridization of poultry, but automatic sexing was possible when the Barred birds were crossed with any other breed. Meanwhile, Japanese researchers developed a system of sexing through examination of the baby chick's vent, and it was common for Hunterdon poultrymen to hire Japanese specialists, armed with magnifying lenses, at hatching time. Today, sex can be determined before the chick is hatched.

Chicken thieves found Hunterdon easy pick-

While millions listened on WOR radio, Jinx Falkenberg of the Tex and Jinx Show tours Kerr's Hatchery in Frenchtown with James Weisel in the 1950s. At the left with Jinx's son is Jerry Zyck, a Hunterdon farmboy who became a *Democrat* reporter and went on to a long career as farm writer and publicist. His book, *Fertile Furrow, 50 Years Long,* is a history of the State Department of Agriculture. (Jim Weisel.)

ings, too! Nothing made a farmer or farm wife madder than to go out to the coop in the morning and find their flock decimated by human predators. Angry farmers got after the Board of Agriculture and the result was rather odd — tattooed chickens.

The featherless web of the hen's wing was coded with an ownership number, which was registered with the state police. Participating farmers nailed bold signs to the tree at the head of the lane: "Warning. Tattooed Chickens Protected by State Police." A surprising success during those early years, the program cut down on thievery and also gave aggravated victims a kind of quiet satisfaction to think of some scoundrel being caught redhanded with a tattooed chicken. A few actually were apprehended this way and successfully prosecuted.

County poultrymen's ties with the state Department of Agriculture and the Cooperative Extension Service were progressing nicely, even though many farmers still retained suspicions of book-learned professors. As one oldtimer used to say during the 1920s: "The more you read, the stupider you get!" Nonetheless, he somehow wound up purchasing a kerosene incubator and becoming so knowledgeable that neighbors who saw him as an ignorant immigrant were coming by the farm to see his set-up.

The modern hen was no cluck or brooder, and poultrymen took their lead from her. The anti-expert farmer who secretly read and followed the latest recommendations was commonplace. Similarly, poultrymen were sympathetic to new state disease control programs that were coming along to help secure the life of their flocks.

In 1925, the state began inspecting hatcheries for BWD, also called Pullorum, a bacterial infection transmitted by hens to their chicks. The infected chicks usually died the first few weeks of their lives

A blood test was used to identify infected breeders to eliminate them. The result was a clean flock of chicks. Hatcherymen could point to Pullorum-free flocks as a guarantee in their advertising.

The program was a landmark of sorts, for it represented the intrusion of a complex state program into private business with complete success and happiness on both sides. Farmers sat on the state Board of Agriculture and supervised the experts. When it came time to regulate themselves, they had no trouble working out a simple,

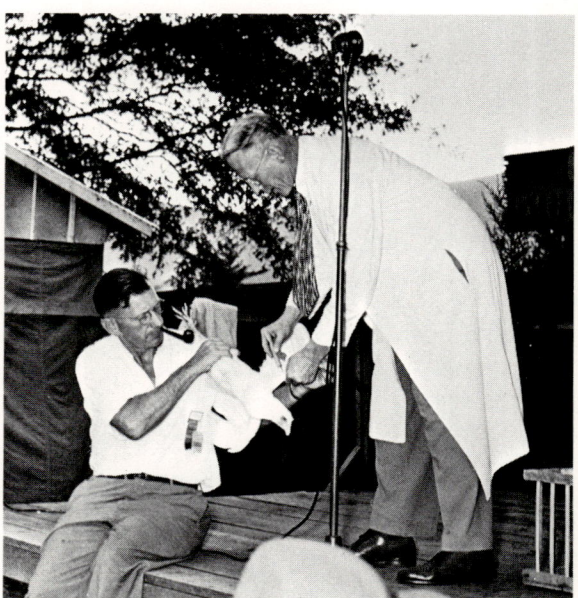

Dr. F. R. Beaudette, Rutgers poultry specialist, shows how poultrymen vaccinate their pullets against disease at the 1949 Flemington Fair. Holding the hen is W. Andrew Cray, who took the first poultry short course given by Rutgers around 1912 and operated a 60,000-chick hatchery near Dilts Corner for many years.

comfortable system.

Not all was harmonious, however, as the pioneers who created and pushed for the new programs were not always sitting on the front porch smiling at all the money they were making. One day, Clifford Synder, the County Board president, put through a phone call to County Agent Ed Gauntt and asked for some help. He sounded mad as a wet hen. His chickens were dying.

"So I go up and I look at the chickens and I open a couple of them up, and I say, you've got BWD," Gauntt recalled of the event.

"'Now, wait a minute,' Cliff said. 'These are Charlie Cane's chickens!'

"I don't give a damn whose chickens they are. I'm telling you, it's BWD, it looks to me.

"'You better be sure.'"

By this time, Gauntt was shaking in his shoes. It seemed impossible that the chickens had BWD. They had all been tested at Cane's hatchery a few miles away in Rosemont. The "experts" had cleared them. True, they were from the state Department of Agriculture and not the educational Extension Service, but to a farmer, all "experts" ran together.

So the experts were responsible! Gauntt was an expert. Snyder had backed those experts for over a decade against farmer inertia, scorn and outright insult. Now the chickens were dying. What was going on? Gauntt drove all the way to New Brunswick and Extension Professor Fred R. Beaudette's pathology laboratory. One of the top poultry pathologists in the world, Beaudette's research led to vaccines for Fowl Pox, Laryngotracheitis and Newcastle disease. One day his work with embryonated eggs to produce vaccine for humans would change the world industry.

"You guys sure don't know much, do you?" Beaudette laughed when Gauntt showed him the obviously BWD diseased birds.

"I told him whose chickens they were," Gauntt said, and the professor put them under the microscope to make sure. Yes, it was so, and Snyder was informed. Snyder called up Cane, who was furious, too. He was a state poultry specialist himself, before he opened his Rosemont firm that earned the reputation of being one of the best hatcheries in the country.

"They'd all been tested for BWD and he had a clean flock, supposedly. But they had used a rapid test method and it had gone bad. Charlie Cane would speak to me," Gauntt explained. "He told Cliff to kill the rest of the chickens and he'd bring him a whole new batch, which he did. But it cost Charlie lots of money."

None of the men stayed angry for long. They were friends, and all three were doing their best for local farming, and having an exciting time of it. But, for a moment, they were looking at each other like the three men who went to sea in a sieve. The changes they pushed and pioneered and risked their careers on sometimes came too fast and drove them to aggravation. They kept on, anyway, and by 1930 Cane and another hatcheryman, James Weisel, equalled Wilson's startling effect on the poultry industry with one of their own.

Wilson had the genius to notice the obvious. Weisel and Cane had the genius to try something that no one thought would work. It was not much fun at the start, a time when doing anything new took guts or lunacy or both. The stock market crash of 1929 had not hit hard yet, but it had frozen everyone's optimism, and it was still going down as 1930 opened.

Cane and Weisel were young men in their prime, the latter only a few years out of Rutgers and working with Kerr as a top flight poultry breeder. Cane had his own hatchery. Both were prominent in poultry circles and both were fool enough to think they could do something useful for Hunterdon poultrymen. That moment came when they were discussing the obvious, and said, "Let's try this and see if we can get it to work."

The scene was a windy, bone-chilling March night as the two men drove home from a state meeting for farm leaders in Trenton. They had heard Warren Oley of the state Bureau of Markets tell farmers about the successful new vegetable and produce auctions in South Jersey. Oley suggested the same could be done with eggs. For sure, a good idea, but good ideas are a penny a dozen.

"You know these fellows at Rutgers will give you the best information and help they can. But they don't actually guarantee it will work!" is how one local farm leader characterized the situation. Nonetheless, Cane and Weisel mulled over Oley's advice.

"My goodness, we ought to be able to have some way of auctioning off eggs in Hunterdon County, because our poultrymen are getting ridiculous prices," Weisel reported. "These dealers go around and offer any price at all to farmers, probably averaging five or 10 cents a dozen less than the eggs should bring."

Small poultrymen were getting short-changed. City buyers came around in trucks and offered them dirt-cheap prices, because they knew these small-timers did not have the time or money to market their eggs better. For the small operator, cleaning, grading, and quality control of egg production took work and hope. The hope was dimming and there remained the possibility of a vicious downhill cycle, where egg quality might drop so much that no one would buy them.

Men like Cane and Weisel would not lose out no matter what, because they were modern and established. Yet, they could help their own prosperity just as much by helping the other poultrymen in the field. So they took off with it.

David Agans of Three Bridges, state Grange master and former state legislator, threw his considerable support into the project. Oley, from the

Poultry Grade AA

Leaders of the Flemington Auction Market at its inception were, standing, left to right: Wallace Suydam, secretary; Newton Gottshall, vice-president; Ed Nief; Theodore Apgar; Clayton Stains, auction master; and Alben E. Jones, State Bureau of Marketing. Seated, left to right, are: Edwin Gauntt, County Agent; William Grossman; Charles Cane, president; James Weisel; and Wilmer Lawrence. Treasurer Percy Niece was absent.

state, and Alben E. Jones, state poultry marketing specialist, were happy for anyone to play the guinea pig with their ideas. Ten of the most prominent poultrymen in the county joined Cane and Weisel on the platform. No one knew whether it would be a gallows platform or a celebration platform. An egg auction for Hunterdon would mean no more desperation selling, they predicted.

The organizational meeting for July 11, 1930, was postponed a few days to attract a larger attendance. Officers and directors of the new cooperative egg auction were elected, and the first trial auction was set for August 1. The Flemington Chamber of Commerce, eager to help its farmer customers, donated six months free use of the basement of the store across the street from County Agent Gauntt's office in the county courthouse.

Charles M. Wooley, then director of the Trenton markets, was set to be the auctioneer at the first auction he had ever handled. A well-publicized pep rally was held in the courthouse two days before the auction. 110 poultrymen attended, but only seven of them decided to pay the modest fee and join. It looked as though the idea was on its way to a quiet and early death.

Ed Gauntt decided to make the funeral procession a noisy and outrageous one.

"I went around and I talked up the auction and farmers kind of held back on the thing. Finally, I said, now look, I'm not looking for work. You birds are either going to support this or we're going to skip the whole thing! This isn't any money in my pocket, one way or the other. I'm helping you, but if you don't want to be helped, just say so, and we'll drop it.

Gauntt reported that at the first auction there were only 39 egg cases placed, representing less than one percent of what Hunterdon's poultrymen had produced that week.

"So I wrote an article in the paper, headlined 'Farmers In Hunterdon County Are Not Interested In An Auction, We'll Skip It!' " Instead of winding up with an embarrassed foot in his mouth, Gauntt succeeded in kicking some life into the idea. "They began to call on the telephone, pledging I'll pledge 10 cases, I'll pledge all mine, and so forth. Then I called another meeting and they came out, and the auction was started and it went right off. The first thing you know we were getting above top (New York) quotations for Hunterdon County eggs!"

If you look at the photo of the first board of directors, and Gauntt, they all look a little glum. Maybe they were wondering if this was not all some kind of pipe dream. But if you look at the decade celebration photo ten years later, you may detect more comfortable faces, though perhaps still wondering how they wound up with the first and largest poultry auction in the United States.

Possibly, the 2,000 poultrymen belonging to the marketing co-op did not care. What they cared about was that their top quality work was netting two or three cents a dozen above the New York market prices, instead of four to six cents below it. It's impossible to estimate how many farm families that extra dime carried through the depression years.

Impossible to say what two young fools and a rude county agent had hatched, but everyone agreed it was worth it by joining the auction. There was very little to lose except the time and effort of trucking eggs to the Nevius Store basement, and paying the $1 a year membership fee. In fact, the rush to join was so fast that by the end of the second auction, Herbert Rodenbaugh, a retired merchant, quit his two-day-a-week job as auction master because he found himself working seven days a week. Clayton Stains, a young contractor from the Frenchtown area, took over, and stayed with the job as long as the auction lasted.

When Weisel came back from a world poultry conference in London and got to the third weekly auction, he found there were 56 enthused members shipping eggs. Poultrymen were getting the news from the ones who were trying it, sitting down and figuring out what two cents or four cents or six cents a dozen might mean to their livelihood, and checking back the following weeks to see if the whole thing had not disappeared like a midsummer night's dream, and then getting their $1 bill out and signing up.

At the end of a couple months, members who found their eggs selling so well were clamoring for a second department of the auction to sell poultry for meat. Poultrymen had no use for the young roosters that came mixed in with the hen chicks, so they raised them for three months and looked for a place to sell them for meat. Likewise, when the laying hens got too old to lay a lot of eggs, their owners needed a place to sell them.

Cane and Weisel marked the first anniversary of their convictions by discussing the new poultry auction idea with the other directors in March of 1931. There had been no cooperative egg auctions anywhere in the country to learn from. There were no poultry auctions, either. In April, at a survey meeting, directors heard members give their pros and cons for the idea. They also heard many prominent poultry leaders estimate the idea would flop. Two weeks later the Flemington Auction Market was having its first successful poultry auction at the Flemington Fairgrounds. Trucks rolled in with crates holding a dozen or so hens. Wooley got up and did his magic, and the livestock dealers rolled out in trucks filled with hens.

As the first year of operation closed in August, the farmers found they had sold a half million dollars worth of eggs. Spurred on by success, the directors purchased the 40,000 square-foot old Empire Cut Glass building on Park Avenue in Flemington in March 1932. Within two years the auction had established a solid base of sales and was growing steadily each year. In another two years, in 1934, the logical thing happened — one farmer brought a chicken crate with two little piglets in it to the poultry auction, and asked Wooley if he could auction them off along with the chickens.

It was the year after the depression had hit bottom with a sickening crunch on farm prices all over the nation. New Deal programs were coming in all over the place to help farmers in one way or another, but the farmers would just as

A fat sow ready for market is taken off a farmer's pickup and wheeled in a cage at the Flemington Auction Market.

Wooden crates of eggs holding 30 dozen each await shipment at the Flemington Auction Market in a storage cellar. Numbers stamped on the end labels identified the producer. Poultrymen who produced top quality eggs became known by bidders and could earn more per dozen than lesser known producers.

soon find the answer in their own organizations. If fair price auctioning could be done with chickens, the piglets proved to a lot of farmers that it could be done with any livestock. The farmers wanted a general livestock auction that could help people with cows, pigs, sheep, and goats, as well.

The farmer-directors of the auction, by now fearless of what they could do, went ahead and the new livestock auction worked. People like Oley and Jones from the state agencies helped with all the expertise they could provide, and took the success story to farmers all over the state to encourage other auctions.

In Flemington, the auction grew steadily through the depression years and by 1940 it employed 57 people and handled $2 million worth of eggs and livestock each year. For Hunterdon farmers, the grey gloomy clouds of the depression concealed a golden egg. Those were years when every man in the state was scrambling to find something behind those clouds.

Some were not so particular about how they found that golden bounty. The egg dealers, livestock dealers, and other middlemen were not all of them happy with the top quality eggs and the fair-priced livestock they found at Flemington's auction. Some thought it might be better to go back to the days when they drove pickup trucks over the dusty back roads in search of a demoralized farmer willing to sell his eggs dirt cheap.

Right from the start there were those who wondered if things might not be better if they could kill the auction or destroy its free-bid quality. So they decided to go on strike, a beautiful idea. A thousand cases of eggs were going through every week. See what those eggs would look and smell like after they had set in the storeroom a couple weeks, losing their quality while every poultryman in the county hollered with anguish. See what those happy country bumpkins would settle for after they had been knocked around a bit by some people with a little more smarts.

"I remember one auction particularly, where the buyers got together and decided they wouldn't bid," County Agent Gauntt recalled. "Charlie Wooley put up four cases of eggs and nobody bid on them. He looked at me. What do I do? I said, try one case. So he tried another lot, one case, nobody would bid. So I said, put up two cases, but nobody bid. They all stood there. I told Carlie the auction's over.

"He got down from the platform and said, what the hell are we doing to do with all those eggs, about 1,200 cases." While the auctioneer scratched his head in confusion, a smiling and silent crowd of strikers began to move in on Gauntt.

"The funny part of it was, soon as the auction was over, soon as I said, you're done, Charlie, there was a fellow by the name of Windy Stryker comes up to me and says, now you let me pick out my lot numbers (favorite producers) and I'll give you two cents over the top quotation." A different kind of New Deal was being offered — one without any competitive bidding. And one based on muscle.

"I said you go jump in the lake! There's not an egg going out of here to any of you fellows; you're not going to get an egg!" All of a sudden the smart operators found out they had no anguished country bumpkins to buy eggs from cheaply. "'We gotta have 'em!' I said, I don't care, you've had your chance, you're done! I just arbitrarily ran that damn auction. Charlie Cane was president, but he was up in Rosemont, so I just absolutely refused to give them a case of eggs. They cried on my shoulder; they did everything. You should have seen them at the next auction. They bid their heads off to get those eggs!" What happened to those 1,200 case of eggs worth $15,000 and sitting in the storeroom and getting old? Gauntt got on the phone to one of the biggest egg dealers in the New York area and told him to expect a shipment of 1,200 cases of eggs. He got the market price for them, a strategy that had been worked out in advance by the directors.

Clayton Stains handled an even nastier strike several years later against the poultry sales. Striking poultry dealers demanded the loan of a meeting room so they could get their independents badgered into cooperation and lay plans for the offers they were going to make to the defeated poultrymen. It added insult to injury to demand a meeting room so they could subvert the free bidding process.

While they planned their war strategy, an employe of the auction market lay in the crawl space under their meeting room and heard every word. The auction was held. Only a couple of dealers defied their fellows and purchased a few crates of chickens. The united dealers had one of their people follow one of the rebels all the way to Somerville and ran his truck off the road.

Poultry Grade AA

The whole effort failed, when an employee of the auction stepped out of the crowd and bid for the remaining 1,200 crates of chickens. Stains had already been on the phone to Philadelphia and had made a deal with a company there to take the chickens. The dealers left the auction muttering to themselves.

"We had 1,200 crates of chickens to change and weigh and feed and water. We started about 3 o'clock in the afternoon, and finished watering them about 4 o'clock the next morning," Stains recalled. "We had Al Dorf, and his brother Paul, and Henry Steps as truckers. I think we had four loads overall. They had a state police escort all the way to Philly. We did that for about three weeks, and then the buyers decided they couldn't get anywhere and they came back. The strike leader later became one of our best friends."

During those golden-egg years, from 1930 to 1940, the cooperation between poultrymen, their leaders, and the state's experts reached a kind of perfection. When the professors from the Cooperative Extension Service visited every month or two to lecture on the new feeds, the new disease tests, the new technologies, they usually found the meeting room in the auction building standing room only. Everyone was there, from the big producer with his 2,500-bird flock to the farmer whose wife had 300 hens.

Mrs. William Davis of Three Bridges was one of those modest producers. "We got a letter through the mail," she recalled, "and they said they'd like Mr. Davis to stop in the office for a talk. We thought they were going to find fault or something, you know. He says to me, well, you'll have to go along, because I don't know anything about the eggs. You grade and case them all and everything.

"So we went in and they said, well, our eggs were of such good quality, we should be getting more money. They put them in the Grade A Program!"

Along with a half dozen directors of the Flemington Auction Market are the men and women who had the courage and imagination to join the new auction in its early days. These "pioneers" had good reason to celebrate. (Charles Cane.)

Poultry Grade AA

This was the New Jersey Certified Fresh Egg program set up by the state in 1938 with the Flemington auction, and the state's four other new auctions. A special processing plant was built outside of Flemington, where eggs were shipped for inspection, and left the building in special cartons labelled premium quality eggs controlled by state inspections. Each egg was hand candled with a light that showed the interior of the egg.

Newspaper advertisements over the state popularized the super quality and housewives paid premium prices. Women like Mrs. Davis collected their eggs three times a day, carefully cleaned and graded them, and kept them in their cool damp cellars where conditions were perfect for storage.

During this golden age there were poultry banquets and picnics with chicken calling contests, and breeders' clubs taking their members all over the northeast to study the newest methods, and Hunterdon poultrymen being looked on as fit material to serve on the state Board of Agriculture, which they frequently chaired.

Hunterdon's 2,000-plus poultrymen expanded their flocks 50 percent between 1930 and 1940. They installed new electric lights in coops to make up for short winter days and give their hens the 13 hours of daylight needed for laying eggs.

Then came World War II, and the golden age was replaced with something else. The 15-year period that began in 1940 with the war was equally prosperous but entirely different. By 1955, the eggs were still coming out of Hunterdon by the millions, yet poultrying as a farm family enterprise was finished.

Door prize winners line up in front of the chalk board in the Flemington Auction Market meeting room. The room was filled each month for a special program on an aspect of poultrying. On this occasion the ladies were invited as well. Two of the prizes were plastic-coated egg pails that resulted in fewer broken eggs than the old wire pails.

A flock of pullets on the outdoor range.

These were years of transition, when a poultryman decided to wind up a prosperous and eventful career in a comfortable way, or shift gears and get in on the ground floor of still another wave of tremendous change in poultrying. During this time, 2,000 birds made a sizable flock, and could mean a comfortable living for a family, quite an expansion over the family poultry flocks of the 1930s. But the period began with World War II, and no one had that much time to think about the changes. The nation was clamoring for more food for emergency war needs. By the end of the war five years later, Hunterdon poultrymen had gone from producing six million eggs a year to producing nine million.

They did not increase their flock size 50 percent to do this. Cane and Weisel and a dozen other prominent chick breeders in the county were simply breeding more productive hens. In addition, the prices paid for eggs were high, so old debts were being paid off, and new improvements were being made in better buildings and

Jacob Oster of Three Bridges and County Agent Dwight Babbitt inspect a hen. Oster's family-operated hatchery often placed first in egg laying contest tests.

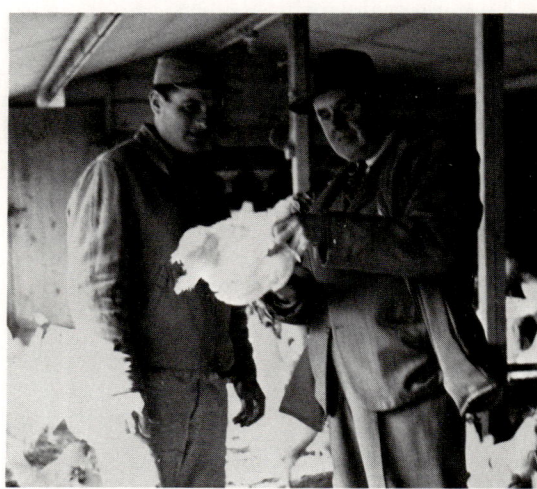

Leaders in Hunterdon, and often in the United States, the County Poultry Breeders Club was in New Hampshire visiting New England hatcherymen when this was taken in 1954. They proved their expertise through tests like those at the Flemington Egg Laying Contest, which placed first in the country that year. Left to right are: Paul Wirtz of Lebanon, president; George Japp of Ohio; Max Treiber of Frenchtown; William Rapp of Farmingdale; John Whetherby and Edward Bean, the New Hampshire hosts; Howard Woodward of Englishtown; County Agent Dwight Babbitt; Jerry Traub of Bound Brook; George Lachenmayr of Whitehouse; Donald DeMott of Flemington; Lamar Sexton of Whitehouse; and Harry Harper of Freehold.

Production Summary of Each U. S. Official Egg Laying Test for 1953-54

Test	No. of Birds Entered	Points Per Bird	Eggs Per Bird	Per Cent Mortality	Ave. Egg Size Oz. Per Doz.
New Jersey (Hunterdon)	611	247.9	239.3	13.2	24.72
Western New York	884	243.8	233.7	8.7	24.86
Florida	936	243.2	235.3	11.0	24.68
Oklahoma	650	243.0	234.4	14.2	24.74
Rhode Island	624	231.9	221.5	11.1	24.92
Connecticut (Storrs)	1,326	231.8	220.2	14.2	25.04
Pennsylvania	793	231.7	220.1	10.5	25.04
Missouri	780	229.6	221.4	13.1	24.74
Arizona	494	225.4	222.2	11.1	24.10
California	520	223.8	213.9	16.5	24.92
Farmingdale	728	214.8	208.7	17.3	24.58
All Tests	8,346	233.8	224.8	12.7	24.79

Poultry Grade AA

equipment. Every possible method was used to run a more efficient operation.

Paul Wirtz of Clinton Township remembers how he studied poultry husbandry at Rutgers University and did a market survey in 1937 to find the best rural area to found a new hatchery business with his brother, Henry. Not surprisingly he found Flemington had the strongest auction. He came to Hunterdon to get in on the ground floor. It takes years to develop a good blood line of breeding hens, and the war found Wirtz well underway. There was a wartime poultry boom and his hatchery was needed.

By 1946 the operation was going well, and Wirtz wrote an article for the *New Jersey Farm & Garden* magazine describing the intensive design and technical ingenuity that went into his three-story Connecticut-style house with its several thousand laying hens.

"Labor saving on the poultry farm is the use of a combination of devices and well-planned practices, taking into consideration both the welfare of the birds and the poultryman himself. No fancy gadget, however, will ever replace a certain amount of personal contact between the poultryman and his birds. I believe the best labor-saving device should be the poultryman's head — his own good common sense.

Efficiency is demonstrated by Paul Wirtz as he feeds hens in the Wirtz brothers three-story Connecticut-style coop in Clinton Township. Every detail had been worked out to make the maximum use of manpower — right down to the scrub brush on the feed and egg conveyor that was used when rinsing out the watering pans. (Paul Writz.)

"Suppose we make an imaginary trip through our three-story laying house, and I'll point out some of the labor-saving devices we employ.

"We are just getting a load of feed. The truck backs up against the loading platform. We load the feed — 15 bags at a time — on our one ton electric hoist and take it to the third floor. Here we dump most of it into bins, total capacity 10 tons. Chutes on the first and second floor enable us to draw out feed as we need it.

"Our first trip in the morning, we feed pellets and collect eggs. We put the pellets and egg baskets on the carrier which runs on overhead tracks, and push through the double swinging doors which require no latching. These doors are at the front of the pen, so the birds have to move only a few steps back to get out of the way. The noise of the carrier on the track signals the birds that someone is coming, enabling us to walk through the pens rather fast.

"We start feeding pellets and collecting eggs in the last pen. While we are there, let's take a look around. There are drop pits taking in all of the back part. These pits are cleaned three or four times a year by shovelling the manure out the back windows into a truck. On one side of the pen are the nests, on the other is an oversized grit and shell hopper, holding over 100 pounds of each. There are several feed hoppers hardly a step away from the carrier. As fountains, we use refrigerator pans with an automatic float set in an 18-inch tile, which acts as a drain.

"We scrub the fountain with a brush and dump the water into the tile. Then we feed the pellets. The birds come out of the nests, making it easier to collect the eggs. The eggs are mostly clean, because we have a deep, built-up litter, kept dry by adding hydrated lime when necessary.

"As we move through the pens, the job of cleaning fountains, feeding pellets, and collecting eggs is repeated. Back in our feed room, we place the egg baskets on our elevator and — after collecting the eggs on all three floors — we take them into the basement to our egg-holding and grading rooms.

"On our afternoon trip we place enough feed on the carrier to feed the entire floor (seven pens), feeding grain on our trip in, and cleaning fountains, filling mash hoppers, and collecting eggs on our way out.

"Perhaps this explanation of what we do will help other poultrymen to reason out ways of

A poultryman demonstrates his automatic pan watering system in a photo taken for the Extension Service. The porcelain pan sits on a tub, and the pipeline supplies water to a fixed level with a shut-off valve. The round tin at his feet is placed in the pan and fills up the middle so chickens cannot wade in it. Clean, fresh water is supplied at all times to the half-grown hens — called pullets — in the background.

saving work on their farms. Labor-saving, to put it briefly, is merely a matter of common sense applied to the poultryman's own habits and methods. If we save only 10 minutes a day, that amounts to nearly three days a year. I could do a lot with that three days. Couldn't you?"

After the war, a great many poultry farmers developed new work habits and new equipment. The result was a postwar boom in egg production all over the nation. The cost of everything had begun to rise faster, but the demand for eggs was there and so were profits. If farmers were adventurous and willing to deal in expansion plans that risked a lot of their capital, they could still succeed.

New conditions tended to discourage smaller producers from making big, new efforts. But any farm family that wanted to could go this way.

The Annual Egg and Chick Show, March 1939, held at the Grandview Grange in Flemington. The man in the center is Stacey Opdyke, a Granger. Featured, in addition to the chicks, are promotional brochures from feed companies. And a demonstration of chick sexing — everything up-to-date that a poultry farmer ought to know about.

The important thing to know was that it was not going to slow down, this new trend towards a more cash intensive poultry flock.

Five years after Wirtz's first article, a second was published, showing his new, square, one-story building containing 27,000 square feet and 8,000 busy leghorns. The man that could take care of the three-story Connecticut-style house with its several thousand birds, could now care for this 8,000-bird flock in the same amount of time! The new building had bulk feed bins that could be filled from a feed truck without human labor. It had automatic mash feeders that took the feed from the holding tanks and fed it in precise amounts to the 8,000 layers. The feeders were long troughs with moving paddles that carried the feed all over the huge 143 by 192 foot building. It had huge air blowers to prevent build-up of stagnant air on hot summer days. It had a furnace to heat the 27,000 square feet and keep winter temperatures from going below 35 degrees.

Wirtz no longer removed dozens of tons of chicken manure from the pits underneath the roosts with a shovel and wheelbarrow. He now used a special pit, nine feet deep and wide enough to fit a tractor with a front-end loader. Cost per hen for the building? Lower than for the Connecticut-style built five years ago with none of these conveniences. Why? Because every detail had been gone over a dozen times by Wirtz, whose second poultry house was two and one-half times more efficient than the first; 1950 was

Poultry Grade AA

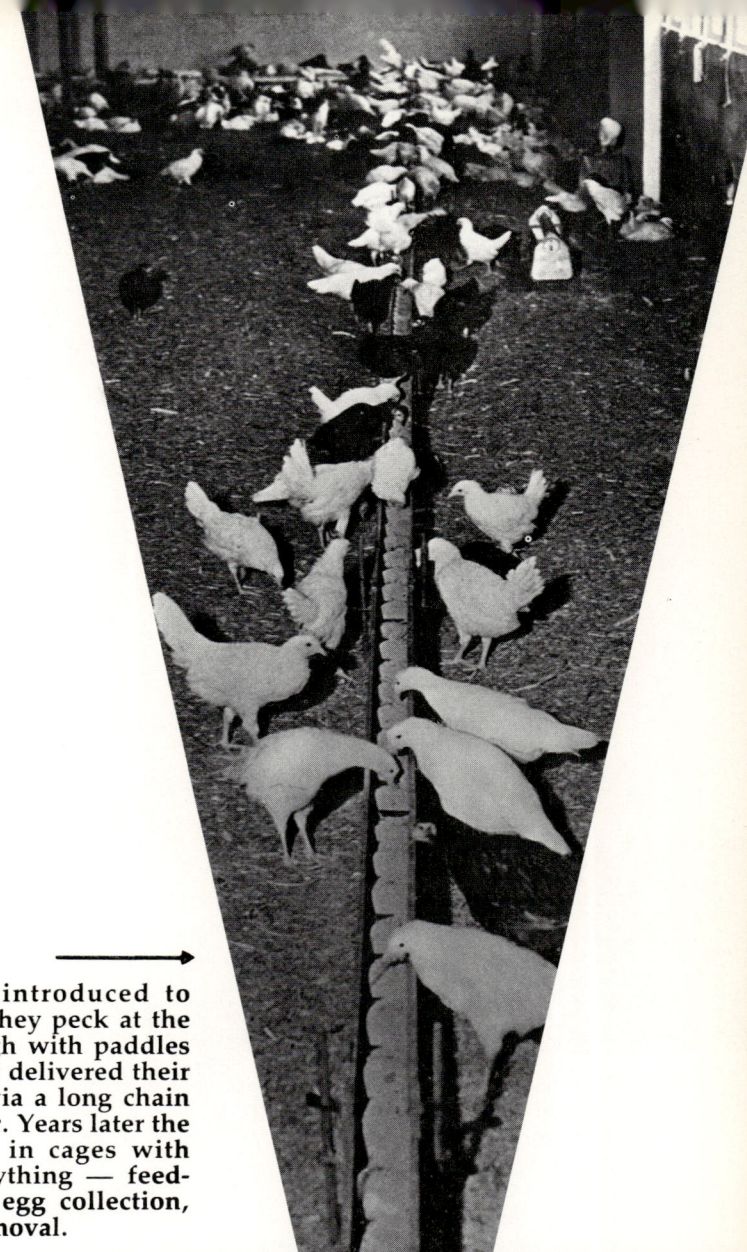

two and one-half time more efficient than 1945.

What happened was part of the expanding economic productivity of the nation as a whole. In 1940, the poultry-egg price index established with 1910 as a base of 100 was standing at around 100, just as it had in 1910. By 1945, it was up to 162. By 1948, it had more than doubled and hit an historic peak of 218.

So had feed costs, land costs, costs of every kind. The money was flowing in faster and out faster. It was like a quiet, broad stream that narrows into a fast moving rapids. New skills were important, and, most of all, one needed to see that there was no end to it.

Wirtz's second house might seem a culmination of the modern efficiency methods he worked on with the first one. But the houses were actually from two different eras, if not centuries. The first was based on design efficiency; everything was done by hand, or almost. The efficiency came from a study of what was done by hand, and then the refined planning of manual labor.

After the three-story Connecticut-style building on the Wirtz farm came this huge, square, one-story structure that cut labor to the bone. About the only time the poultryman needed to enter his "egg factory" was to collect eggs from the walled-off nesting area.

Chickens are introduced to automation as they peck at the long steel trough with paddles which have just delivered their ration of feed via a long chain driven by motor. Years later the chickens were in cages with automatic everything — feeding, watering, egg collection, and manure removal.

Poultry Grade AA

In the new hen house, hand labor was avoided like the plague. The entire feeding operation ran off a dutiful and efficient time clock, controlling the automatic feeders. Manure removal went 10 or 20 or 50 times faster with a tractor doing the work. And automatic waterers fed fresh water 24 hours a day.

When the cold spells came, thermostatically controlled fans kept the air from being stagnant, and the automatic furnace came on if needed. Only the eggs were still being picked by hand. And out in the room where they were taken for cleaning and weighing and packing, high speed cleaning and automatic machine weighing were coming into their own.

Eggs arrive from the hens in wire pails, to be inspected and polished by Mrs. George Pearce and her daughters, Peggy Ann and Mary Jane, of Whitehouse Station. At left is a 1940s machine egg grader, a clearer view of which is the one below, right, operated by Robert Crane of Pittstown. The eggs roll down the track at right and are lifted one by one onto the looped scales by a lever. Extra-large eggs tip the first scale and roll down, while the next scale drops the large eggs and so on.

Leslie Black of Sandy Ridge, an Extension Service man, was pioneering in washing methods. No more little piece of sandpaper to scrape off dirt flects and an egg scale that held only one egg at a time.

Would it be possible to have automatic egg-gathering? Tiny metal hands that reached into the nest and plucked the freshly laid eggs? No doubt there were men all over the east coast egg market lying awake at day's end and wondering how it might be done.

Wirtz's new building was a part of this new era. What would happen to the smaller family farm, with its couple thousand laying hens and now obsolescent set-ups? They could hold on, though only in a delaying action. Egg prices were flying high, and instead of going the expensive innovative way, much lower costing improvements could be made.

Around 1950 there was a strong influx of city people and displaced persons from Europe who had the capital to erect a moderate-sized cinder block coop that might be as effective as Wirtz's 1945 coop, or a little more so. Egg prices were good enough to pay off the investment in a few years. But they only had until 1955 to do it.

Between 1950 and 1955, Hunterdon's egg production zoomed up another 50 percent. By the latter year, it was all over, and automation had won the future.

Oscar Grossman of Frenchtown, whose father had stuck his neck out with Cane and Weisel in founding the auction market, put it simply: "There was still money to be made. In a good year, a poultryman could pay off the bad years. But only the larger producers tended to have the money to hold out during the bad years. The smaller ones were out."

This was because in 1955 egg prices began going up and down from year to year. It was a reflection of the new, automated industry, and also there were plenty of eggs for everyone. No more lean war years to remember. Consumer tastes might shift towards other foods.

At this point in time, the small poultry farmers were laying plans to leave the business, if they had not already. It might take two or three years for a poultryman to see that the writing on the wall of modern life was not going to dissolve, but by 1960 people were not kidding themselves anymore.

"Congress should ask, should the family-type farmer have a role in the economy of the country or should efforts be made to preserve the family farm?" Wirtz stated bluntly when interviewed by a newspaper in 1959.

George Lachenmayr over in Whitehouse Station, a neighbor of Wirtz, was even blunter:

"This is a real depression in the egg business. The worst I have seen in my 30 years in the business. What to do about it — there is no answer to that. When it gets worse, the farmer will just be wiped out. That is what comes naturally."

The federal government took one look at the high producing automated operations that could produce trillions of eggs, another look at the small farm family that could produce only a fraction of that, and a third look at the "consumer" who always tended to vote favorably during election years if food prices had been low. Should federal money be spent to help hundreds of thousands of small farm families continue doing the fine egg raising work they were doing? Keep the industry one of open opportunity for anyone willing to work like the blazes? No.

The large farms of the future were not going to be in Hunterdon, because the area was becoming urbanized and land prices and building prices were high. The southern states were more fertile, with cheap land, cheap labor, lots of open spaces, and no one to complain about odors. Yet, some men loved farming and the area so much they were not going to quit.

One was Lachenmayr, who in 1959 had 16,000 laying hens. He worked 10 hours a day, seven days a week. So did his wife. So did their children. He could not get good labor. New businesses and industries were moving in to the county, siphoning off the available workers. Lachenmayr said of those days:

"You know, you shovel the manure out from a house 400 feet long and it's got 15,000 chickens in it. That's a job. Now who the hell do you hire?

"The younger fellows got so they wouldn't work with a shovel any more. I sometimes made fun. I showed them how it was, I said, there's only one thing — that shovel's got no motor, and that wheelbarrow's got no motor. You've got to push it, see?"

Push a wheelbarrow loaded with 200 pounds of chicken manure? Nobody laughed. And Lachenmayr went crazy. "I put the whole house in cages! I put 15,000 cages in!" Cages equals total automation. Each chicken had a square-foot sized cage. The chicken eats from a mechanized feed trough, just outside the cage, and it drinks from a similar trough.

Its golden egg rolls down the wire floor of the cage to a trough with a conveyor belt, which goes to the egg room where women wait to clean and grade it and pack it in cases, using semi-automatic machines. The manure? The shovels

A modern post-war chicken coop is emptied of dried manure and litter by a tractor with a hydraulic scoop. Straw or other litter was spread on the coop floor and, as it became covered with droppings, more was thrown down and a layer was gradually built up.

all have motors on them these days.

Cages had been around for years when Lachenmayr made his move. Everyone was afraid to try them, even Lachnemayr. He'd tried 500 on a free trial basis years earlier and they'd worked well, but he got rid of them. Now he was filling up one of his long coops with cages that engineers had been fine tuning for efficiency.

"I was the first big sale for the manufacturer who made cages. The Agriculture Department, the Extension Service, they all were here and looking, they all thought I was nuts. Everybody thought I was crazy to put cages in. They couldn't see it. Not even the doctors and all the high-credit guys in the Extension Service, who couldn't see anything in it. Oh, Oscar Grossman, he hollered like hell he would never put cages in. But he put cages in, also. Everybody's got cages."

That's where the story of family poultry farming ends in Hunterdon. Perhaps George Lachen-

Mrs. Werner Frank of Stockton stands in the family's poultry house with pails of eggs she has collected on a wheeled cart. After the hen lays an egg, it rolls down the tilted wire floor and comes out in front.

mayr qualifies as the last real fulltime family poultry farmer. Today, at the age of 79, he gets up early in the morning, has breakfast, and drives down to the family's farm near Ringoes. He puts in 10 hours of work a day, seven days a week. He has one full-time man to help him. He has a number of women who tend the eggs coming off the conveyor belts. Thousands of eggs an hour roll off the belts. Lachenmayr has 20,000 communal type cages that each hold several hens, 90,000 in all.

The hen is so highly bred for productivity, seemingly impossibe 20 years ago. The hen is cared for by an automatic complex of machinery that involves 108 electric motors.

Lachenmayr is a happy man who looks 20 years younger than his years. And he isn't getting tired.

"I'm a young fellow," he laughed. "You hear those fellows saying, oh boy, next year I got it easy, I get pensioned off, I go to live in town — and two years later you look around and the guy isn't there anymore. So if you are physically healthy and there is nothing wrong and you stop working, everything stops. You've got too much time, you eat too much, maybe you drink too much, you've got it too easy, you are invited here and you are invited there, and it's just no good for you!"

Today in Hunterdon, Lachenmayr has 90 thousand hens and the Grossman firm has 100 thousand. The two have 60 percent of all the laying hens in Hunterdon County. Add a couple of other large operations, and you come to a 1977 flock size estimated at 326,000 hens. Only Salem County has more chickens in New Jersey — around 411,000 hens. Hunterdon has always been a leader in poultrying and has remained near the top. It even has about 75 farmers engaged in raising poultry in small numbers, usually as a supplementary income.

If the reader is fortunate enough to visit one of Hunterdon's remaining poultry operations, large or small, he or she will probably find the contented clucking of the masses of hens curiously tranquilizing — they are always contented, even in cages.

"I always enjoyed working with them. They are beautiful creatures," Paul Wirtz still says of his past years as a hatcheryman.

"Mr. Customer. You are the most important person ever to enter this store. You are not dependent on us — we are dependent on you." So reads the sign in George Lachenmayr's egg handling room in Whitehouse Station, where he works with his son. The store is gone now, but Lachenmayr's operation near Ringoes is still going strong and is much larger.

VII
Dairy Farming

"Well, it's pretty hard to tell someone how to milk a cow. It's simply grabbing hold of the teats, pulling and squeezing at the same time. At first, it's a difficult process, but it's pretty much like riding a bicycle. After you once learn, you never forget. Only thing is, if you haven't done it in a good while and had to milk very many, you might think your wrists were going to drop off before you were done."

Here's how it had been done since cows were domesticated, in a familiar scene at Lloyd Wescott's former Mulhocaway Farm north of Clinton, a modern dairy barn for the early 1940s. The cement floors made cleaning easy and the windows provided ventilation during the summer.

Dairy Farming

So says Howard Case of Three Bridges, a heavy-set man who spent his working life with dairy animals and was comfortable with the work.

If you look at 100 poultrymen, you'd see mostly trim, light-weight men. But if you look at 100 dairymen, you'll find the majority to be heavy muscled individuals. That's because a chicken weighs two pounds and a cow weighs well over half a ton. A person's extra weight and muscle comes in handy. There are times when a cow has to be pushed around.

"When I started, I bought my first couple of purebred calves, and Dory Dilts down here had a purebred bull. We didn't have a bull, so every time a cow came in heat, I'd have to lead her down to Dilts' place. But the animals weren't trained to be lead. They'd have you up the bank and down the bank and through the bushes and everything. And they always picked the stormiest day or else a Sunday to come in heat, and either she wouldn't go at all, or she'd run like thunder," Case recalls.

It's the same with delivering calves and handling bulls and emptying a huge barnful of hay every winter to feed a dozen cows. So for every light-boned dairyman — and there are some — there are more than a few heavies.

The great American philosopher Henry Thoreau once commented that he had seen many a fatigued and careworn man going down the road of life with 15 acres, a house, a barn, and a herd of dairy cows on his back. Milk is a luxury, Thoreau implied. Life itself is a luxury and a gift. The European peasants and farmers who became Hunterdon's dairymen brought this understanding to the new world with them. Dairying was their charm, and to own a cow was prosperity indeed.

In the cold, dank winters when feet got soggy and bones got chilled to the marrow, to have a cow that gave warm, rich milk was like heaven itself, for babies, children, and adults. That's why there were cows in Hunterdon County as quickly as early pioneers could bring them in.

It was difficult to raise a cow in the wilderness, however, and she wouldn't give much milk, and it often tasted like garlic and herbs. Cows just wandered in the woods and the meadowlands and were marked with their owner's brands for retrieval, just like in the so-called Wild West a century later. They could be pretty lean and rangy. It wasn't enough to love their milk. When you called the cows in, they simply did not come unless they knew you cared, too, by having some warm bedding and good food for them. Yet it was worth it to have that milk.

You had to be there to appreciate the sound of calling home the cows, as this gentleman demonstrates at a cow calling contest at the annual Dairyman's League picnic in the 1930s. Having cooperative cows who came home when called saved a long trip to the meadow.

By the time the Board of Agriculture was founded in Hunterdon in 1886, this kind of devoted dairying had occupied men and women for a long time. Early pioneers knew the ropes. And the rules haven't changed much, either. If you've ever heard a dairyman talk about work, here's what he means, either in 1776 or 1976: Before you open your presents on Christmas morning, you milk the cows. Before you go to church that evening, you milk the cows. Before you go to your New Year's Eve party, you milk the cows. After you come home from your New Year's Eve party, you milk the cows. When you get sick, your wife milks the cows. When you are both sick, your children milk them. When you are all sick, a neighbor comes over and milks them.

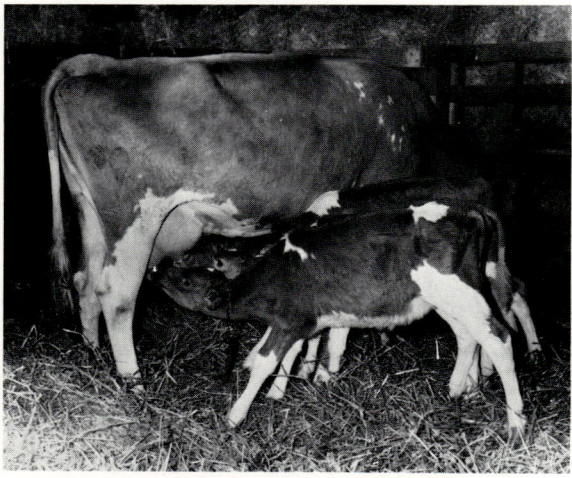

It's mealtime for these three calves. Once they leave their mother for grass and forage, a biological mechanism causes the udder to dry up. The same is true for cows milked for human consumption — unless they are milked regularly and completely. After about a year, a cow begins to dry up anyway, but giving birth again will restore the cycle.

You milk the cows regularly because, if you do not, the cow might get sick and be spoiled for milk production forever. Or perhaps she just stops giving milk and you have to let her udder dry and breed her again and wait a year for the new calf and the milk again. For a new calf will start the milk coming again. Indeed, the cow's milk production peaks a few weeks after calving, and then decreases steadily over a period of a year or more. Hence, a cow has to have a calf about once a year for maximum production.

As a result, dairying has always been regarded as a special commitment from the turn of the century to the present. A farmer can't make trips to town or spend the day working with another farmer very easily because he had to be in the barn milking twice a day. A hired hand to help out? Sure. But the hired hand problem has been another eternal and unchanging situation in dairying. First, he has to like the cows, too. If he doesn't, he will be insensitive to their tender feelings and some of the temperamental ones will stop milking.

Finally, you will have to explain to him why he should work for you for a very modest pay when he could do better working in town or renting his own farm. Most of the men who have been hired hands down the years have had a special love of working with animals and plants, for it was never the monetary rewards that attracted them.

Dairying has strong spiritual qualities. The housewife who reaches into the refrigerator for that plastic coated paper carton is the culmination of the dream. The milk is for her children. "Drink up. It will make you big and strong."

It's easy to laugh at such conundrums. A person may spend five times more money on soft drinks and junk food, but when he or she becomes a mother or dad, there is a sudden realization that they want their kids to have something better. During the Korean War it was learned that dangerously fatigued and emotionally drained soldiers returning from the front recovered rapidly when given fresh milk. Nothing else worked as quickly or as well. It was a part of their heritage and it symbolized energy and comfortableness in a physical way, in an emotional way, and yes, in a spiritual way, too.

The spiritual quality of milk may be the one factor that makes its history in Hunterdon understandable. Dairying is full of contrasts and paradoxes, the most striking being that the dairyman pays you for the privilege of producing your milk; you do not pay him. In other words, if he invested his money in banks or stocks instead of in a milk factory, his income would rise. If that sounds amazing, it is only secondary to the excellence that dairymen have achieved the past century in doing their job well.

The best estimates of a hazy past claim there were about 13,000 cows in Hunterdon in 1870 and they produced about 600,000 gallons of milk each year. There were still about 13,000 cows 100 years later. But that same number produced 16,420,000 gallons of milk in 1970. Somehow 30 times more milk came out of those udders, due to the stimulus of the country's economic growth, especially the growth of the cities.

The changes began in earnest after the Civil War, with the railroads and the canal linking the city to the thousands of small dairy operations in the country. Before that, milk marketing was a small-time operation.

To have milk for your family you needed a cow and a bull. It was helpful to have a couple of heifers coming on. All were needed to insure a steady supply of milk. The result was production of 10 times more milk than a family could use. Some was sold to neighbors. Some was made into butter and carted to the general store for barter. Some was made into cheese, which keeps much better than butter at non-refrigerated temperatures. In this way, country milk appeared in the city as cheese and butter.

But fluid milk spoils in a few hours if not refrigerated, and so it never got very far from the farms on which it was produced. By 1867, though, all this had changed irrevocably — milk was being delivered daily to homes in the town of Flemington, Hubert Schmidt discovered when the Board hired him to research their roots in 1940. More important, it was being shipped out of the area and into New York City as fresh fluid milk. Dairy operations in the urban areas were limited, milk was in short supply, and people wanted a hundred, a thousand times more milk to drink.

The railroads brought drinking milk, and butter and cheese to the city. To Hunterdon they brought change, although first not much because only farmers with an ice house for cooling, and location near a railroad, could ship fluid milk to the city. Nonetheless, from 1870 to 1880, estimates of milk production in Hunterdon doubled, and several thousand more cows were put on.

The first big change was the creation of creameries which could locate near farms and instantly make butter or cheese or pack the cream in ice for quick shipping by rail to a city ice cream maker. Sergeantsville was first with a creamery in 1881, farmers creating a stock company and putting up $3,750 for construction. By 1883, F. S. Holcombe of Lambertville reported to the state:

"We have two creameries in our county, one located in Sergeantsville, the other at Locktown, both in Delaware Township, and only four miles apart, doing a good business, and having a ready sale for all the butter and cheese made. Our county is selling large quantities of milk, several farmers putting it in quart air-tight cans and shipping to Jersey City. Enormous quantities are shipped from Whitehouse Station on the Central Railroad."

The new industry lifted the dairy herd as a money-maker, from a small change earner to a big dollar input. There's not much money in selling the homemade butter to the general store. There is money in leaving all the milk off at the creamery and having all the cream used like this and then sold for a good price in the city.

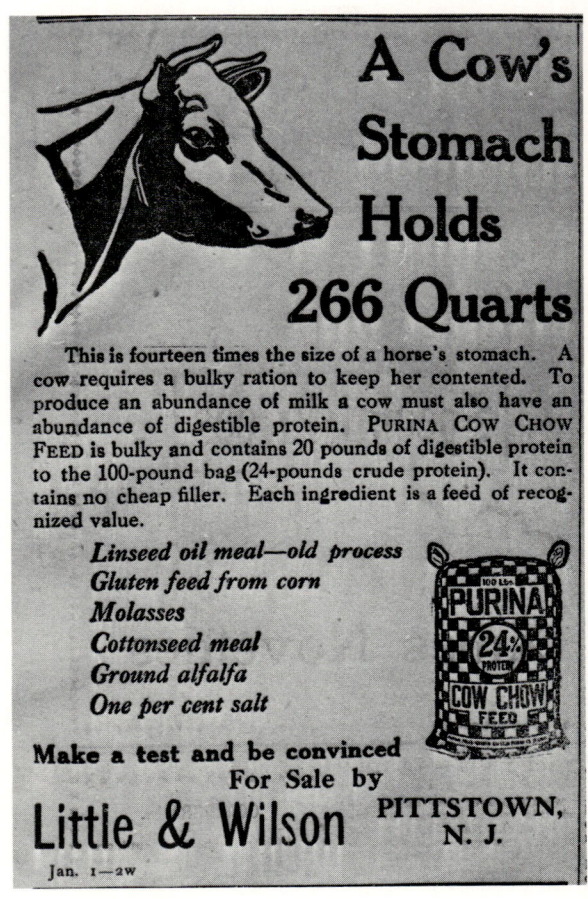

A dairy herd could now become the major income earner for a farmer. And the farmer agreed in turn to pursue incentives for quality, whether it meant improving the cow shed or perhaps having a cow bred to a Holstein bull, a new breed brought into the county in 1871.

In 1887, the Board wrote to the state: "There has been great progress made in the keeping and management of live stock for the past few years. Formerly, in travelling through the county and seeing stock which had been badly kept, it was quite a common thing to hear many farmers complain that their cattle had wintered badly and many of them had the 'hollow horn,' in fact the entire animal had the appearance of being hollow. But since farmers have found out that the best must be made of everything, they find it pays to be more particular in breeding, raring and caring for their animals."

Four years later, in 1891, farmers began to establish a system of rewarding the quality producer of milk. G.W. Hockenbury, at the Locktown Creamery, reported that a centrifuge had been installed to separate out milk fats from fluids and measure the "butterfat," as the cream was called. This meant measuring the cream content of the milk by percentage, since some cows gave milk with more cream in it, and only cream mattered for butter and ice cream.

Hockenbury reported the richest milk contained an average of 6.04 percent butterfat and the poorest 3.88 percent. The farmer with the most butterfat received $1.56 for his hundred pounds of milk, and the farmer with the poorest, $1.01. That's a 50 percent premium. If it had been a five percent premium it would have been enough to send dairymen scrambling to feed and care for their animals better. But it was 50 percent because there was 50 percent more cream. The high cream producer did not boost the overall price to reward the low cream producer. Incentive for cream production was the system, because cream was worth a lot more than milk.

The new system must have spurred a lot of questions from farmers on bettering production, for in 1896, Hockenbury summarized the methods in a paper he delivered to the Board of Agriculture:

"The first essential thing for the dairyman to do is find out 'where he is at.' I will admit that it seems like a great undertaking for the average dairyman to do this, but I feel sure if anyone will undertake the work, he will be amply repaid for doing so . . . Allow me to say right here, that I believe it is the lack of systematic figuring on the cost of production of the various farm crops that is in a great measure responsible for the financial embarrassment of so many of our farmers today."

Hockenbury went on to examine the cost of producing a quart of milk for cows of different

Samuel Komisar of Ringoes demonstrates the washing of a modern bulk milk collection system. The rows of metal and rubber tubes are the teat cups that are attached to the cow's udder. They do the milking with cycles of compressed air imitating the farmer's hands.

breeds. He analyzed the cost of feeds at present market values, figured yearly depreciation of a cow based on purchase cost and sale value of an old cow sold for beef, which " . . . leaves $19.63 as the yearly net profit per cow which certainly should be an incentive to dairymen to crowd on a full head of steam and try to reach that mark. But someone says you have not allowed us anything for our work, but it is conceded that the manure account will balance this item and that is the reason it was not counted."

"The "manure account" probably sounds like a joke to a nonfarmer, but manure has a tremendous fertilizer value, even in this modern era of commercial chemical fertilizers. It can do much to make plants healthy and bountiful and every farmer an expert in recycling — something new to American industry or the American people, but not to the plain dirt farmer who has often been popularly pictured with hayseeds coming out his ears. Such a man knew how much he paid to produce a quart of milk to one hundredths of a cent.

He most certainly knew how vital recycling

Dairy Farming

manure was to his prosperity. And probably he could even tell you how many pennies it cost him if he berated a temperamental prize-producing animal. The profit margins were too narrow.

Hockenbury and his expertise, as well as creameries in general, marked the rise of the modern dairy and the modern specialized farm. By 1909 there had been creameries like the one at Locktown for 30 years, and nearly 30 scattered over the county. They had established and accelerated modernization and now were going to be swept away by it — in another decade most of them would be gone and the buildings turned into fluid milk shipping stations. The report for 1919 explained the situation in terms of a complaint.

The fluid shipping stations existing then were "becoming so exacting regarding sanitation as to drive many out of business or to patronize the creameries . . . as one dairyman tersely put it when he said 'they want certified milk at the lowest prices paid wholesale on the general market for common milk'."

What the reporter was revealing was that creameries had in 10 years become obsolete and forgotten. Only the hard-pressed dairymen who could not meet the high quality fluid standards tended to use them. Those higher standards took care and patience but they led to higher milk checks. And this was vital in an underpaid industry — so vital that the creameries were abandoned with hardly a sentimental glance backward.

Yet they were still valuable since, to a recycling expert like a farmer, everything is turned to value. Their value was to act as a cushion to the blow of modernization. The new improved dairy buildings were not something that a man avoided out of laziness but because they required a good bit of money to build. A dairyman who needed five years to raise the money could sell to a creamery during those five years.

Creameries did not need to be as particular about milk quality. As local historian Ken Myers put it, "They didn't like it but they would take a can of milk if the top hadn't already blown off from the fermentation pressures building up inside!"

Sanitation was going to be a big factor. It's no longer a matter of fresh milk twice a day, any stuff that gets old being fed to the animals for its high protein quality. Or you put it in the spring house, which is 50 degrees and helps extend its useful life a few hours more. Or you make cheese. The ideal from now on would be to put fresh milk into a sealed container, cool it, and ship it as fast as possible to the bottling plant and then on to the user.

Marius Nielson lifts off a can full of warm milk, while his daughter, Marie, tends the horses in this 1920s scene. By this time the Pittstown Creamery had closed and had become a shipping station for the Dairymen's League, where milk was transported by train to city processing plants to be bottled for consumers.

Dairy Farming

There were new scientific methods for checking quality, testing for communicable diseases in cows, and treating the milk properly to preserve it. The dirt barn floor gave way to the new concrete floor. Washing the milk pails and utensils in the kitchen gave way to a "milk house," where washing went on more efficiently, and where milk waited prior to shipment.

By around 1920, farmers began buying Delco electrical generator-motors for their farms and attaching them to a refrigerator they could use to cool fresh milk. Farmers who were careless about removing manure from the animal stalls daily could throw down more straw and muddle through. But that was poor sanitation and no longer tolerated.

James Pauch of Lambertville uses wrenches to show repair and maintenance accessibility of his new bulk milk tank. Milk was pumped from the cow through the stainless steel pipe and into the tank, where it was cooled immediately and later picked up by a bulk tank truck. After each milking, Pauch disassembled the pipe, hooked it to a washing pump, and rinsed the entire system with boiling water and solvents.

A young milk maid attaches the automatic milkers to the udder, a process that also requires hand-stripping the remaining milk, cleaning the udder, and replacing that cow with another. This continues until the entire herd has moved through the parlor. The jar holds milk before it is pumped to the bulk tank in the milk room.

Dairy Farming

Most of the new rules were reasonable. Others, however, were the outgrowth of scientific speculation on subjects not well understood. To do such-and-such might help prevent disease contamination. Or it might not. Either way, the farmer would pay for it. Board President Clifford Snyder summed up the dilemma in the humorous creation of the milk house on wheels.

Snyder and others observed that one milk inspector of a dairy barn would holler and complain that the milk house was too close to the cow barn and might pick up airborne bacteria and odors blown from the barn or the manure pile. The next inspector who came along might complain it was too far away from the cow barn and the milk might become contaminated as you carried it to the milk house. But the milk house on wheels solved that problem permanently, for no matter how quixotic their demands, the inspectors could be satisfied.

However, the realities were harsher than the humor. During the 20s and 30s one dairyman became so frustrated with a milk inspector jumping all over his proud set-up that he grabbed the man by the nape of the neck and dragged him face down through the manure pile.

Snyder and the other Board of Agriculture men had considerable influence in Trenton, where they went, hat in hand, to beg the state not to revoke the man's right to be a dairyman as punishment. When the new TB testing came in, the state did not buy them a new cow if tests showed that one of the herd was sick. Normally, a cow found to be diseased was sent to the butcher.

The state offered compensation, but it was only enough to cover the replacement value of a poor cow and did not begin to cover the loss on a good one. Loss of cows with TB was short-lived, however, since the regular test and slaughter program essentially eliminated the disease in New Jersey. But, then, a program came along to eliminate cows with brucellosis or "contagious abortion," as it was called. This, too, was short-lived, because an effective vaccination was developed. Thus, the gains were great for public health, and for the dairyman, but there were some dairies destroyed or almost destroyed. As one farmer recalls:

"We started farming in '36 and in the fall of '37 we lost pretty near all of our cows in TB tests. We lost 12 the first shot, then we lost five, and then I think it was six or something like that. Before we got straightened out, we almost quit farming before we got started. I went out and bought some replacements and then some of them went out with TB and then I was nearly licked. What they seemed to think was we had a 'spreader' in the herd, where a cow is rotten with TB but won't react to the test. We had one yellow cow, sold her for beef. When they opened her up she was rotten with TB. So she went for soap. When the butcher came back, he squawked like hell at me. I told him the cow was his, he bought her. We lost 22 head altogether."

So the "spreader" was found and instead of folding, Margin Stout and his wife held on to their farm near Pittstown, not only enjoying a long career in dairying, but seeing a son become a field representative for the American Holstein Association. Their story multiplied gives some idea of why farmers were finding their world had changed. Perhaps their criticalness towards vague sanitation regulations helped refine the quality of the system that was evolving.

The milk the consumer drinks today comes from cows tested and found free of a variety of possible disease. It is cooled minutes after it comes from the cow. It usually runs in stainless steel pipes that are flushed and cleaned after each milking. It is pasteurized to kill bacteria. Cows are routinely treated with the most modern antibiotics, and receive a better diet than most people. All to keep them healthy. Most of it had been envisioned in the 1887 Board of Agriculture report that exhorted farmers to "make the best of everything."

That best began with the cow herself, and her companion bull. When John T. Ellis imported three Holsteins from Europe in 1871, it was a matter of pride to do so. The men who created today's Flemington Fair were back then organizing animal shows with entries mostly from farmers anxious to show the best. The huge majority of farmers who did not have the money for that sort of fancy simply looked on with approval at the fine animals. But now, in the following century, they were going to treat every cow and bull like championship material. As the Hunterdon *Democrat* chronicled:

"It was in December, 1919, under the leadership of Fred Totten, then Master of Ringoes Grange, that the first meeting was called to set up a herd improvement program in Hunterdon County. (Under this new production testing program, a man was to come once a month to weigh the amount of milk each cow gave and test the amount of butterfat.) The meeting was held in the pool room at Ringoes Hotel, and 21 consented to join, including Thomas McCandless, Joseph T. Haines, James Lambert, H.D. Bellis, Hart LaRowe, Frank Bodine, James Stryker, and Charles C. Bond.

"At the outset, 250 cows were put under test by Thomas W. Borjesson, who came down from the state of Maine to take on the new assignment. While Borgesson was a capable tester, he established more of a reputation for consuming buckwheat cakes, and because it was the farmer's responsibility to feed the tester, it became something of a contest among farmers' wives to see who really could fill the tester up.

"A second testing association was established at Flemington in September, 1920. Among the charter members were H.E. Deats, Roy Schomp, John Van Doren, Clifford Snyder, the late John Tine, Sylvanus Apgar, William Hoppock, Theodore 'Dory' Dilts, and Howard Case."

Stanley Douglass of Pittstown was the tester for the new Flemington association, and he remembers well being carted by wagon and sometimes by car from farm to farm. He had to measure the butterfat of each cow and the pounds of milk produced that day, morning and evening, and the amount and cost of the feed eaten.

Douglass recalls: "I'd been a farmer, I'd been through a short course in New Brunswick, dairying and general farming. In those days your production was so low. If you worked on a good or a fancy dairy farm, you would milk cows that would give twice as much, ten times as much milk as the more average cows were giving.

"We thought then, and New Brunswick told us, that you could get a farmer working on the notion of working for 'gold' at 10,000 pounds of milk a year per cow, an excellent average. In those days you had only three or four herds in the county that ran up to 40 cows, and there was one herd with only three cows."

Ten thousand pounds of milk is about 1,428 gallons per cow. The average for Hunterdon's milk production for 1920 was about 450 gallons. The herd improvement farmers wanted that gold enough to pay Douglass $3 a day to come by and test each cow in the herd. He would stop each month and they could look over the records and "find out where it is at," as Hockenbury had recommended in 1891.

While Douglass was busy spilling sulphuric acid on the oilcloth covered kitchen table ("That wasn't so good!") and being fed and boarded in the guest room for the night, his host-employer was looking over those butterfat and milk figures and getting excited.

Out with the low production cows. Save that heifer from the top producer; she may produce well, too. How much would it cost to invest in some high priced feed supplement such as cotton seed meal? Those hotshots from the county Board have been talking silos to store corn for 20 years now.

The experiments would be made. Slowly the cows would respond to them as the months passed. Douglass would come around again. He would weigh the milk again. He would test the butterfat again. The results would be in.

This DHIA (Dairy Herd Improvement Association), as it is called today, was that road to gold. It gave the dairyman a scorecard. He could take that expensive feed supplement and prove the dollars in profits it made him. And of course he could tell that old timer so-and-so down the road who said it was nonsense — he could tell him how many dollars that "nonsense" earned. It was no longer some hotshot expert telling you what to do. It was a man you went to school with, and he was going for gold!

Following the establishment of the first test groups, milk production for the whole county went as follows in five year increments: 445, 477, 628, 651 gallons per year average, the county average for 1935, when there were 1,828 cows under test at 73 farms. That represented only 10 percent of the county's cows and dairy farms. But just because a man may have been too miserly to spend $3 to have his cows tested doesn't mean he was too proud to try all the successful experiments his neighbor tried.

The year after Totten got the Ringoes test group going, the experts from Rutgers were called in for four dairy feed demonstrations in the county. The best methods were described to farmers in detail. Printed brochures were available. And, like as not, there was a county Board man sitting quietly in the background to see to it that the "expert" didn't somehow alienate the crowd or make a fool of himself.

One farmer recalls such a demonstration at Flemington High School, where the expert was a young fellow who got a little rattled in front of the farmers. He was hand-mixing a scientific supplement for heifers and kept adding too

Mrs. Anna Hammell fills a special test tube with a milk sample for routine testing. In the 1950s, she was a supervisor for the Dairy Herd Improvement Association's Unit No. 2 and the samples were part of the systematic improvement of the county's high-producing dairy herds.

DHIA tester John Frazee of Annandale records the weight of an average feed supplement ration that Flemington area farmer William Wagner feeds his cows. Note the typical stable of the 1930s, with individual stanchions, concrete floors, and electrical wiring. The whitewashed walls were redone each spring as part of the overall sanitation effort.

much of each ingredient like a harried housewife who doubles the flour because she put in too much baking soda.

"Why, man, is this for a heifer or is this for an elephant!?" Snyder cried, and broke the tension with laughter. There were 17,000 cows and 2,000 dairymen in Hunterdon during the 30s and Snyder didn't want them deterred from progress by derisive stories going the rounds about "experts."

There were other things spurring farmers on, as well as the desire for prosperous incomes or the fear of poverty. The Mount Airy Dairy Club was founded in 1919 for the sons and daughters of dairymen. Its purpose was to have each member buy a purebred heifer, raise it to maturity, and sell it to pay off the loan of money for the purchase. Or even keep the cow as "foundation" to start a small herd. By 1924, the annual report of the club noted that fathers of five of the youngsters had replaced their grade (non-purebred) bulls with purebred ones. What it added up to was, that, in 1924, John Van Doren of the Ringoes test group had one of his Holsteins produce more milk than any other cow in the state had ever produced. The following year the farmers in the Ringoes group added another 100 cows to the test group.

During this period there was another kind of farmer who was rubbing his hands happily — the fellow who liked to breed quality cows and bulls to sell. He could point out a good looking bull, and show official records of how many gallons of milk his mother gave, and how much his daughters were giving. Things fell into place rapidly. The modern cow was being put together and the modern dairyman was learning the ropes.

Electric milking machines were introduced in the 1920s and a few daring farmers purchased them along with home electrical generating plants to run them. But it would be two decades before they became the rule, and the always innovative Fred Totten liked to laugh at the recollection that he had avoided them entirely until his son Kenneth had badgered him into getting them for the two-family dairy.

The last step in putting together the modern cow was the bull. Purebred breeders, like William Phillips and Herman Schick near the Delaware River knew all about bulls, and what a superior one could do for a herd's milk production records. But it remained to take this knowledge to the nonspecialist dairyman, and such was the vitality of Hunterdon's dairy farms that this was begun at the height of the depression with the formation of "bull rings" in 1934 and 1935. (Bull rings had been in existence since the turn of the century, but did not enjoy widespread practice in Hunterdon until the 1930s.)

"Babbitt, the county agent, and Professor Enos Perry of New Brunswick, the dairy specialist there, helped us a lot with the ring and its purpose was to be able to buy better sires than an individual could," Harold Everitt of Flemington recalled of those first rings. "So we went together

County Agent Dwight Babbitt looks on as Flemington's first bull association shows of its expensive, purebred bull. At right is Harold Everitt and the man holding the animal is William Wagner. The others are Fred Van Doren of Ringoes and W. C. Voegtlen of Lebanon. The group had four bulls that were rotated from farm to farm to diversify the breeding.

Dairy Farming

A farmer drives a Holstein cow into a cattle truck from the Neshanic area. The "A.I." on the truck stands for Artificial Insemination, reminding customers of the high quality of the animals for sale.

and bought four bulls and changed them around. Each year we'd switch them around to a different farm. These were Holsteins.

"The other members of the group were William Wagner, who lived right near me, and Fred Van Doren, who at the time farmed down near Wertsville, and the other man was at Lebanon (W.C. Voegtlen). Oh, we borrowed money, even, and we paid what we considered to be big prices for animals at that time. We bought them mostly for breeders in New Jersey. I was using purebred Holstein cows, and the other members of the bull ring were, too, and of course we were members of the cow testing association here. In this way we raised our own replacements pretty much, and we tried to build the herd up that way, that was the idea. It worked in general, now and then you'd get a freak that wasn't any good, but generally, you could build up your production by breeding.

"Babbitt always promoted this, raising your own replacements. I learned this when I was quite young, because I started out buying cows, and if you bought cows from some cow dealers, well, I soon found out I wasn't gypsy enough, they were always a little smarter than I was."

Two of the reliable cow dealers around the Flemington area were Jacob (Jake) Dvoor and Barney Berkowitz. Dvoor came to this country in 1914 with little money in his pockets and settled in Three Bridges. He moved to Flemington in 1919 and through hard work prospered. He soon brought his parents to Hunterdon County. His is the story of many immigrants of the day. Community-minded, Dvoor helped many young farmers get started. His sons, Herbert and Melvin, have carried on the family cattle business.

Berkowitz, who emigrated from Russia about 1900 and first settled in Freehold, moved to Flemington in 1915 and for many years his 64-acre farm at the corner of East Main St. and Route 31 was the location of his two businesses, the Flemington Horse and Cow Market and the Flemington Packing Co. Weekly cattle auctions were held there, where Berkowitz also operated the county's only kosher meat market. He was a charter member of the Flemington Elks and a founding member of the Flemington Jewish Community Center. His wife, Dora, resides today in Raritan Township.

Cow dealers were hard bargainers, or they would not have been able to stay in business. They had been importing cows to Hunterdon since the 1890s, bringing in the best they could find in the Middle West and Canada. That saved a farmer time and money from having to raise his own replacements. Many farmers could not have survived without the dealers. And many another was saved from having to leave farming during hard times by receiving credit extended over long periods of time from these men.

Bull rings made it possible to raise high quality replacements at home, and that could be well worth the effort. Beside the Flemington ring there was the North Hunterdon Cooperative Bull Association, with William Phillips Jr., Sylvanus Apgar, William Hoppock, Nelson Boss, all from the Milford area, and Howard Stout and Arthur

Dairy Farming

Wilson from Pittstown.

Farther north was the Mount Grove Cooperative Bull Association, with Fred Teets of Cokesbury, Richard Stevenson of Califon, and David Teets of High Bridge.

Quality or not, there was another problem — the bull himself — on the 1,993 farms that had a dairy in 1935. Herman Schick of Milford remembers the time a herdsman from another farm came by to pick up a purebred bull. The fellow, in a jaunty mood, a pipe in his mouth, assured Schick there would be no problem loading the animal on the truck. He knew how! "After one look at that bull, his pipe began to go up and down in his mouth like it was going to fall out," Schick recalled.

Everitt recalled.

The nose is one of the tender parts of the bull, and the theory was that the bull would come along quietly because pulling on the ring in his nose hurt. In actuality, if the animal became too upset then the hurt just made him angrier. You then had 2,000 pounds of angry muscle on the other end of a six foot pole. If you hung on too much, you might get thrown through the air. If you let go, then there you were six feet away from an enraged bull. That's a big reason why it helped to be heavy-set.

"I remember one or two men who got killed by bulls," Everitt said. And so did every other man who handled bulls remember. They were always dangerous. But there was no answer to it, except

A man with a bull staff guides "Progress Oral Premier." The staff was hooked to a ring through the bull's sensitive nose, which hurt when tugged.

Quite simply, bulls were mean, onery, and dangerous. And you could tell if one was in a nasty mood just by looking. The man with the wobbling pipe was not a coward; he was just wondering how long it would take that bull to break him in half.

"The bulls weighed around 1,800 to 2,000 pounds. It was a dangerous business when they were big, and sometimes got a little mean, but we used a ring in their nose, and a bull staff to handle them with. It's a long rod, about six feet long that hooks into the ring in the bull's nose,"

to be careful. Then, again, there might be an answer. It came as a surprise, straight out of a science fiction novel.

Professor Perry turned up the answer when he took a leave from his job as Rutgers Dairy Specialist to go to Europe. He made his discovery on a small island off Denmark. Stanley Douglass remembers: "Well, E.J. Perry brought it back from Denmark to Babbitt, and Babbitt got to Clifford Snyder, and Clifford Snyder got to Dick Schomp and Dory Dilts, and it was just a group of men in there who did a lot for Hunterdon

Dairy Farming

County. Hunterdon County wasn't the most forward county in the state at that time, but that was '38 of course, and they'd begun to go."

There were two possibilities evident to the leaders: 1) This is going to make us look like damn fools; or 2) This is going to revolutionize dairying in Hunterdon County, the state, the nation, the world. They were proud men and doubtless still smarting from being the last county in the state and nearly the entire nation to get a county agent. So they bought it, Perry's Danish discovery.

"It" was artificial insemination, whereby semen was obtained from a bull with the use of an artificial vagina, then cooled, diluted and split up into a thousand separate samples. Each was used to breed a cow in heat. One ejaculation of semen could rarely be extended beyond 150 individual ampules, so there would be thousands in the life of a bull — hundreds during any one week of his life. Big purebred breeders had been fooling around with the idea for years and never got it to work well. Now, the Board of Agriculture was going to steal their thunder in the name of the small dairyman. William McIntyre, who followed Babbitt as county agent, remembers the early reactions:

"There were a lot of people who thought this was a most unnatural thing. And of course like any new thing, 'Well, I'm not going to do *that* to *my* cows. I don't know that I'm gonna try that, we'll just wait and see what happens.'"

But, men like Van Doren who had tried herd testing and bull rings, were ready to try more.

"It was a big thriller so far as I was concerned, the way dairy farms in New Jersey came to the rescue and said, yes, let's try this out, if it has worked all right in Denmark, why can't we make a go of it," Perry recalls. I just went over there to study anything about Denmark cattle and feeding I could, and I just bumped into this at a cattle show. I met a county agent over there, who said, 'You must visit our province, we have something to show you.' They had been operating quietly for 13 months. And after 10½ of those months they began to get calves. They had 60 or more calves by the process. They found their farmers were happy because they could get the service of the most outstanding bull in the whole country and they could multiply his use a thousand times by dilution, by using a diluter in the preservation of the semen, and by keeping it cold, down around 38 degrees."

Perry returned home in the fall of 1937 and the Hunterdon County Dairy Committee of the Board met in December and unanimously voted to repeat what Demnark had done more openly. Hunterdon dairymen were active in the New Jersey Holstein Association, which also agreed to support the project. Similarly, dairymen in Warren and Somerset Counties were invited to be in on the ground floor of this new service to farmers. Babbitt's letter to farmers in February, 1938, reads like a routine note on another farm demonstration:

"As a result of considerable interest being shown by many dairymen throughout the county, an effort is to be made to organize a program of artificial breeding of dairy cattle for this area."

On March 24, those "many dairymen" met formally and 45 agreed to pay $5 to join the program. A managing committee was elected, composed of Clifford Snyder as chairman, W.C. Voegtlen of Lebanon, C.V.N. Davis of Somerville, D.W. Amerman of Neshanic and George Edgar of Belvidere as members. J.M. Nevius, state Holstein treasurer, served as treasurer.

They set an informal goal of 1,000 cows enrolled in the program and three days before that meeting they already had 900. All Perry and his people had to go on was what the Danes had told him. The procedure was technical. If you did not get the details right, the first attempts would be a failure, and the whole program would be in danger of losing steam and failing.

So, on April 8, the Hunterdon Board voted a $500 loan to borrow the services of Dr. K.A. Larsen of Denmark as its first inseminator. Snyder reportedly remarked to his fellow Board members, "Well, here's $500 we may never see again, but I think it's wise." Now that the initial excitement had worn off there was time to remember that everyone was putting his reputation on the line.

Dr. J.A. Henderson was completing his post-graduate veterinary work at Cornell in cow sterility and was hired to handle the program full-time at $2,400 a year. He started work May 16 and worked 364 days for his salary, with Christmas day off. Babbitt later wrote of the events that followed:

"Dr. Larsen arrived about May 1st and helped get the project organized. Arrangements were made to use the famous 'Alice' bull, which was jointly owned by P.O. Van Nuys of Belle Mead and the Experiment Station, plus 'Career,' both mature bulls, and a third young yearling called 'General.'

"They were labelled H-1, H-2, H-3 in that order, and arrangements were worked out with Mr. Van Nuys and the Experiment Station to house them on the Van Nuys farms and have the breeding work for the three county area center out of this headquarters.

"After suitable opening day ceremonies at the Van Nuys farm on the morning of May 16, Henderson and Larsen and county agent Babbitt started out over the three counties to breed the first cows to be bred in this country through a cooperative organization by the new artificial insemination method.

"According to our incomplete records, the first breedings that day were made at the farms of Fred Meyer in Somerset County, Kingman Brothers at Three Bridges, Clifford Snyder at Pittstown, and at Hans Schanzlin and Son at Montana in Warren County.

"There were some great comments made about this 'crazy' system of breeding cattle. Some, although they tried it, voiced doubts that it would work, and it took nine months to convince them that a normal calf could be the result of such 'funny business.' "

By July 1, 199 animals had been bred, and 70 percent of the cows had conceived and were pregnant. Newsmen and farm leaders from all over the United States were coming to see what was going on.

Lloyd Wescott, who had started to develop a Guernsey herd north of Clinton, had just purchased an outstanding proven sire, and wanted the maximum number of his cows bred to the bull. So he offered the use of the bull to the artificial breeding unit provided they would breed his cows. The extra semen, of which there would be a great deal, was made available to the new organization. Jerseys and Brown Swiss were added at a later date.

By October of 1938, there were 2,120 Holsteins and 359 Guernseys enrolled in the program and a second veterinarian was hired. Finally, on February 15, 1939, Dick Schomp of Stanton went out to his cow barn and found one of his artificially inseminated cows had given birth. It was a calf and it was normal, and it meant that the dairy industry in much of the world was permanently changed. It might have taken large numbers of Hunterdon dairymen 10, 20, 30 years to get around to using purebred bulls for their herds, but in less than 12 months the number had gone from a scant dozen men using bull rings, to a large group of farms that had over a thousand

A merry-go-round type of wheel draws the animals in a circle at the Mulhocaway Farm north of Clinton. The line from the bull's nose-ring to a clip on the turning exerciser kept the animal moving, a safer methods than having to round up dangerous bulls out exercising in the pasture.

cows in the program. Cows were being bred to not only purebred bulls, but to top quality purebred bulls. Dairy herd upgrading had been moving along steadily but rather slowly for a half century. Now it was going 10 times faster, 100 times faster, 1,000 times faster. It was the beginning of a new world and Hunterdon County was the first in the country to offer this to farmers.

A local veterinarian who started his professional career with Hunterdon's early artificial insemination effort is Dr. F. Bennett Duke of Clinton Township. Shortly after his graduation from the Ontario Veterinary College in 1945, Dr. Duke came to the county, following, among others, Dr. Jack Hamilton, who now lives in South Jersey, Dr. Jack H. Beattie, and Dr. Douglas Reed. Duke recalls that the bulls were housed at Wescott's farm and the veterinary team would travel to farms throughout Hunterdon, Warren and parts of Somerset counties with quantities of semen. Duke, who worked with the unit into 1947, was recently named "Veterinarian of the Year" by the Northwest Jersey Veterinary Society.

As the demand for the service grew, bulls owned by various breeders around the area were added to the program. It soon became apparent the operation could only be efficient if all the bulls were concentrated in one area. That summer 17 farmers put up $100 each to build a bull barn to house nine bulls and provide a small office. Wescott rented the land to the group for $1 a year. And in between running his own farm, he wound up the informal host for farm men and women who came from all over the country and all over the world to look and learn so they could adopt the new method.

Meanwhile, the war was coming on and governments everywhere needed more food to feed their armies and their workers at home. If Perry had not made his trip when he did, then Denmark would not have been accessible until after the war because of the Nazi invasion. This new

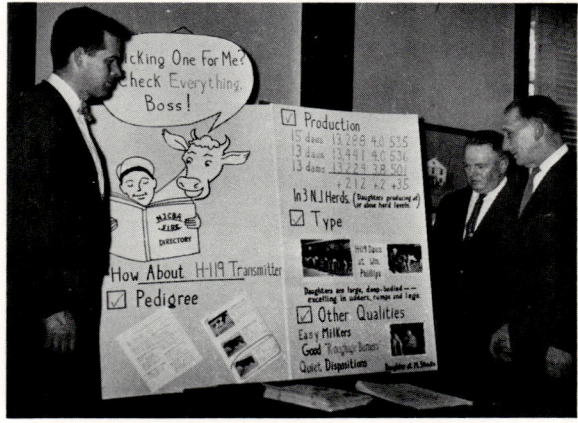

New Assistant County Agent Calvin Wettstein, at left, and Margin Stout and William Phillips, at right, examine the simple display "selling" artificial breeding from the New Jersey Cooperative Breeding Association.

A herd of Holsteins at the Margin Stout farm outside of Pittstown lines up for this group photo in the 1960s. They are the product of selective breeding, scientifically-grown feeds, and quality sanitation.

Dairy Farming

miracle meant more than giving aid to the war effort. Milk production for Hunterdon rose steadily from 1940 to the present. While this is only the average, leading dairymen went even further.

Margin Stout was one of the dozens of Hunterdon dairymen who farmed during this period. He was glad he did not stay licked with his TB problems of 1937, for it gave him some busy and exciting years: "At one time I was involved in almost everything there was in the county. One week I had eight meetings in only seven nights. School board, fire company, county Board, church, and a little bit of everything.

"The state Holstein group, the county Holstein — we helped start the Holstein Club in Hunterdon, which now is part of the Central Jersey club. They have the Black-and-White shows (Holstein showings) down in Flemington now. The first show was in our meadow. I started the thing in 1960, was the first president, had the first three shows here," said Stout, whose father had started the cow testing records in 1932 which had become part of the whole quality breeding effort.

"The daily records you keep on your milk production, you used more or less to cull your calves. Then when you got into the purebred business, you used them to improve your herds and to sell your cattle. One bunch of heifers we sold went to Japan; they shipped them all the way over there."

Dairy Farming

Stout sold his herd in 1968 when the power lines took part of his farm. He has never really stopped being a farmer, however. "The milk records today, well, when we started farming if you had a 12, 13 thousand pounds (of milk per year) cow, you had what you called a pretty decent cow. Now they're getting up in the 30 and 40 thousand pound cows! When I sold the cows I had a herd average of 16,000 pounds of milk per cow, and now ten years later they're getting up around 20,000 pounds herd average."

As to the 1980s and beyond, there will be more developments in technology. Scientists are in the process of perfecting ovary transplants. Hormones are used to make a cow shed more than one egg when it comes into heat. They can shed a dozen or more, but usually four to six. Thus, the cow is artificially bred to a great bull, given the hormones, and after five days the eggs are flushed out of her system and examined under a microscope. The fertile eggs are then taken and implanted in "host" heifers.

It's an expensive process, but for a cow with high production records and offspring who also have high records, the process is worth the trouble because it multiplies the possible offspring. The modern dairyman lives in an era when the best cows are having dozens of offspring, and as for the bulls — Paclamar Astronaut had 50,000 sons and daughters.

All of the developments really come out of farmers treating their cows with the greatest care and affection. They hope for and receive rich reward for all, as this old Christmas rhyme from Betsy The Golden Guernsey promises:

> Cud I udder to your ear
> This friendly message of Christmas cheer
> Of peace and contentment and hope so
>   dear
> There will be more cream the coming year!

Hunterdon's heritage in this long dream of richness has come entirely from other places and countries, because it is such a widespread dream. And it has done its share in paying back that debt.

George E. Miller of Cherryville and his family show off one of their Holsteins in 1963. Because such animals require regular attention, every member of the Hunterdon farm family had a hand in their care.

VIII
Crop Farming

Dairying and poultry raising have been the mainline of Hunterdon's diverse farm history, yet they rank second and third to another kind of farming that utterly outclasses them in importance — crop farming, the first here and elsewhere, for without plants there is nothing.

Plants are so important that they are noticed by people about as often as fish notice the water they swim in. A person may spend a whole life taking plants for granted until one day on vacation he finds himself in the middle of a western desert where there is almost no plant life for miles. Then he may begin to feel that he knows what it is like on the moon, and why human life is so close to plant life.

Yet anyone who has ever been hungry will understand something of plants, for it is several times easier to create a meal of plants than it is to raise meat and poultry and milk to go with it. Any person who wants to understand more need only take a small seed the size of the head of a pin, place it carefully in the ground, water it, then watch and wait. If he or she has the patience of a farmer, a plant will appear of the smallest and most fragile sort. It will grow slowly, then faster and faster. Finally, the plant will mature and bear fruit or seed, what is called food. All out of what looks like a grain of dust.

From that kind of experience it is only a short distance to being a farmer, who multiplies the one seed by a million or more. Then come the cycles and vicissitudes of life that no one controls, what insurance companies call "Acts of God" — wind, rain, sun, moisture, dryness, even the cycles of the moon, all in different quantities and qualities, and forever changing.

Crop Farming

The Grangers, as "Patrons of Husbandry," have a popular symbol for all this that they have often used in their produce exhibits at the Flemington Fair. It is the "cornucopia of plenty," pictured as a winding horn that begins at a point, and then expands to a large and open conduit disgorging fruits, vegetables, grain, milk, and eggs.

The cornucopia means literally "the horn of plenty." The word comes down to us from Greek mythology. It is a positive symbol for the men and women who look at the growing processes, which include floods and rains and drought, as well as tornadoes and hurricanes and ravenous insects, molds, fungi, plant diseases seen only through a microscope, and the beautiful but somewhat greedy deer that defoliate corn patches, soybean fields and backyard gardens.

The history of crop farming in Hunterdon has been a proud one, and it has always received fond attention. When the Capners, who lived here before the Revolution, wrote home to England to others coming over, they sent long lists of materials to bring, and always specified the best.

Plows made here then were not the best, and the new settler was urged to purchase a couple in England to bring along. Other reports in those old letters told of bounteous harvests of all sorts. The trees were cut down, and long before the stumps were removed, there were hills of corn growing among them. Meadowlands near the streams provided the first grazing ground and hay land, which was quickly sown with perennial European seeds. In the two centuries before the Board of Agriculture got its start, the infinitesimal seed of pioneer settlement grew into a complex farm society that had the beginnings of modern agriculture in it.

The forests had been eliminated, leaving only wood lots on unusable land. Open fields were left, with fences to control the animals. The small towns were there to supply goods and market the produce. The larger streams were dotted with mills to lessen the labor of grinding grain into meal. There were kilns to bake the limestone and make it good for curing acid soil.

There were huge barns big as apartment buildings to store the hay and fodder. There were smokehouses to cure the meat, springhouses to keep the perishable foods fresh, and root cellars to store the summer's garden produce. There were dozens of special industries to serve the diversity of the farming of the time. And in 1828 there was even a blacksmith, John Deats in Pittstown, who solved the plow problem by patenting a Hunterdon County plow that his son, Hiram, built into an extensive business.

Mechanization had advanced to a surprising degree, and chapters can be filled with descriptions of the farm implements of the time. There was a simple reason for this that anyone considering a bushel of whole wheat flour can understand. As flour it is ready for a farm wife to turn rapidly into bread and food. But it started out as a handful of seeds.

A south Hunterdon farmer, dressed in his best white shirt and suspenders, maneuvers his best team of horses for the photographer. In the course of a day, he may have plowed two acres, with as much as 40 or 50 acres to go before planting. (Kenneth Stryker Collection.)

Crop Farming

Sutphen Wilson's Daybook

March 6, 1901
6 went to store, very cold
7 litel water
8 went to Lambertville
9 dull all day
10 dull, raw, and cold
heavy rain at night, brooks high
11 greas some harness
12 tras (threshed) weat
13 got in corn

April 6
6 rain in afternoon
7 dull, Susen Lise was here
8 fix chicken yard. cold
9 thrash weat, cold
10 went to mill, windy
11 plowed, cold
12 sowed oats
13 plowed, warmer

May 6
6 plowed sod, cool
7 plowed sod, warmer
8 plowed sod, dull
9 dull and rainy
10 rain most all day. sifted dung
11 dull all day
12 nise day
13 dull till noon

June 6
6 finished planting corn
7 heavy rain and wind
8 got in corn, cool
9 went to circh (church) cool
10 help Elwood plant corn
11 funeral Mary Anwarmen
12 work in corn, very hot,
    90 in shade
13 work in litel cellar

July 6
6 done noting, shower at night
    90
7 dull, Amos was here
8 dull, litel rain
9 finished corn
10 cut weat
11 cut weat, finished
12 dul
13 hold (hauled) weat

August 6
6 heavy rain at night
7 trim fns (fence)
8 plowed ½ day
9 plowed, hot
10 plowed
11 nise day
12 rain till noon
13 plowed hot

September 6
6 hold (hauled) lime, hot, 90
7 sheid corn, hot, 92
8 nise day, cool
9 got fosfate (fertilizer), cool
10 got fosfate, shower at night
11 trash weat, tuck chickens
12 finished rye
13 tuck corn away

October 6
6 nise day, cold here frost
7 hust (husked) corn, warmer
8 tuck hens to town
9 hust corn
10 hust corn, hot
11 hust corn
12 dull, litel rain
13 hust corn

November 6
6 tuck chickens to town, cold
7 finished dung, cold
8 got brand, cold and dry
9 went Lambertville, cold
10 cold high wind
11 kild pigs, tuck pigs away,
    rain a litel
12 litel rain, got dog
13 done noting, cold and windy

Dec. 6
6 got horse shod, cold 8 (above zero)
7 went to town, cold
8 dull all day, warmer
9 cold at Clint's
10 dull, a litel rain
11 helpd Elwood holl (haul)
    in stock
12 went to woods
13 Mr. Young was here.

Crop Farming

Thus runs the daybook of a Sergeantsville area farmer. Weather was recorded because of its importance to crops; the main chore of the day was given; important events like funerals and help to neighbors. Wilson's terse, phonetically spelled words make his life sound 'dul,' but they were just a record book, and one, incidentally, in which 'nise days' were recorded.

First, the ground has to be cleared and the weeds regularly rooted out, or else the harvest will be mighty thin. Then the seed must be sown — and quickly, too, at the right time. Mother Nature takes over, and suddenly one day there is a stand of waving grain, ready to be harvested.

Again, speed is necessary to avoid the rains and the losses of a late harvest. So the harvest was cut with scythes and bundled with ties of rye straw. Then the grain needs to be extracted from the heads. Each stalk of wheat has a head full of a dozen or two dozen grains of wheat. It's easy to break one open by hand, rub, and separate the wheat from the chaff. But it takes a long time to make a loaf of bread that way, unless you have special tools and implements. Thus, in a paradoxical but fruitful way, the basic life of crop farming and plants has always been intimately connected with tools, machinery, and sophisticated skills.

Until the 1920s and 1930s in Hunterdon, wheat and other long stalked grains were separated by what was called a "thresher" and was pronounced "thrasher." It was a highly complex machine that first threshed the heads of grain loose, and then ingeniously separated them from the stalks and broke them open, letting the kernels of grain out. What may come as a surprise, however, is that the first working threshers were perfected in the 1820s — and even Deats manufactured one locally.

They were beautiful machines and to see one in operation was a marvel — iron chains clanking and grinding slowly, wooden panels shaking and clomping, fans turning up a hurricane of dust, loud noises and shakings and rattling and a gigantic draft horse who walked patiently on a wooden tread mill and created that whole orderly chaos. They can still be seen today at the annual fair of the Rough 'N Tumble Engineers.

During the modern era after the Civil War, the first non-horse machine used was the steam en-

Farmers were always attaching machines together to combine operations and this rig threshes the grain, bales the straw, and elevates the bales to the loft. The barn, on the old Walter Wagner farm, in now the site of a root beer stand on Route 202-31 south of Flemington. Chickens can be seen feeding on grain that would otherwise be wasted.

gine, and it was pretty rough and tumble in its workings — hence, the name of the Society. A 20- or 30-horsepower machine might power a thresher the size of a tractor trailer — and somewhere in that gigantic shaking cloud of dust and noise you would find a small chute with a 100-pound bag under it and trickling into that bag a stream of precious golden wheat.

If you look inside a 1980s modern grain combine, you will see the same basic process with only a few differences. The thing is on wheels and runs down the field cutting up grain and throwing it into its mow. There is no more extraneous noise, replaced by the high pitched whine and powerful rumble of the best modern industrial machine design. And the wheat comes out of the cornucopia end in a raging torrent enough to bury you in a minute!

But at the start it was horse power, then hand power, and next steam power. The farmer of the 1880s was a highly skilled mechanic and craftsman, whether it was the way he cut wheat by hand with a grain cradle, or the way he used the cultivating equipment of his day with a skill that almost made the machine part of him.

Machinery was only one part of his life in crop farming. He was equally a horticulturist. If he was one of the many who despised "book learning," it meant that he learned by himself and from his neighbors. Some of the neighbors, by the way, read books, so no area of knowledge was ultimately ignored. He tested out his knowledge by himself, adapted it to his farm, his fields, the local weather patterns and soil conditions, the things that make every farm in Hunterdon different from every other.

Variety was the keynote in the late 1800s, and it was not unusual for a vigorous orchardist to exhibit at the fair or Grange events, displaying several different species of apples. With two dozen different kinds of apple trees, it was virtually impossible for all of them to fail. One would be drought resistant, another resistant to too much rain, a third to late frost that kills the budding flowers on all others, and a fourth to stand up against an early fall frost that ruins most others.

Crop farming was, and is, pure gambling. Perhaps the reason moralists always attacked gambling at cards was that it was such an unimaginative and unproductive form of gambling compared to crop farming. When card players gamble, all but one loses, and the one who wins winds up with a bunch of losers for friends. When farmers gamble their labor and toil and money, and throw seeds on the ground like the profligate son throwing money, everyone stands to win.

As the new Board of Agriculture prepared its first report on crop conditions for the state Department of Agriculture in 1886, a major change was underway, from diversity towards the modern "specialized" farm where only one or two crops would be grown.

The first big expression of specialist farming in Hunterdon County was peaches.

Peaches led thousands of farmers on wild chases for profits that ran up and down from year to year. The general rule seemed to be that for every decent but not outstanding year for a peach farmer, there were three or four or five years that were either the wildest boom or the most disheartening bust. It's the nature of specialization in a free-enterprise society. In 1886 the Board crop report read in part:

"H.D. Duckworth, Pattenburg, N.J., sends his report of peaches as follows: Planted trees 15 feet square, and planted 1,465 trees; the year that they were 3 years old gathered 700 baskets, net gain $585; fourth year, 1,000 baskets, net gain, $1,050; fifth year, 3,400 baskets, net gain, $1,700; sixth year, 2,400 baskets, net gain, $1,300; seventh year, 1,900 baskets, net gain, $1,200; eighth year sold then on the trees in the orchard for $600.

"Two years used barnyard manure broadcast; for two years used Lister Brothers ammoniated dissolved bone — about one ton each season. The other years of bearing did not use anything."

Duckworth's orchard contained a little over eight acres. In his eight years of enterprise, he could have paid off a 100-acre farm purchased at $40 an acre, and had thousands of dollars of capital left to boot. It was a stirring reality, and a look at the chronology for peaches shows some of the things that happened with it — the mention of 23,000 peach trees near Quakertown being a rough census figure for 1882, while seven years later in 1889 there were an estimated two million mature bearing trees, and an estimate that two million young replacement or expansion trees had been set out that spring.

The industry literally multiplied by 100 in seven years.

And then there were the poor years, like 1891: "The year taken as a whole has not been a pros-

The peach boom was over when this photo was taken, yet orchard crops remained the major income item for dozens of farmers. They were collected at central places — such as in Lebanon — and shipped by rail. Today Hunterdon orchards still provide farmers' markets and roadside stands with peaches, apples, and pears. (Hunterdon County *Democrat*.)

perous one for Hunterdon County, on account of the almost entire failure of the peach crop. The crop in the county has run as high as 1.5 million baskets; reducing this to probably 10,000 baskets makes the average peach-grower feel extremely poor."

By 1895 there had been too many bad years. Peach trees all over the county were falling to the axe, and the remaining growers were an advanced lot: "I look upon the dead and neglected orchards, however, with a feeling akin to satisfaction, knowing full well that the poor fruit raised by slovenly growers will no longer compete with the luscious product of the careful orchardist . . . "

The reporter stressed the importance of careful growing and scientific management of diseases of peaches. He estimated correctly that the peach industry of the past decade was on the way out. By 1899 there were only a million trees of bearing age. Then the San Jose Scale, an insect that affected the trees, became prevalent, and only growers who could spray their trees regularly could produce. By 1909, there were only 300,000 trees. The downward spiral of numbers continued over the years.

Meanwhile, the modern grower was evolving, the man who read the Hunterdon Board reports, which contained detailed instructions on spraying and fertilization and growing. He was the man who attended the Board-sponsored institutes, and could question the speaker on specific problems he had. He followed the advice faithfully, for if he didn't he didn't have even a faint chance of prospering, and what kind of gambling is that?

Dr. C.W. Larison of Ringoes had been a pioneer in effective peach growing in the 1850s and had also advised farmers on another matter: to consider truck crops for fast rail shipment to the cities.

Thus in 1887 the Board reported: "Thomas R. Hunt reports 10,000 quarts of strawberries grown on three acres of ground, and 8,000 quarts of raspberries on four acres. He considers these good crops but says 'prices were too low for any profit.' He fertilizes his ground with William, Clark & Company's bone meal from 800 to 1,000 pounds per acre, and says he has raised many crops of small fruits that paid him well."

And in 1891: "Owing to the failure of the peach crop, many farmers in the southern part of the county planted tomatoes quite extensively, for the purpose of supplying the cannery at Lambertville. There were put up 510,000 cans of tomatoes of a superior brand, now selling in New York and other markets, where they bring the best prices."

A farmer might gross $7 per ton with tomatoes, with a yield of as much as 10 tons an acre.

Truck cropping, the term used to describe vegetable farming, had tremendous potential in Hunterdon that was never fully developed. A major reason was the farmers' inability to establish a stable market for sales to the city wholesalers who came out to buy. Peach Exchanges had succeeded in producing some kind of moderate stability, but basically prices fluctuated even more severely than with other farm crops.

Instability could be tolerated during the years Hunterdon grossed half a million dollars a year in peach revenues. The huge profits from a good year might pay off part of the farm and tide the family over several years of hard work and no monetary reward for it at all.

But, except for the peach boom, the growing of small truck crops and orchards remained in the hands of enthusiasts who could risk years of failure without discouragement, or hard-eyed realists who were willing to stay with the activity and endure the bad years because the crop suited them or their land.

For most of the county's crop producing farmers, the wave of the future lay in developing their dairy herd quality, and expanding their poultry flocks, which would grow continuously in the decades past 1900. That meant producing the major crops of corn, wheat and hay, along with related grains and grasses to feed those cows or chickens. These were the dominant crops in the

A Hunterdon farmer holds a spectacular variety of corn 12 foot high with ears nine feet from the ground, out of the reach of nibbling deer. Though the tall varieties were impressive, what was important was yield in bushels per acre and smaller hybridized varieties proved the winners over the years.

Crop Farming

1880s and remain so today with the addition of soybeans as a harvestable seed crop, plus the multiplication of different kinds of grasses and other fodders to supplement hay as a feed.

Hay and straw were important crops also because they were steady export items sent to metropolitan stables to feed the horses that made the cities run. A major market had built up in the 19th century and it was doomed to extinction by the 1920s. County 4-H Agent B.F. Ramsburg recalls, during his term in Hunterdon, Brevort Conover telling him how a number of farmers in the Croton area specialized in supplying timothy hay to the old hay press at Pittstown, where it was baled into huge bales. As the horse declined, so did their livelihood, and they were forced into other kinds of farming.

There was a lot of supplanting going on. The century began with highly effective and efficient methods of planting, harvesting and hauling to market. Despite this, however, the changes kept coming. Specialty crop growing very frequently leads to insect damage problems, and these were being ingeniously attacked, leading to changed methods. And the scientists who had studied plant breeding in the 19th century with great success were continuing with new developments in the basic grains and fodders. The development and use of the too heavy and thus limited steam engine was now being followed by the new and much lighter internal combustion gasoline engine.

The needs of the population fed by Hunterdon farmers were changing rapidly, too, as the population mushroomed and a greater percentage of the people were prosperous. As a result, farmers found themselves in the middle of many exotic and interesting times. Arthur Danberry of Ringoes, born in 1908, recalls growing up on the farm operated by his dad, Calvin, and grandfather, David Hill:

"They got along very well with very modest means, because there was very little cash flow in those days. You're speaking about the time leading up to World War I. Things were poor economically until the war came along. We did general farming, a small dairy, 12 to 14 cows, and wheat, corn, oats and hay. We hauled the loose hay to Three Bridges to a hay press, and from there it was freighted to the city for horses.

"There were flour mills for wheat along the South Branch of the Raritan. I remember Higgins Mill at Higginsville, which was burned down by arsonists during the war. We had a wonderful market for wheat; wheat went up to $4 a bushel during the war; they just couldn't get enough.

Flemington in the 19th century. Today, the Prospect Hill Apartments stand in the cornfield and the old elementary school in the background, right, is the site of the Flemington-Raritan School complex. Tilled fields run all the way down to Park Avenue in the background, and the only sign of modernity is the telephone line along Capner Street in the foreground. (Kenneth Stryker Collection.)

Crop Farming

They always say, food wins a war, and the fight was on then to produce as much grain as possible. The wheat raised in those days, if you got a yield of 18 bushels to the acre, you were doing well. Today your average yield is above 40 bushels."

Danberry's early days as a farm youth were filled with the practices of the 200-year-old diverse farm. There was the grocer who came around once a week to barter necessities for your farm eggs. There was the mill that ground the wheat to provide you with flour. There was some pork to sell, as well as that raised for the family larder. The real "grocery" was out in the garden growing and later in the cellar in rows of home-canned food. You might even slaughter a beef animal or old cow and make your own dried beef, or salted corned beef.

Danberry suddenly found himself going to Flemington High School and taking the new vocational agriculture courses. And when he got out in 1926, he became a super-specialist of the time and went to work at custom grain threshing with his dad. "We kept changing as the new machines came out. The last horses we sold we traded with Schomp Brothers in Flemington for a Case Tractor. The tractor cost $800 and we got a $125 allowance for the team of horses."

"There was a very interesting thing — we were doing this custom threshing in 1928 and everybody had plenty of money and the bills were paid, and it was a surprising thing. But the 1929 crash came and farm prices were going down, and by 1930 we could hardly collect our threshing bills. No one had any cash. It just dried up."

The custom threshing the Danberrys did was the usual practice. One operator owned a thresher and the steam engine or tractor to power it. It moved from farm to farm. If the sheaves of grain had been stacked near the barn, only five or six extra men were needed to feed the machine, bag and haul the grain, and stack the straw — the last a terrible job in the dust and dirt. If, however, the sheaves were still in shocks in the field, a larger crew of a dozen or more men and about six teams of horses and wagons were needed.

Farmers would join together and move from farm to farm with teams and hired men, threshing for themselves and their neighbors. Preparing the mid-day meal for a group of dust-coverd, sweaty men was always an enormous task for the housewife, but an event enjoyed by the men. Often the wives joined together to help one another.

For the Rinehart family in Franklin Township, machines, especially new ones, ran through their whole history of three generations and into modern times. John Rinehart bought the family's farm in 1896 and was followed by his son Arthur and by Arthur's sons, Jack and Bob, who farm the land today.

Arthur remembers his father telling of his start in farming and how the year 1896 was full of unusual things. One day John was down in the cellar with the dog operating a treadmill to churn butter when the doors to the outside steps flew shut with a mighty crash. He went up the steps to find out what was going on. There was a tremendous noise outside.

Forcing the doors open, he saw the old barn spinning around in the air, coming down with a crash in the onion patch and then going off up in the air again. He shut the doors and stayed in the cellar. It was a mini-tornado. Hunterdon has them occasionally to the present day. They usually don't kill anyone, especially if the people remain in the cellar.

But John Rinehart loved unusual things and he wound up training as a steam engine operator, and ran the electric plant for Clinton Town at times, and sometimes the huge engine that was used to collect ice from a farm pond on Kingtown Road. He had a peach orchard toward the end of the peach boom. Arthur remembers how the peach wagons headed for the station at Landsdown would back up the hill a half mile all the way to the Rinehart farm like modern auto owners waiting for gas.

Sometimes they bought peaches for $2 a basket and the farmers came home rich, and other times, no: "I took a load of 100 baskets to Annandale once and they offered me 10 cents a basket, so we let them go, didn't bring them back, because what the harry are you going to do with 100 baskets of peaches?"

As young Arthur Rinehart grew up, he found himself following his father's diverse interests. He learned about the horse trading business and the care and nurturing of horses. "We got rid of the horse and bought a pair of mules, and then we got into tractors, got the first tractor being sold, an International Osborn about 1919 or 1920. It was called a Steam Mogul. It ran on either kerosene or gas and when it got warmed up, it made steam. It had two round discs, narrow wheels down in front that came with the plow. You'd put this gadget on, drop the two discs down into the furrow the plow was making, and then you could just sit there and ride, you didn't have to steer it!"

The Rinehart farm was run by a mixture of self-guiding Steam Moguls and plain work by hand or even a team of horses still. The Mogul could plow reasonably dry soil, but in the wet the giant steel wheels would bog down. And for cultivating it would crush the corn, so you would go back to horses or mules that moved more delicately through the rows. And to harvest the corn before the first frost, the father and son would go out to the field and cut down the corn stalks by hand, "because if you cut it after the frost, those corn leaves would dry out, be worth little or nothing for feed, and catch you on the neck and cut and scratch something awful."

John Rinehart would cut a square of corn four hills by four hills and begin bundling the stalks with rye straw instead of twine — preparing the straw was a rainy day and wintertime chore. Meanwhile, Arthur would be cutting three rows out from the square on two sides and passing that cut corn to his father, who would continue bundling it in shocks.

In October they'd go out again to pull the corn from the shocks, husk it and throw the shocks into bundles of four each. The husked corn got hauled in with a wagon and put in a slatted crib to dry. Later the shocks were brought in and heaped in a 10 foot high pile by the barn. "You'd either run the shocks through a chopper and use them for bedding for the cows, or you'd put molasses on them and feed them to the cows — there was a little food value there, not too much," recalls Arthur. "You'd get a barrel of molasses, mix it with a little water, put that on the chopped up stalks, just like ensilage, let that set overnight, and the next morning when you went to feed the cows they were glad to get something like that."

Ensilage, or "silage," was something special. The progressive dairymen built tall cylindrical silos used to store the ensilage of chopped green corn and other fodder. The corn would be cut while green and hauled to the silo, where a machine would chop it up and blow it into the silo. There it would be stored with most of its food value intact, many times more than with the dried stalks.

William Phillips of Milford remembers his changeover from tractors and horses to just trac-

John A. Rinehart's Mogul chugs massively along with a two-share plow at the family's farm in Franklin Township. The huge flywheel kept the power output of the steam engine even, and the machine could outwork a horse anytime. It used kerosene, which was less expensive than hay in the early years of the century.

Crop Farming

tors in the mid 1930s. By that time, tractors had rubber tires that didn't crush the soil and get mired like the old steel-wheeled tractors. But Phillips' dad told him that you'd never get rid of the horses entirely; you needed them for a few special things like cultivating, or pulling the grain drill that planted your seed.

"I said, 'I have a notion, Dad, to part with the last team,' " Phillips recalls. They were a very good team of farm horses, about seven, eight years of age. He said, you'll find out that you can't farm all of this farm by tractor; there's some things you still have to have a horse to do. You just can't do it."

So Phillips kept the team, although he still found himself doing nearly everything with the tractor. One day after the horses had been left unworked for a long period of time, he hitched them up to drill wheat and found out the expected — the horses almost collapsed from exhaustion since they had not been used and kept in working condition.

"I drilled a half day and it was a hot day, and my nephew came down to the farm. He says, listen, you can't drill with that team as hot as it is, you'll kill them. I said what are we going to do about it? He said, I'll come down right after lunch and we'll saw the tongue off that drill and put a tractor hitch onto it, and hitch the tractor to it. That's what we did. About 10 days later I sold this team of horses for, would you believe it, $60 for the team."

The Danberrys had gotten $125 for their team a few years earlier. The dollar value of a horse was plummeting. It was a universal experience in the 20s and 30s, selling the last team of work animals, then getting onto this amazing device that rumbled and chugged and jerked like a mule when you let the clutch out too fast, but just went plugging along indefinitely.

No more barnful of hay to feed those big horses! Gas instead, for but a few pennies a gallon!

The gasoline engine was the most revolutionary new machine of the century for crop farmers. Tractors could be made light and small enough for chores like cultivating after all. And the old thresher that was stationary because of its heavy steam enging could grow wheels, and start a new line of machine design going.

The new harvesting machines rapidly proliferated into a family. By running a long steel shaft to the tractor "power take-off," they could be powered devices. The previous harvest machines were "powered" by the turning of the wheels that supported them, and this severely limited the work they could do. It was hard on the horses, too, that supplied the power.

These new machines always had bugs, but always worked well enough to be worth the trouble. The farmer who wanted to wait several years might get the same machine in a perfected state,

Three fine horses are shown off by Margin Stout, right, of Milford and his father in the old family snapshot. Strong but delicate creatures and easily ruined by poor care and attention, horses were the mainstay of farming. And, for men with daring in their blood, there was "horse trading" and the races at the Flemington Fair.

Crop Farming

but he also risked finding that design of machine already outmoded and a new design — with bugs — ready and waiting for him to try out.

The average farmer in Hunterdon County used to look at every horse he saw with an appraising eye. Now he was looking at machines the same way. The ones his neighbor was using, he might even borrow to try out. Then there was the Flemington Fair and the top state fairs — Syracuse in New York and Harrisburg in Pennsylvania. He'd also read *New Jersey Agriculture,* a magazine put out by Rutgers, and any of a half dozen similar commercial magazines for farmers. He'd talk to the equipment dealers, who always had to be ready to quote hard facts if he really wanted to sell.

One of the more interesting promotions by an equipment dealer came from Van Zandt near Hopewell, a dealership popular in the south county. Farmers were rejecting the new rubber tires on tractors that showed up in the 1920s. They cost a lot more and the old steel-wheeled models worked better, they thought. They didn't even believe it when the dealer said no, they work much better in soft ground and have much better traction.

Van Zandt got together a steel and a rubber-wheel tractor, got the use of a long field on the main road, and invited the farmers for a demonstration. The two tractors started off at the roadway and headed for the opposite end of the field a half mile away, plowing. As they headed back, everyone could see the rubber-tired tractor was way in the lead. It had more pull. So did Van Zandt after that, when the dealer told a customer the rubber wheels were better.

It was nearly impossible to induce a farmer to part with six months' or a year's profits to buy a new machine unless he knew it would work. But the inducements were always there. The finest team of horses would plow about two acres of land a day, and that meant 50 days plowing for a 100 acres of cropland. The average 1920s and 1930s tractor pulling a double-bottom plow might do an average six acres a day. Plus, a farmer could work on into the night, since the tractor didn't tire as quickly as horses. Fifty days of work reduced to 15 or 20. With today's gigantic machines, he can plow 20 acres in a day.

Besides the power take-off spindle at the rear, the tractor had a large belt-driving pulley at the side. In addition to the miraculous field machines, the area around the barn could have portable power enough to resemble a factory with a dozen separate engines.

The ensilage chopper-blower that ran the fodder into the silo could be hooked up by a heavy, yards-long drive belt to the tractor.

A two-bottom plow, powered by a rubber-tired tractor, rolls down a field of hay making short work of the job. More than anything else, tractors with a plow changed the face of Hunterdon and the rest of the nation. Faster than horses, they didn't get tired or sick, didn't break down, and cost only pennies a day to operate. The driver checks to be sure the shares are plowing to the right depth.

Those old hand-run corn shellers were now turning into belt-driven, high powered machines that would eventually produce a 100-pound bag of shelled corn in a couple of minutes.

Even the Civil War hayfork that ran on tracks in the hay mow and carried hay up could be powered by a tractor now, with an ingenious slip-clutch that a ten-year-old kid could operate.

Yet crop statistics for the 1920 to 1930 period were poor. Corn planted each year dropped 40 percent and wheat dropped 25 percent. Part of it was the agricultural depression of 1920-24, and the lagging years that followed. It also appeared that activity was shifting from the field crop to the barn and poultry building, since these activities were increasing from 1920-30.

The records suggest that for dairying, crops that produced shelled corn or grain were being diverted to fodder crops. Thus, the corn and green fodder planted for ensilage rose from 1,705 acres to 3,325 acres, and the high quality perennial alfalfa fields were increased from about 2,000 to 3,000.

The depression decade of the 30s gave the conventional crop farm statistics a boost back, however. Federal government stabilization programs made it possible for the crop farmer to know he would get a decent price for his crop, and he, in turn, became involved in restricting acreage to avoid useless surpluses.

The new crop for the 1930s was soybeans. They could be chopped for cow fodder or harvested like grain, and the pea-sized beans sold on the market. In a decade's time, plantings went from 600 to 3,000 acres. The crop was popular because it had that old-fashioned diversity built into it, and its most charming use was for "green manure" — the roots put nitrogen back in the soil because they were nitrogen-fixers, and then plowing the crop under as green manure added more high quality organic fertilizing elements. Farmers were going from a low cash-flow system to a high cash requirement, and anything to slow that trend was a life-saver. With soybeans you were manufacturing your own fertilizer.

The other way to get fertilizer was to go easy on the fields. Different crops required different nutrients. Farmers rotated their crops, planting a different one in a specific field each year, a method that had been developed in the 19th century. For example, the following schedule was common for a twenty-acre field as part of a five-field, 100-acre farm: 1923, mid-September, plant winter wheat and timothy and top-seed red clover February or March; 1924, July, harvest the wheat; 1925, summer, harvest two cuttings of clover with timothy mixed in with it; 1926, summer, the biennial clover is gone, harvest one or two cuttings of timothy; 1927, spring, plant corn, use some fertilizer, cultivate for three months, harvest in fall; and 1928, spring, plant oats, cut in June, mid-September, plant winter wheat, clover, timothy again.

Such a farm each year, given adequate weather, would produce 40 acres of hay, 20 acres of corn for grain or ensilage, 20 acres of wheat, 20 acres of oats. Each of its five fields would be at a different stage of rotation.

Manure from the cows or the chickens or any other of the farm animals was always used when available. It was spread on fields that had their crops already harvested. Or piled in heaps where it would compost itself rapidly and then spread in the fall or early spring. Then it was plowed under.

A farmer during the 1930s looks over his tractor-converted manure spreader with pride. He's facing the business end — whirling paddles that fling the manure evenly over the field as a conveyor belt moves it along into the blades. Next, the farmer plowed the manure under to rot into the highest quality organic fertilizer.

The spreader was a big wagon with chain-driven paddles that dragged the manure towards the back of the wagon where spinning blades hurled it all over the field. For several decades it was the prankster's symbol of defiance. Many of those years you could drive into Flemington the day after Halloween trick or treat night and find an empty spreader parked on the county courthouse's front steps.

The major difference between the crop farmer of the 1920s and of the 1930s was that a man following all the most progressive practices and using the newest machines was a "leader" in the 1920s. Ten years later he was part of the large majority. The "progressive" farmers had won their county agent, and had gotten the large majority to be progressive.

Lime was a key element for over a century in restoring fields that had grown too acid. A farmer at the turn of the century might drive a wagon all day to a lime kiln or processing plant, fill it up, and drive home. By the 1920s, the feed mills were offering lime, and it was available in other ways. "Unslaked" lime had to have water poured over it to make it usable. A farmer might

farmers doing it then. It was a truism that the best methods were always used by a small percentage of farmers, and the job was always to reach the large majority with those methods.

Crop variety tests and demonstrations sponsored by the Board of Agriculture and conducted by the county extension agents were an important part of the changes and the improvement in crop production. Research at Rutgers and other agricultural colleges was aimed at creating new

A Hunterdon farmer kneels by the results of the corn demonstration he planted for the Board of Agriculture to show its members. "N.J. Hybrid" and "Ohio Hybrid K-23" are on the small signboards.

hire a local truck owner to go down to the U.S. Steel plant below Trenton to pick up a load of the lime that was created there as a waste product.

Fertilizers of both natural and man-made sorts had been sold for a long time, as lime was, but were used sparingly because of their cost. But a man who hooted in derision at the regular use of fertilizer in the 20s might be putting 100 pounds an acre on his corn in the 30s. A common mixture was an inert substance with two percent nitrogen, eight percent superphosphate, and ten 10 percent potash in it, and it was called by the standardized code name of "2-8-10."

Later these amounts would be doubled, tripled, quadrupled, and there were even a few varieties of crops. Hybrid corn, higher producing lines of wheat, oats, barley, soybeans, red clover and alfalfa, as well as better strains of hay and pasture crops were being developed during these years.

Rutgers crop specialists such as H.R. Cox, Carlton S. Garrison, Robert Briggs, John Baylor, and others would bring new varieties to the county agent for trial on local farms. With the agent's help, a farmer who participated in the tests would plant different varieties of a new selection along with his usual crop. Only a small area 100 foot long and 20 feet wide planted in a part of the field where the soil type was uniform would allow an accurate comparison. The agent and the soil specialists would come by and harvest the samples.

Then would come the Board's annual meeting or special crop meetings, and the season's results would be reported and publicized. Ultimately the practice resulted in a State Crop Recommendation summary each year of all the tests and demonstrations. In Hunterdon, the Board Newsletter would often feature the latest news at the time when farmers were placing their seed orders. When a farmer stopped by to ask the county agent for planting advice, the summaries would come out.

Results were favorable to the farmer, usually. One year the results showed Yorkwin, a soft white winter wheat developed at Cornell, to be absolute tops. The wheat looked beautiful, like puffed rice, the kernels were so large. Unfortunately, the following season when farmers were planting it was terribly wet. The soft kernels absorbed all that moisture, sprouted, and grew five or six inches long in the heads before farmers could combine it! The earlier used and harder red varieties didn't sprout quite as fast, so there wasn't much loss there. Luckily, by this time the county agents had a lot of good friends who had tried earlier recommendations and found them workable — so they were willing to understand that the new variety only held good for a "normal" season.

Probably one of the most significant advances in the history of agriculture in the world was the development of hybrid corn. Large organizations have developed closely inbred strains, each with a particular quality. The seed planted by the farmer was the result of a first cross of two hybrid strains, called "hybridization," greatly increased production. Hybrid corn is a concentration of all the desirable characteristics of several strains to minimize variation and thus enable the farmer to produce a more uniform crop. An acre that once yielded 40 to 50 bushels, might produce more than a 100 with hybrid corn. Today, a combination of hybridization, improved soil management, and better fertilizer can lead to as many as 300 bushels of corn per acre.

As the years passed, more and more of the seed companies began to breed and sell their own special varieties of hybrid corn seed, and

No one had much money in the 1930s, not even enough to construct a storage building for corn. So, Harry Britton, among others, bought a few rolls of inexpensive snow fence, laid down some scrap lumber for flooring, and, presto, a corn crib.

Crop Farming

Neat piles of corn are inspected by farmers in a corn demonstration about 50 years ago. Rutgers and the Board of Agriculture encouraged volunteer farmers to grow "test" varieties side-by-side to enable the comparison of quality by everyone.

they began to enter their varieties in the local corn tests, which grew in size and complexity. Dr. John Anderson, Rutgers corn breeder, would coordinate any commercial samples, and pass them on to the county agents in Hunterdon and elsewhere. Sometimes 20 to 50 different hybrids were tested. The local crop grower learned what were the best hybrids for Hunterdon, and the seed company breeders got back important information on the strong and weak points of their newest combinations.

Perhaps more than anything else, this whole program speeded the day when farmers would begin to realize the magical number of 100, the number of bushels of corn per acre. First there was another problem to be solved, the nationwide one of soil erosion. Hunterdon had the lucky opportunity to be leaders in the development of the solution.

In 1937, the *Democrat* carried a story, entitled "Dr. Evaul reports on progress of soil erosion work in Hunterdon where 190 farmers were adopting new methods on 15,000 acres." The project, which involved controlled drainage, was crucial. Aerial photos showed that 93 percent of the county's farmland needed work done on it, and 25 percent of it was rapidly losing priceless topsoil in severe washing.

How Fred Totten of Ringoes became "guinea pig" for never-before tried federal programs in large-scale land conservation is recounted in the Board of Agriculture narrative. The program was a pioneering venture in the use of modern bulldozers and earth moving equipment to create improved field drainage patterns. Hunterdon had the newest things going for it, in soil protection as it had in other farming areas. But Earl Hartpence of Stanton, who grew up in the Ringoes area, recalls another side to the story:

"You know Harold Holcombe's farm at Mount Airy? When they first started in conservation, they came around. His father's name was Charlie, and they started talking to him about putting in drainage terraces and he kind of started laughing. What are you laughing at?, the fellow said.

Charlie said, my father was practicing that when I took over the farm, and I'm still practicing it, he said, and we don't have the fields wash as a result, he said. You fellows are about 50 years behind the times!"

They were a half century late, and twice as necessary as a result. And probably the good-natured gibes of Charles Holcombe helped farmers in his neighborhood realize that the new "textbook" miracles were not going to destroy them, because they'd been stolen from the book of commonsense by one of their own kind a half century ago.

By the same token, popularization was vital in Hunterdon, since otherwise a farmer could live next door to the Holcombes for 50 years and not realize that they had learned how to prevent soil erosion and increase production. Popularization and progressiveness were sometimes hectic and sometimes had the air of opening the Sears Roebuck "wish book" and wondering what to give yourself for Christmas. It could be quite gratifying when it worked out well.

As World War II came into view and the decade of the 40s began, there were going to be different changes coming along. In some ways, events looked the same. The war production effort emphasized human food stuffs, and two huge lima bean threshers wound up in Hunterdon with participating farmers hauling the whole plants to the threshers and coming home without the beans to use the green plants for

The first load of vines filled with soup peas is fed into a special thresher that had been trucked to Hunterdon to boost productivity during World War II. The truck has just collected a load of the vines at the J. Alfred Rinehart farm in Franklin Township.

Crop Farming

forage.

By that time, Arthur Rinehart of Franklin Township was dairy and crop farming with his son, Jack. They wound up using the same machinery that Arthur and his father had used during the first war: "During the World War I, we got into the soup bean business, producing navy beans, those little ones. I know it was during the war because I remember the troop trains going down along the valley, there were two or three going by every day, bringing men from out West into New York. Ironically enough, the same machine we used to cut the beans in World War I, we used with the lima beans in World War II. We rebuilt it to make it go on a tractor."

The device had special blades that cut the bean

Local high school girls load a truck of tomatoes near Cherryville in 1942. With all except fulltime pre-war farmers off to war, women helped harvest crops that otherwise could not have been grown.

With male farm labor at a minimum during the war, these young women made the difference between a several hundred acre tomato crop in Hunterdon and none at all. Despite the back-breaking work, the novices in the photo are all smiling, perhaps because they knew of their contribution to the war effort.

bush an inch or so below the soil — before it branched out in a dozen different directions. This made collection easy, though, as Arthur recalled of World War I: "If you didn't gather those beans up right away the next day they'd be all gone and people in the area would have soup beans enough for their whole winter!"

Thus, it certainly seemed that the old virtues of diversity and flexibility were still being applied the way they had been for decades. And were having an important effect in contributing to the war effort. Something fundamental had changed by 1940, however, even though it was not yet visible. There had been several decades of intensive innovation on every level of activity from machine to man. Innovation towards "going all out." Towards new machinery. Towards cash operations. Towards listening more closely to the leaders and the experts.

It was all thrown into the war effort like leading canned goods into a large pressure cooker. And by the end of the war, there was a new world that wasn't anything like 1925 or 1935. The tremendous pressures to produce during the war were half-strangled by shortages of gasoline, farm equipment and rubber tires. Then the war was over, and the pressures that had built up got a full boost with plenty of gas, tires, and farm equipment.

But the real element that transformed the situation was the one farmers never considered because it was outside their sphere of operation. At the turn of the century, 409 square miles of farmland were reported for the county, and in 1940, only 297 square miles were reported. Towns had grown, new, wide highways had been built, and the less productive farmland had been sold to people who were not farmers and did not farm it. With the war over and its subsequent economic boom, new people began streaming into the county.

In the meantime, competing crop producers over most of the nation did not have this growing problem of finding land to use, and meeting the new taxes. So on a national scale, crop commodity prices tended to be geared to their lesser need for income. It had always been rough for farmers everywhere to make a living in changing times. Now Hunterdon farmers were entering a stage where the situation was measurably rougher.

The response was pragmatic and unavoidable: up your pace of development, use less labor which is too expensive to hire, produce and produce and produce. Or produce another way, by going to work in one of the new industries in the surrounding area while keeping the farm active. In the Rinehart family, that meant Jack's younger brother, Robert, leaving farming, and Jack himself making changes.

"It was interesting. We had started building up our chickens in 1938 because we had the auction market to use, and then we did like a lot of other people. I still had the chickens on the farm, but I worked in a factory 12 years on shift work. So I was tending chickens and working out during that period."

Because the farm was also a home with many rich personal associations, many farmers did that rather than consider selling their land. Those who stayed and hung on did not go easy on changes. William McIntyre of Lebanon was County Agent Dwight Babbitt's assistant during this period before he became agent himself in 1959. The crop growing changes that dairymen made in producing cow fodder were an example of the similar changes that occurred with every type of crop farming. As a young agricultural expert, McIntyre remembered them well:

"The big changes were in mechanization and crop rotations and this whole matter of grassland farming. That was a part of our continuing conservation program — it worked in beautifully with our dairy and crop programs.

"New things were coming out — pasture management research at the college with grass silage, the work that Carl Bender did with various crops, the work done up at the Rutgers Research Farm in Beemerville by Claude Eby and other men.

"It resulted in a lot of changes and improvements in crop varieties for pasture, grass silage, and hay. And it all led towards a more profitable operation with less labor demand. It's a lot easier to make silage than it is to make hay. It's harder to feed silage sometimes, but you don't lose as much of the crop. So grass silage came into the picture along with pasture improvements, and rotational grazing."

The rotational grazing was applied to the 20- to 40-acre "pasture" field that most dairymen kept for summer grazing for their animals. It was the last field to receive this attention. The pasture fed the animals somewhat during the summer, but even a small 10-cow herd could trim the grass down to the roots by July, and after that all you had was a 20-acre yard for the cows to exercise in.

Crop Farming

A two-foot-deep row of sun-cured hay is gobbled up by this postwar baler that produces a cylinder-shaped bale weighing 40 pounds. The rectangular baler was more popular, but of late the cylinder baler has made a comeback. The evolution of machinery has been continuous since this scene in 1947.

The first work in earlier periods had dealt with planting the pasture with better quality grasses and lime it to correct acid soil, and even the occasional use of fertilizer.

That was now being supplemented with rotational grazing, where a forage crop was grown. Cows were fenced into small portions of the field

An old stationary baler takes hay and reduces it to densely packed chunks the size of a steamer trunk in this 1930s photo of workmen at the Mulhocaway Farm north of Clinton. It was easier than working with loose hay, especially when filling the loft which a dozen cows and a couple horses could empty out during a long, cold winter.

Crop Farming

and ate the crop there while other areas grew. Then they were released into another portion, and so on. This kind of rotation was necessary because animals grazing a large field will trample more of the plants than they will eat.

"The County Board sponsored the State Green Pasture and Forage Program to encourage farmers to improve their use of those soil conserving crops for livestock and dairy cows," McIntyre noted.

"Efforts were made to extend the pasture season on both ends using Balbo rye. This crop would green up in March and if the field was not too wet, cows could get two to three weeks of early pasture before bluegrass got started and if planted in early fall — say September — it would be ready to carry the cows a couple extra weeks into the fall.

"Ladino clover and bromegrass or orchard grass were combined to take the place of bluegrass that slowed down when warm, dry weather came. To fill pasture gaps in the July-August period, sudangrass was a very useful crop.

"Before field choppers were available and popular, efforts were made to have the cow do

An eye for quality is cast upon hay samples by Lloyd Wescott, second from left, and his dairy manager George Schellenberger. To the right are Orville Barrick and George Miller, at the Fourth Annual Dairy Institute at the Stanton Grange in 1951. The difference between top quality and second-grade hay could mean the difference between a slim profit and none at all.

her own harvesting. The Green Pasture contest gave a farmer a chance to judge and be judged on how well he or his neighbors succeeded in the management of these new pasture-foraging methods."

McIntyre continued:

"The hay crusher and hay drying was looked at, too. You chopped hay and blew it on top of ducts that you could force air through and keep it from heating up, and dry it out rapidly. We had several farms that were trying this, and we'd have demonstration meetings at the farms to show others how it worked. And we'd go out with an extension engineer and help farmers design those systems to fit their operations.

"One of the early ones was Norman Fulper and his sons near Lambertville, and they used an 'Ohio' system. A big duct ran along one side of the barn with a large fan run by a diesel motor. In addition to moving the air through the hay mass, it used excess heat given off by the diesel to warm some of the air and to help dry the hay.

"The duct was so big you could actually walk through it, and it ran along the barn to smaller ducts about two feet high and one foot wide that went across the barn floor. They were raised a couple inches from the floor, and the air came out through these and went up through the hay and dried it. It worked beautifully and it was a case of using the power to make it work. A number of set-ups like this one went in.

"Then we got the hay crusher. Loose hay or chopped hay is a pain in the neck to handle, and it's difficult to dry when you pack it into bales. The crusher could squeeze the stems and crack them and the hay would then dry within a day or so. This cut down field drying time by at least a day, sometimes two, which meant the difference between getting a quality hay crop and not getting it — if the rains came too soon, you'd have to dry all over again, and lose a lot of food value.

"During this same time, field choppers and self unloading wagons for silage became popular. And we got sorghum coming in as a forage crop as well as corn and sudangrass," according to McIntyre.

These dealt with the production of the highest possible quality of ensilage, plus good summer feed. Instead of grazing cows on a field of good forage and thereby losing a significant portion to trampling, farmers would go out with the chooper, chop a wagonload, bring it back, and feed it to the cows in daily rations. Pastures became obso-

David Perrine of Lebanon measures the depth of spoilage of his grass silage in a "trench silo," graded so that rain would run off the caked top layer and seal the rest of the fodder. The mixture of grasses underneath stayed green and retained their nutrient value. A trench silo cost a fraction of the tall cylinder that was normally used to store silage.

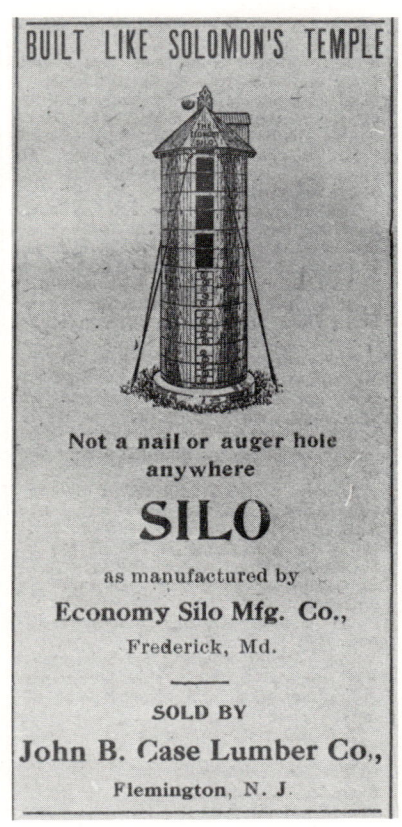

lete and the parts that were plowable were turned back into cropland.

These changes in crop farming methods helped keep dairymen in Hunterdon County. For the two-decade period following the war, as the cost of operation for a farmer or anyone else soared, the dairyman's price per quart of milk changed comparatively little. The rising costs of land taxes and machinery were paid for through more efficiency in producing the expensive feeds that cows need to make quality milk.

Each improvement was measured precisely in terms of the ratio of cost to benefit in output. This was true for the crops raised for dairy, the grain crops for poultry, and crops raised for sale as commodities. The 80-pound bags of 2-8-10 fertilizer that were dumped into the planter-fertilizer hopper in the 20s and 30s were replaced by bags with high content formulas like 5-10-10 and 15-15-15 and even 20-20-20. Pounds per acre of fertilizer for a corn crop might go from 100 per acre in the 30s to 500 pounds per acre in the 40s and 50s.

Farmers no longer spread a few tons of lime with their small spreaders every few years. Now they called upon GLF or another feed dealer with systematic regularity, who came over with tractor-trailer-sized vehicles and spread many times more fertilizer in a few hours. This saved the cost of the bags, and the costs of spreading. All this was preceded by an extension soil test to insure the right amount.

After applying 500 pounds an acre of fertilizer on corn, it was then "sidedressed" with 150 to 200 pounds an acre of 40 percent nitrogen during the growing season when cultivating. Or liquid nitrogen by the tank was applied at much higher speeds than when cultivating. The nitrogen was injected into the soil near the corn as the vehicle sped down the rows.

Perhaps the most interesting and controversial post-war change was the intensified use of pesticides. DDT was an early wonder chemical, credited with saving thousands of lives in malarial countries by killing mosquitoes. It has since been replaced by other pesticides that have fewer residual effects.

Lloyd Wescott of Rosemont remembers with humor how the first time a farmer sprayed his cow stable with DDT (first removing all milk and feed to prevent contamination), the flies disappeared like magic, and stayed away. But, then, after a while the survivor flies came back and this time were not wiped out by the DDT, because they were the rare few who were resistant to the spray! And they soon multiplied into the previous numbers of flies.

Farmers quickly learned that a great deal of subtlety and care was required to make pesticides and herbicides work. Probably their widespread success among farmers was due to the highly pragmatic and trained nature of the man who has to deal with 100 different factors that may help his crop or harm it. "You take the average farmer, he didn't buy a lot of spray he didn't need," Earl Hartpence noted. "And he found out if you put too much on, it injured the crops."

Of all the groups using specialized scientific developments over the decades, farmers have probably the best record of careful usage. Hartpence recalled with annoyance being required to take a "test" to prove he was a careful worker when new government regulations came along to tighten up pesticide security.

"I don't think one of them who gave the test was over 24 years old. I doubt if they'd ever sprayed a field in their life. But they thought they knew how. I'd been spraying for 25 years and so had the rest of the farmers there!"

Historically, the first sprays used extensively in Hunterdon were of crude oil from Oil City, Pennsylvania. Men like Arthur Rinehart used it at the turn of the century to combat the San Jose Scale that appeared on apples and peaches. Sprays that came along after the World War II were light-years ahead of the oil spray in sophistication. Nowadays sprays are both highly selective — may knock out only one kind of insect or a few kinds of weeds — and produce is double-checked continuously by the federal government for contamination.

Despite this, accidents occasionally occur in the use of the sprays. As McIntyre once put it, the responsibility for this is a joint one: "When people get to the point where they'll accept a few harmless spots on their produce, farmers will be happy to cut back on the sprays."

One big spray was the one that eliminated having to cultivate corn. During May, June and July in Hunterdon, tractors could be heard chugging away endlessly, keeping the weeds down so the corn would grow. All of a sudden three months of repetitive work was replaced by one tractor operated at high speed, using a 20-foot-wide rig, spraying the ground when the corn was six inches high. The end product was virtually no

2, 4, D herbicide is applied to a cornfield by this early spray rig, another postwar development. The use of sprays was a labor-saver for farmers who before had to cultivate out the weeds.

weeds and more corn and grain per hour of work and acre of field.

During the 20-year period, from 1940 to 1960, land planted in corn in the county went down 20 percent, but bushels of corn produced went up 50 percent. Bushels produced went from 36 an acre in 1940 to 48 in 1950 and then 68 in 1960.

American industry is held in awe the world over for its creation and continuous development of "automation" and "assembly lines" to increase manpower productivity year after year after year. Yet, a study done a few years ago comparing the industrial output growth to the productivity growth in American agriculture showed that the average farmer and his wife and kids increased farm productivity faster by far.

"Big industry" is supposed to be the most efficient way of doing anything. It is not always the case. Small farm families fighting for survival are just as efficient, adaptive, and inventive. All of this was now in sharp focus after the World War II.

The horse that plowed two acres a day was bumped by the tractor that did six. And the tractor was retired after the war as more powerful engines were added that would pull a three-bottom plow through 11 acres of hard ground in an average day. Today, a six-bottom plow will turn over 20 acres in a day.

By 1960 all of these changes in Hunterdon and throughout the country had produced another tip-over into a new world. On the national level, the government had failed to create viable crop production and price control measures and had settled for ineffectual ones that piled up billions of tons of surplus government wheat in makeshift bins such as mothballed warships. On the local level, the number of farmers had dropped and gotten much older in average age, and the county's farmland was down to 238 square miles, and further land was being lost at an alarming pace.

Farming was over in Hunterdon as a major industry, and likewise in the rest of the state. But through cooperation of farmers and nonfarmers, the Farmland Assessment Act passed in 1964 came along to severely slow the flow of farmland into urban congestion.

Farmland assessment was the result of a court ruling that ordered tax assessors to assess land regardless of its use at its highest possible value, which a developer might pay for it to sub-divide it and cover it with houses. This ruling literally kicked many farmers off their farms. Those in metropolitan counties or in rural counties near residential or commercial or industrial sites were forced to sell to get out from under an impossible tax bill. In some places the resulting tax was many times the total net income of the farm. It was an impossible situation for agriculture. Farmers proposed an acceptable amendment to the state constitution by working through the County Board of Agriculture, state farm organizations, the College of Agriculture and the State Board of Agriculture.

It was aimed at saving open spaces in the Garden State. Known as the Farmland Assessment

Fallow farmland was beginning to create problems. One of the answers was the growing of Christmas trees, which would yield a cash crop in five years or so. Here two men demonstrate pruning techniques to keep the growth even and full.

Amendment, it was strongly supported by much of the non-farm population of the state. Under the act, farmland is assessed at its agricultural value based on its productivity and use in farming. The very best soil used for cropland is assessed more than poorer land for the same use. There are five classes of land ranging from Class A, the very best, to Class E, the poorest. Soil survey maps can spot these types. Uses range from the highest of cropland through pasture to woodland. The farmer is still taxed at the same rate as any other landowner for his home, barns, out buildings, and any other land under and around these buildings.

So the act stopped the rapid demise of farming and gave it a new life. And thus it came about that men who can remember spending all day cultivating an acre of corn with a corn plow came to see their sons or grandsons operate the thousand-acre corn patch. More accurately, around 800 acres is about the popular optimal size the county's remaining crop farmers operate with.

Jack Rinehart and his brother, Robert, are one of the remaining farm family teams, and Jack believes farm assessment is the reason they're in business today. "Farmers sold a bunch of smaller dairies out and other farms, and investors bought some of this land. The land had been farmed under farmland assessment and grain was the logical thing to give them a qualifying income on the land.

"A lot of the land we are using belongs to investors, syndicates even, and they're only holding it until a big buck comes along. I would think that we just happened to be ready to move in on this thing at the time. People wanted to farm, and the machinery was getting bigger, and the commodity prices warranted it, so you actually had a combination of maybe three things in this.

"I think farmland assessment has had a good effect. The investors didn't have to farm those fields; they could just let them grow up, and a bulldozer could clean that field instantly. So maybe the first two or three years they were a little bit slack obtaining farmland assessment. Then some of these people began to get (huge) tax bills and they began to look for somebody to farm the land!"

This change occurred gradually over the past two decades. With the Rineharts, Robert returned to farming in 1962, and went in with his brother on a 25,000 hen egg laying flock which they built up over a period of years.

"'And as we were growing with the hens, we were also growing a lot more crops. In 1974 we went out of the chickens and went with the grain. Right now we're farming approximately 800 acres with a little hay included — 500 acres of corn, 135 acres of wheat, 250 acres of soybeans. Ha, if I tell people what we're doing, they'll think I'm bragging, so we just don't tell them everything."

What is actually being done in farming can be a surprise to nonfarmers, since farmers change so much faster. Melda Snyder remembers when her husband died in 1967 and she prepared to take over running their 530-acre farm. She had their

The farmer grabs the bale just before heaving it onto the elevator. Inside the top loft, another man stacks them neatly for maximum storage.

A one-man factory moves down a field of wheat with a machine called the "combine," which came into use is Hunterdon in the 1930s. Steel knives cut the wheat, a conveyor belt moves it into rotating blades that "thresh" the heads of wheat loose, then a long railed platform shakes the stalks out of the machine. The grain is conveyed to a storage compartment.

Always a cash crop, trees for lumber are loaded onto a tractor-trailer flatbed with a bulldozer. By this time, the 1960s, Hunterdon had a fulltime forester, Otto Kunkel, working out of the Soil Conservation Service. He pre-marks the trees to be logged for farmers so their woodlots can be cared for with scientific precision.

banker come out one day to review things and evaluate them in terms of money. Together they looked over the farm's large collection of modern farm machinery.

"What do you think all this is worth?" she asked him with a slight smile.

"Oh, $10,000."

She told him that any one of the tractors alone cost much more than that amount.

He apologized profusely.

That was during the crossover period into the present time. Today's prices have inflated like anything else, and the machines are larger, too. A machine to harvest grain and soybeans cost $40 to $84 thousand dollars. It cuts a swath 10 to 15 feet wide, completely processes the grain, and dumps it into a truck that follows it through the field. The operator rides in an air-conditioned cab, drives with power steering and operates the controls and adjustments of the machine with hydraulic linkages.

A farm child can still operate the big machines the way his granddad drove the steam tractor when he was a kid, but farmers are very careful about letting others use their machines, since a single mistake or a second's slowness in response can do a thousand dollars worth of damage.

The basic heavy duty farm tractor lists at about $35,000, according to the Rineharts. It pulls a plow with six to eight shares, and it can plow a 20 acre field in less than a day. When the field is harvested, it no longer goes to the mill and is sold — prices are lowest at harvest time and the buyer of grain reaps a rich profit by holding it till later on in the yearly cycle.

Over the countryside one can see large cylindrical steel buildings that are the farmer's grain bins, holding sometimes tens of thousands of bushels, and containing expensive forced hot-air drying equipment. Many have been financed with loans from federal government programs designed to help farmers hold their crops for the best selling time and thus avoid losing out at harvest-time.

The investments involved are huge and the risks are as always the purest form of gambling — a farmer may gross $25,000 during a good year at harvest time, and during a year of crop failure he can pour $10,000 into a 100 acres and get nothing but dust.

When it's time to plow, there are 800 acres to plow, and harrow, and plant. No, you can't wait until next week because a four-week-long rainy spell is predicted. Do you want to get your crop in late and lose it to frost because it's not finished growing? Or maybe try some early maturing corn, and take a chance?

Hunterdon farmers do not worry too much about competition for the big money they may be

Crop Farming

making. It isn't so big, really, though if they are careful they may be able to support their families and avoid losing their shirts. They do that by using the latest methods, as usual. These involve hybrid seeds and fertilizer applications and soil testing, all calculated by a computer, and a businessman's knowledge of accounting.

Hunterdon's present Senior County Agent Calvin Wettstein remarks that after half-a-century of sharing knowledge, the farmer is unlikely to tell what his net profit was for a year — in fact, he might not know — but he will share all of his other knowledge willingly.

"This the second year we've run a three-day crops economics course. Three day-long sessions. Somerset Agent Nate Repair and his son, Jon, who's now in Mercer, and I, ran it," said Wettstein. "We had some 20 farmers involved and on the middle day we would have a farmer in to talk. Last year it was Everett Hill of Clover Hill, this year it was Ernest Kuster, south of Flemington.

"And we'd sit all day long and pump questions at him. We'd hear him first on how he operates. Then the rest of the time those other people are pumping questions at him — 'How did you make that decision on that size combine?' — 'Why do you grow oats at all, you know, it's a marginal crop?' "And he produces figures to show you why he does things like that.

"And how many businesses do you know of where they share like that? Would you get a bunch of paper companies together to share their techniques? That's an amazing thing about farmers. They love to talk. They won't tell you how much money they make, that's getting a little bit too nosey. But they'll talk about their practices, their decisions, how much they are producing, everything short of that. The sharing is unbelievable.

"Farming is competition. We all have a little competitiveness, there's a competitive nature in all of us that surfaces — when somebody else is doing a really good job, or just bought a six bottom plow, you may go out and buy a seven. I know a few fellows who play that game, but on the other hand, they talk to each other, they exchange ideas!"

That's how farmers get along in business. They compete, beat the other guy, then tell him how they did it so they're on an equal footing come next spring. As they ride down the field with the door to their air-conditioned cab open, they smell the fresh earth turned over by the plow, smell the perfume the hot sun raises from the earth, smell the different scents of a season — rain, morning dew, dryness, plants growing. And they look over the fields they know so much about and beyond them to trees, houses, more fields.

They see the sights and fragrances of their fields change slowly through the varying season, and know every one of them from last year and the year before. But they don't talk about this aspect of it. They talk about commodity prices and equipment deals. Or they lay awake nights thinking about what it feels like to lose $70,000 this year if the bad weather continues.

The *American Agriculturist,* a venerable farm magazine, once explained it all in the humorous story of the farmer who was asked what he would do if he were given a million dollars.

"I'd farm and farm and farm 'til it was all gone!" the man replied.

He didn't entirely mean that, of course. He could not really express his real reaction, for perhaps it was too close to the fragrances and sights that the fields infused into his life and which he never spoke about. But the story does help to explain why, so long as there is farmland in Hunterdon County, there will be men and women and children to farm that land.

Beautiful but greedy, a herd of deer romp through a cornfield already plucked clean by a modern corn picker. In some areas of the county, deer remain a nuisance and the crops they feed off tend to increase their numbers.

IX The Auxiliary Forces

You rarely hear a farmer call himself a farmer, just as you rarely hear a banker call himself a banker. Both are too busy being what they are to talk about it much.

But, for the farmer, there is another reason. If a farmer is a man who farms the land, who is that seven-year-old kid leading a team of horses pulling a walking plow? Who is that woman with two 40-pound buckets of mash walking through the chicken pens?

South Main St. in Flemington looks different today from what it did many years ago when Liz Smith posed with her prize milk cow. All it took in the summertime was a small pasture and a galvanized pail to make a little money selling fresh milk to your neighbors up the street. (Kenneth Stryker Collection.)

Down by the South Branch of the Raritan, a favorite meeting place after school or after chores, with or without swimming togs and often including a bull who snorted and pawed the ground near discarded clothes.

Who does the most work on the farm? The woman gets up at five in the morning to get her husband breakfast before he goes out to work, and washes the dishes at 10 in the evening after he has had his evening meal?

Who is it who cares for the children in the thousand ways they require, washes the clothes, does the shopping, and keeps the house an attractive, comfortable place to live — and then takes on some "light" work, like caring for a thousand laying hens, to help keep the whole farm prosperous?

What about the kids? What do they do the 10 hours a day they're not in school, or the 16 hours a day in the summer? They have fun, of course. They go swimming in the river and sneak home in the bushes at nightfall because there is a mean looking bull near where they left their clothes. They ride around on their bikes, play with other kids, but they also follow mom and dad and older brothers and sisters around and envy their grown-up things and events. They wind up in a 4-H project and learn the skilled care and reliability needed.

Before you know it, they're helping mom clean eggs in the cellar, and getting to drive the one-mile-an-hour hay wagon during harvesting. They listen and watch and talk and do some of the numberless skills and chores of the farm. It is another kind of play, they think. But by the time they are ten years old they may be doing 10 or 20 hours or more of work a week that would need to be done by an adult. Because of this there rarely have been farmers who bragged about what hard workers they were, and how they put the farm operation together with nothing but the sweat of their brow. It is a family operation and the rest of the family may be doing as much as the head of the family. He and his wife may make the crucial decisions and do the hardest or most hazardous work, but the others overlap his work activities in a harmonious way.

Conflicts occur as they do in all families, but they are generally built-out rather than built-in. Mother doesn't want the heavy field work. Dad doesn't want her thousand lighter chores. And the kids get bored with repetitive jobs, which, nonetheless, develop stamina and endurance for adulthood.

Farm parents understood the problem, so they spent a lot of energy seeing that education was adequate to the times in which their children would be adults. The farm environment may be ideal for a child to mature in, but the farm community was not satisfied with the way American society of the time was complementing that environment. W.W. Case of Frenchtown, Board of Agriculture secretary, gave some of the reasons in his 1907 report to the state board:

A father and son show off their hybrid corn. Once all the official words and definitions are stated, what the real meaning of 4-H comes down to is adults teaching, working, and sharing with the younger generation.

"It is high time that our educational authorities were waking up to the need of teaching agricultural science, expecially in rural districts. For the last 30 years our education has all tended to wean the country boy and girl away from country life, with the result that the more education the child receives of the kind he now gets, the more he despises the dirty fingers and blue overalls, and the more he admires the white hands and natty appearance of his city cousin, who sits listening to the click of a telegraph sounder 16 hours at a stretch or who keeps books in a stuffy office at $8 a week.

"An experience of 26 years in the school room compels me to the conclusion that no more than 10 percent of the work in the school in the past — except, of course, the ability to read, write and reckon — is of any real value to those who expect to stay on the farm and become farmers.

"And most of our brightest boys, and those who have the best advantages, especially, recognize that their schooling has tended to every end but country life and act accordingly — while in after years they regret having left the farm.

"More than one young man has frankly stated on leaving school 'after all my study and pains in acquiring an education, I have learned absolutely nothing of plant life, growth, development, requirements of food, pruning, propagating, budding, etc.' and he is at the mercy of every commercial fertilizer agent in the country, as he knows nothing of what a fertilizer should contain, nor the requirements of different crops to obtain a full maximum crop at the minimum expense of fertilizer."

In other words, farmers believed that 90 percent of the education their kids were getting was subverting them away from country life. The commonsense reaction was to get farming courses into the schools. Rural leaders in Hunterdon followed national legislation and developments closely, as much of the rest of the country participated in a wave of concern over rural education.

The first solutions were the simplest — school clubs, where the kids might have a home garden project, then get lessons during or after school on gardening, and finally have a grand festival with contests, blue ribbons, proud parents and all. The wave of adult sentiment culminated in the Smith-Lever Act in 1914 that created the extension service for adult education and led to the Smith-Hughes Bill in 1917 that provided federal aid for vocational education in high schools.

By this time, the Hunterdon Board of Agriculture was in the throes of its own reorganization, and sent a resolution favoring the Smith-Hughes Bill to its national legislators at its December 11, 1915 meeting. "The meeting was then adjourned after which the members went to Flemington High School Auditorium where the school children of the county were having exhibits of the contests held throughout the county."

By 1918, Flemington High School had started the first vocational agriculture course in the county. Sherman Tharp was appointed temporary emergency 4-H leader during the war to organize more of the new youth clubs through the schools. Club Secretary Frank J. Smith reported on the Flemington School's new farm club in 1919 as one "for boys of the high school who are interested in agriculture and who desire to take an active part in the advancement of country life."

The club had 20 members, each of whom had a personal project ranging from chicken and livestock raising to gardening and crop raising. In January of 1920, the Hunterdon *Democrat* ran a three-line headline of the size used to report disasters, or perhaps peace in this case. It said:

>
> Hunterdon County Boys
> Win First Place Judging
> Dairy Cattle At Trenton

They won first in dairy cattle judging as a team, first place by an individual, and third place in the overall team averages in different kinds of contests. Clarence Alles of Flemington was the first place individual, and the contest was a step towards an "active part in the advancement of country life," just as the club promised. During 40 years of farming in Raritan Township, Alles was a master of Grandview Grange, overseer of the State Grange, a director of the Flemington Fair, Raritan Township Committeeman and Clerk, chairman of the Flemington National Bank Board, member of the County Tax Board, and Hunterdon Medical Center trustee.

Meanwhile, the vocational courses at the county's high schools reached interested youths, but that was not enough. For one thing, it was commonplace into the 1930s for young farm boys to quit at the eighth-grade level because their labor was needed on the family farm. Similarly, farm children were ready to begin serious and advanced projects long before they reached high school age at 14. As a result, the 4-H became the central group in terms of organizing young people and teaching them systematically about farming.

The first clubs formed in 1918 resulted in fair exhibits that year and the next, but there was little systematic attention given to the clubs at first. By 1922, the state had named Charles Oliver 4-H leader-at-large, and he began to cover Hunterdon part-time. He was followed in 1924 by B.F. Ramsburg, who would cover Hunterdon and two other counties to the end of 1926.

In the winter of 1923, at the home of young John Williamson of Mount Airy, one of the first dairy clubs in the state was formed with the 4-H leader-at-large's help. In 1924 the junior judging team of the Mount Airy 4-H Dairy Club came home with the state trophy. And the following year, animals raised by three New Jersey 4-Hers were sent to the National Dairy Show in Indianapolis, where they won four first prizes out of a possible six.

The 1926 agent-at-large, B.F. Ramsburg, came back to Hunterdon as a full-time 4-H agent for the county in 1936 and stayed to 1960. He replaced Brandon Wright, who worked out of Flemington from 1930 to 1936, covering Hunterdon and two other counties. By February 1936, Ramsburg was able to drop the others and concentrate all his effort on Hunterdon. The county demanded the best of its salaried experts and, judging from Ramsburg's report for his first full year, they received it:

"During the year the agent spent 100 days in the office and 165 days in the field. There were a total of 672 farm visits compared to 125 the previous year. 415 office calls and 288 telephone calls were made. 130 news stories were written, and 1,401 individual letters were written. Held nine leader training meetings with an attendance of 371. Held four method demonstration meetings and 148 result demonstration meetings with a total attendance of 2,642. Held 14 other meetings of an extension nature with an attendance of 7,995. And 719 meetings with an attendance of 16,560 were held by local leaders but not attended by the club agent."

The dairy club enrollment was increased 50 percent that year and two new communities started clubs. Poultry and vegetable clubs were developed. Two forestry club rallies attracted 1,174 4-Hers and parents. Ramsburg also made 72 visits and held two meetings for County Agent Babbit. "We considered ourselves as members of a team," Ramsburg said. "Anytime he could do something to advance my program,

The Flemington Chapter of the Future Farmers of America in 1942. Along with the 4-H, the FFA provided an opportunity for the young farm boy to establish confidence in himself and his work. Eugene Brokaw, fifth from left in the back row, still farms in Hunterdon county today.

Doris Everitt of Ringoes shows off her first-prize Ayrshire, "Strathaven Major Snowflake," at the 1937 Flemington Fair. The Fair contests were the high point of the year for the young people who raised their own pedigreed calves as part of their club activities.

he did, and anytime I could do anything to advance his, I did."

Darlene Teets, kneeling, presents a Holstein calf for her parents, Mr. and Mrs. William Teets of Lebanon, to the two girls winning in the show. Barbara Davidson, left, came in second, but won the animal because first-place scorer, Susan Lambert, had won a calf the previous year. Scores are based on showmanship, fitting, record-book quality, and the animals themselves.

"We would work with any organization. Most realized they could call on us for anything. Say, one of our young farmers, a club member, would come in and say, 'Gee, I'm over a barrel, could you help me get a poultry program together for the Grange? I'm in charge of the program, I forgot about it, and it's only three days off.' I would call one of our poultry specialists to help him out. He also knew that I would come to him if I were in a jam, and he was very willing to help me out. All the organizations felt that. We had a wonderful working relationship.

"In fact I urged one of our adult leaders, who moved here from another county, to start a 4-H Club in the community. Where will we meet? she asked. I said I think we can get the local Grange Hall, so I introduced her to those folks. She told me afterwards she was astonished at the cooperation she'd received. These adult leaders were responsible in great measure for the success and achivements of the 4-H program."

"4-H stands for the four-fold development of youngsters — head, heart, hands and health. I always believed one of the best character-building activities a youngster could engage in was a livestock project, whether dairy, sheep dogs, pigs, cattle, chickens, whatever. They had to be cared for seven days a week and you learned early to take responsibility."

Once, while in New Brunswick helping with a horse club program that was expanding rapidly and featured contests for fine horses, Ramsburg had to explain to a publicity man that the horses did not matter. "I said, listen, we're not interested in developing blue ribbon horses. We're interested in blue ribbon boys and girls. Sometimes a youngster can't afford to have a blue

A judicious eye is used by Roger Everitt of Ringoes as he displays a heifer early in his farming career in 1939. Today, he is a partner in D & R Equipment of Ringoes, a business that sells and maintains gigantic modern machinery used by crop farmers.

ribbon horse, but you can still make a blue ribbon youngster out of him or her if they have the will and ability to take up the program."

The 4-H dairy program was augmented by the statewide Frelinghuysen Loan Fund for youngsters who wanted to raise a heifer. "I know one father who said he thought it taught his kids grit, because they never saved any money," Ramsburg explained. "But after they bought those animals, you couldn't pry a nickel out of them. They were saving their money to pay back on the animal and cut down on the interest charges."

Shows, fairs, and all public events tended to feature contests and judging. "People think you're having that for entertainment to the public . . . but you're doing it primarily to develop the youngster. For example, we had a farm boy in the vegetable garden project, who was in his early teens and interested in gardening. He raised practically the family's entire garden. The first time he showed at Flemington Fair, he didn't qualify for a single ribbon. But he learned from the judging and later won 10 first prizes at a local garden exhibition."

Record-keeping is an important part of 4-H. In the dairy program, Ramsburg developed a program where the youngsters kept a record of feed eaten, the cost of the feed, and the growth of the animal. They drew a graph line against a line of how much the animal should grow normally over the months. These records showed the exact feed cost of raising a heifer.

This was done so well, Ramsburg said, that the state Dairy Extension Specialist for adults would quote the records as proof of the usability of

A group of 4-Hers with dairy projects gets a lesson in judging the qualities of a cow's body structure, with four Mulhocaway Guernseys as examples. Over the years training in the 4-H dairy programs was so thorough that the records youngsters kept of their cow-raising projects were used as research data by Rutgers University.

extension programs. They had been carefully tested and here was the proof in terms of cost of feed and value of the animal grown. Similarly, many parents who had not taken the time to follow the most advanced feeding and care methods were inadvertently educated by their youngster's 4-H project.

The 4-H junior leader program is a crucial part of 4-H for older teenagers in modern Hunterdon. It teaches them how to organize and run clubs and how to serve in the various offices and work posts.

"When we first talked of starting the junior leader program, one of our club members asked, well, what does a junior leader do?" Ramsburg continued. "I told her what the program was designed to be. She said, well, heavens, any 4-H member worth his or her salt would do that! You don't have to have a title.

"The youngster who said that was Beulah Van Lieu, president of the Mount Airy Dairy Club. She was an excellent president. I remember they were having a 30th reunion, a special event, and she organized the thing in about ten minutes. She'd say 'now your father is president of the board of education, so you see about getting the school auditorium. And you, Gus, your uncle runs the store that has ice cream, so you arrange the refreshments.' Then she ended up with, 'Now you kids who haven't been given a job to do, you be here to pass out programs and act as ushers.' She had everybody involved and it took about five or 10 minutes. And a lot of the others did the same sort of work. An adult couldn't have done it better, and I think at the time she was 16 or 17 years old."

Over the years, Ramsburg found one of his principle allies in 4-H was Major Edward Allen, manager of the Flemington Fair from 1910 to 1947. "The 4-H program was built up here at the fair. There was a state appropriation for the 4-H exhibits and Major Allen was responsible for getting the original appropriation. Whenever we went to him and suggested something new that would cost more money because the appropriation didn't cover it, he was always willing to work it out, if it could be afforded."

In 1929 adult dairy exhibiting was dropped in favor of a 4-H dairy program. The following year with Ramsburg's predecessor on the job, exhibits were added in 4-H forestry, poultry and eggs, and garden displays of vegetables and flowers. 4-Hers gave demonstrations of the club's activities, and displayed the record books they used to measure their progress.

By 1932, the 4-H Dairy program at the Flemington Fair rivaled the one at the state fair in size, with youths throughout New Jersey invited to

The Teen Egg Contest in 1951, sponsored by the Home Economics Agent, produced a large array of desserts and other dishes, which judges had the pleasure of sampling. While more than one of the girls may have had a 4-H animal-raising project, there were clubs that developed expertise in homemaking, too.

The Auxiliary Forces

contribute. Before long, sleeping accommodations and a commissary had been set up for youths who were caring for their animals on exhibit. The growth continued after World War II and the state dairy show was held there in 1947 and the first state sheep show in 1956. The first horse show was held in 1959 and the first state horse show at the 1961 fair.

Though all the shows involved tremendous labor and logistics, there was never much money involved, since much of the work was done by adult 4-H leaders and the young people themselves. Thousands contributed their labors and resources over the years, and Major Allen never tired of getting the fair's limited income to accommodate them all.

Ramsburg recalled the last time he saw Major Allen: "I took him to a 4-H baby beef sale at Trenton where he bought a steer. Coming back, we were talking about next year's fair, and I said, well, Major, I think we ought to do so-and-so and maybe we can take on something else, and so on. He said, well, that sounds very interesting. You go ahead and develop your ideas and we'll see if we can't put it together. He died a few months later, right around his 85th birthday. That was the kind of person he was — he never looked back. He was always willing to consider a new idea, and if it had merit, you didn't have trouble getting him to back it."

As a result, the modern Flemington Fair has as many or more 4-H exhibits than the fairs of 30 or 40 years ago, and likewise the modern 4-H and its programs continue to prosper. Over the decades, the adult club leaders have been the backbone of the program's success in Hunterdon. One of the dozens of leaders is Mrs. Beth Perry of Whitehouse Station, who created the Hunterdon 4-H Sheep Club and ran it from 1948 to 1968. Some of her experiences and comments provide an idea of what modern day children learned.

The monthly Saturday club meeting was often held in the Perrys' living room. An average of 40 young people from 10 to 21 years of age would be seated around the floor. They loved the congestion, and there was no time for boredom — the "demonstrations" covered highly technical subjects and took concentration, such as telling the age of a sheep by its teeth, what to do at lambing time, shearing, how to fold and roll a fleece, proper feeding, hoof trimming, worming.

Mrs. Perry discovered that adults who recom-

A youngster receives a prize calf for his winning showings in the Flemington Fair 4-H show, with Lloyd Wescott making the presentation.

The first 4-H baby beef contest for Hunterdon at the 1939 Fair, with Shirley Kuhl (now Mrs. Shirley Brokaw) and her stepbrothers, Walter and Theodore Bauer of Flemington, the only 4-Hers to enter. William Skelly, animal husbandryman from Rutgers, presented the awards.

mend segregating kids by sex and age are shortchanging them. "I know some leaders would say 'Oh, you can't manage those big kids. Well, you give them something to do, and then you don't have to manage them!" she said. "I can remember riding along in the car with a lot of kids, when I heard one say a word or something. An older boy whom I knew had a terrible 'mouth,' (but never around Mrs. Perry), said to the younger kid who said something, 'We don't use this kind of language in this club!' That made him feel like a big shot because he could tell the little ones what to do. And the little ones were all trying to be good because of the older ones, and the older ones had to behave because the little ones were listening!"

It worked the same way for individual teaching and special help. Don't ask for volunteers for demonstrations and projects, Mrs. Perry recommends. The kids who are a little shy will only learn to be miserable do-nothings. Instead, make them miserable by appointing them to give a demonstration to the others. "They will usually feel miserable beforehand, and always feel proud afterward," she said. Learn each youth's special talents, so you can give them a push when a project comes along that requires that talent. Also, get any parents with talents and time to help when you can.

Be glad if you have a mixture of rich and poor youngsters, according to Mrs. Perry. Each learns "how the other half lives" and learns living in friendship with people from different backgrounds. Narrowness and provincialism are thus avoided. Mrs. Perry still smiles about the little boy from a wealthy family whom she sent to the refrigerator to prepare a snack for the whole group. He came from a home where the butler and the cook did everything. "They never let me do this at home!" he chortled happily.

Variety makes the whole experience a rich one, meetings in the living room on cold winter days, having your own animal at home that you care for warm or cold, going to barn meetings in warm weather, meetings at friends' homes, special personal projects and demonstrations, a Christmas party, and, of course, the Flemington Fair.

"I've had parents who worried about their kids showing at the fair. I tell them, listen, they all go

Two 4-Hers relax with their equally tired show cattle at the Flemington Fair in a photo that might have been snapped last year were it not for the 1940s cars and trucks. Some things don't change. (Rutgers Unviersity.)

down the midway once, they lose all their money on the games, and that's the end of it, that's it, it's short. Then they all hang around the sheep barn or the cows or wherever their animal is, and they have a grand time together."

Discipline needs to be balanced. "Whenever I had to bawl out a kid — and sometimes you have to come down pretty hard on them — I always made a mental note to find something in that kid to praise. I would wait, and then the least little thing that he did that was good — and they all do something good! — I would try to compliment them. You have to give them both sides."

The "generation gap" does not exist when there is a mixed group of kids and adults of all ages. Mrs. Perry recalls the time the group was putting on a skit at the Stanton Grange, when, instead of popping a paper bag behind the scenes to imitate a gun going off, one boy lit a cherry bomb. The noisemaker walloped everybody's ears and probably shook loose several decades of dust from the curtains. Mrs. Perry jumped up and ran to the back of the hall where Richard Schomp from the Board of Agriculture Executive Committee was sitting. A Grange member overseeing the loan of the hall, Schomp had the reputation of a precise and even severe person. No nonsense at all, so Mrs. Perry wanted quickly to get in an apology for her kids before Schomp blew a gasket. Instead, she found him clutching his sides with laughter. He loved kids and understood them.

Today, 13 years after having retired from the Sheep Club, Mrs. Perry still receives random visits from her ex-club members, who have children of their own, and want them to meet their 4-H leader. She thought of the club work as primarily a character-builder and the sheep as secondary — but she finds that many more of the youths than she estimated now keep sheep as adults. Then, of course, there are LuAnn McKinney, Walter Knight, Malcolm Kram, and Richard Jakimer — they were so impressed by what they learned as youths in the 4-H that today they are licensed veterinarians.

Mrs. Perry's experiences are repeated dozens of times over, for the county currently has about 50 4-H clubs like hers. Joe Buchel of Clinton Township took over when Ramsburg left in 1960, and in 1978 Ray Nichols became the 4-H Agent

The Auxiliary Forces

Frances Anne Williams of Sergeantsville shows off her perfectly groomed animals at the Fair in the early 1960s. With her are Dr. and Mrs. Thomas L. King and son, Fred, from whom she acquired the sheep.

Despite increasing urbanization, one of Hunterdon's farm traditions that continues to flourish is the 4-H. Here pre-4-Hers, called "Preps," enter their personal pets in a Fair contest. No. 2 contestant appears less concerned about his frog than does No. 1.

for Hunterdon. There are 850 youths in the modern club program, plus another 120 in the 4-H Prep Club Program for kids from seven to nine years old. Finally, there are 125 adults volunteering from a few hours help a month to a few hours a week.

Just as Ramsburg in the 1930s learned "people here are so helpful," Nichols reports it is not unusual for a parent who's just discovered the program to tell him, "You meet such nice people in 4-H."

"It is a great way to get to know the people in the rural part of your community," Nichols says. "Although increasingly fewer kids are going into the traditional farming career, a lot who are involved in 4-H projects are going into careers related to agriculture."

Today's clubs cover a wide variety of rural-suburban subjects: electricity, nature study, herpetology (snakes and such), gardening, five dairy goat clubs, two twirling clubs, swine, square dance, sheep, small animals, veterinary science, three dairy clubs, three beef raising clubs, beekeeping, six homemaking clubs, eight horse clubs, and a special club for the residents of the Hunterdon State School near Clinton.

Thus, the program that was originally developed for farm children has been transformed into one that provides important out-of-school learning for thousands of nonfarm children as well. Just as with the Granges, which regard anyone interested in growing things as qualified to join, so is any youth interested in learning by doing invited to join the 4-H.

* * *

As for the women who worked on the farms and bore the farm children, the mythical farm woman that follows is being described by her most appreciative admirer, the mythical Hunterdon County farmer.

A Special Agreement
When Matilda and I were married — what! Did I forget to mention that? No Matter. You knew and your readers guessed it long ago. When we were married, or very soon after, we entered into a special agreement. Matilda was not to meddle with my affairs, nor I with hers. In plain Frogland language she was to mind her business, and I, mine. You will not think that of much importance, John, for various cynical reasons of your own; but we have found it to come in handy very often as we jogged along.

That kind of agreement should not be made of cast iron. Something a little more elastic works better and lasts longer. Ours was too stiff at first, but we soon discovered the weakness resulting from too much strength, and remedied the defect.

Yes, we have lived up to the agreement all these years. Of course Matilda crowds over the line at times. How could she help it? And who would want her to help it, anyhow? But when she sees how angry I am or might possibly become, she scurries back — or pretends to, which amounts to precisely the same thing. When circumstances push me over a little — it is always circumstances and not personal inclination as you must know — Matilda puts on that injured look and says in most impressive pedagogic tones, 'Philander Martenis!' Then it is my turn to hurry back, and

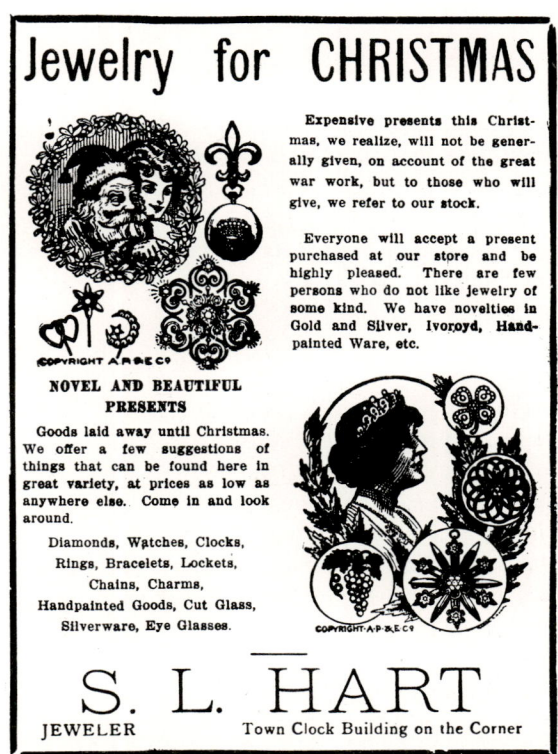

everything is lovely as before.

Some people get rich by keeping agreements and some by breaking them. We cannot claim to have got rich by either; but there has been no little satisfaction in living up to our bargain. Perhaps this trifle should not be mentioned at all, John. I don't believe I would, only that some think there is none too much smoothness in farm life at best, and even hint the same holds true of married life in general.

Three weeks and nothing but rain, rain, rain. Things were going badly enough. No wonder that morning was particularly dark and gloomy. Shut out both physical and financial sunshine and there is a deep blue tinge to the blackest cloud.

When circumstances have worked one into just the right condition, it is as natural to pick up morbid notions as to breath, and one somehow feels that it is much more important. One does not mean to keep them, of course. But did you ever try to let go of a "live" wire?

Conditions were all right on that particular morning. Crops had been poor the previous year and the prices low. Yet Matilda and I had kept our courage up — at least she had. Things would certainly go better this year.

Now, with the corn rotted in the ground and no possibility of replanting in time for a crop, things looked worse instead of better. Two such years would ruin us. Running expenses on the farm are relentless as death.

The morning chores all done, I wrapped myself in the big buffalo robe for a quiet hour in the haymow. Was it to think, or to keep from thinking? It is much the same. Only somewhat harder to keep from thinking when you don't want to, than to keep at it when you do.

Rain, rain, rain! It sounded doleful for a time. Then it lost its splash and patter; it became rhythmic, musical, dreamily delightful. Soon came a fitful sleep with dreams of debts and duns and failing crops and empty pocketbooks.

"Philander! Philander-r-r!"

I was wide awake and hustling out of that cozy nest. "What is it, Matilda?" I asked, rushing about as if in great haste to get something done. It is doubtful whether Matilda was badly fooled by the ruse.

"Come down right away. Mr. Barton is here and wants to see you."

By this time I was half way down the ladder, feeling very sheepish and eyeing Matilda to see if she mistrusted.

The Auxiliary Forces

Honeybees once had a small but strong place in Hunterdon's agriculture, as seen by the long rows of contest entries being examined by judges at the Fair. There are still apiarists in the country today, and on a spring day, when the wildflowers and hay fields are in bloom, the bees can be found at work fertilizing flowers and increasing crop yields.

For a few cents a column inch of type, women from communities all over Hunterdon sent in these reports each week to the *Democrat* and other papers in the area. They'd collect news from neighbors and thus establish an identity for their rural crossroads and see to it that all the good social news circulated far and wide. It gave an unusual breadth of reporting to newspapers that could not afford to hire full-time reporters.

That was very foolish. It made no difference if she did mistrust that I had been asleep in the daytime, even though that was enough to brand a Frogland farmer with a lasting mark of disgrace. And it was all the more foolish because you can never find out anything by watching a woman.

"He has come to buy the brown yearlings," she whispered, coming close to me at the foot of the ladder. "He will give forty dollars, and that's a good price. Let them go, Philander."

That was a little too much. Matilda had gone a long way over the line and I told her so. No matter what was said. I gave her to understand that selling steers was not a woman's business.

Matilda looked hurt — under such circumstances, the meanest thing a woman can do. Why couldn't she look mad? Now she had me at a disadvantage, and I must make the best of a bad situation.

"Barton would beat me down to the lowest cent!" said I, putting particular stress on 'me.' "Don't you suppose he knows I'm in a tight place, and has come over to make a few dollars out of my necessity?

"And then there's all that pasture in the lowland. Steers may as well be growing into money on that as not. Losing both ways is a very poor shift for raising money, Matilda."

I thought she would look convinced and humbled. It takes a man a long time to find out that he can't convince a woman, much less — but no matter. She didn't look that way.

"Don't take a cent less than forty dollars, Philander," said she with a provoking disregard of all my efforts.

"He'll give it, I know. And Mr. Allen says we can pasture two cows for him at two dollars a month. Steers

wouldn't grow into money much faster than that, would they?"

"Matilda!"

"Come along, Philander. Let me boss you this time. We'll raise some ready money and be none the poorer for it."

It is doubtful whether Matilda knows to this day how glad I was to be bossed that time. Have you ever realized what a comfort it is to have somebody force you into doing what you wanted to do all the time?

We sold the steers for forty dollars. We pastured Allen's cows for something over twenty. We made several lucky turns during the summer, and it wasn't such a bad year after all. Since that time I have been saying "we" much oftener than ever before.

Yes, John, Matilda got over the line badly that morning; but it was all forgiven long ago. When I learned how much pains she had taken to manage those deals, and all for the sake of getting me out of a foolishly blue streak, I crowded over on her side a little, just to show her how mean I felt; and that time Matilda didn't care.

Sometimes I fancy she has been taking greater liberties ever since; but it is all right. Our agreement has never once been broken — no, never!

* * *

They started with a crank, the old Model-Ts and As, but the women of the day were strong enough to start one as well as the men. (Hunterdon County *Democrat*.)

Mildred Saums of Three Bridges climbs onto a John Deere after her "other" job at the Flemington Auction Market. There was still enough daylight left for tilling the plowed field with a harrow and, with labor short during World War II, women kept the farm going.

This excerpt from an unpublished novel by 1915 Board President Egbert Bush tells something of the story of the farm wife in adversity and at her best. It also tells of the respect women have always been held in by farm men, and how different it was from the city customs. For the model for the 19th century middle-class was the rich, strong businessman and his beautiful but nonfunctioning wife.

The model for farmers was instead one or two rather friendly and good natured people with distinctive personalities, working to survive together. The husband was identified to the outside world as head of state, but often the title was merely ritual and the hand that rocked the cradle ruled from behind the throne. In urban society, Philander would be the ineffectual, henpecked fool. In farm society he is simply a good farmer surprised at the ingenuity and affection of his wife and receptive to it. Compared to *her* urban counterpart, the farm woman and wife has had opportunities that were harder in some ways, but richer in others.

"We were poor, but we always had a good time. We'd go over to the neighbors to listen to the Dempsey-Tunney fight on the radio, and go sledding in the winter, and swimming in the summer. We and the neighbors were like a big family. I'll never forget my mom saying those were the best years of her life," one ex-farmboy recalled.

To raise a family that happily were the riches

The Auxiliary Forces

Mrs. Max Gutzwiller of Copper Hill tends the spring garden in front of her farmhouse on what today is called Hampton Corner Road, near Flemington. Onions, peas, lettuce, radishes, beets, carrots, tomatoes and cucumbers were a typical planting. In addition, the cornfield might have a row of sweet corn plus pumpkins and squash that liked to grow among the stalks.

The average farm woman with a small family might can 1,000 quart-sized mason jars in a summer, with time left to cultivate the large farm garden. Here judges from Rutgers look over the products of such labor at the Fair.

This is what most farm-family dinner tables looked like in the 1930s and 40s. The cook is Mrs. William Phillips Jr. of Milford. Digging in after a hard day's work are, from left, William Phillips Sr., Roy Egerter, a hired hand, Mrs. Phillips Sr., Shirley Phillips, Mrs. Phillips Jr., her husband, and Orville Weider, another hired hand. The high-chair is occupied by the youngest member of the family.

that many farm women reaped. The farmer managed his fields and his animals, and the wife orchestrated the life of the family. A basic part of her work dealt with producing and preparing food. Edna Smith of Ringoes recalled some of the routines of a mid-summer's day, when wheat was being threshed:

*Up at 5 a.m. to help with the men's chores of milking the cows and feeding the hens so husband Horace could turn to the harvest chores earlier.

*Prepare ham and eggs for the team of up to eight men who arrive at nine for the threshing.

*Start the big midday meal of meat and potatoes, vegetables, fresh bread, pies or pudding for dessert.

*Finally, tend to canning, berries, which come ripe in June, July and August, and items from the family garden, which is in full production from mid-summer to fall.

When the old cast iron wood stove or the modern kerosene range wasn't going full blast to prepare food, it was raising clouds of steam all day with canning. It had to be done immediately and continuously for days and weeks on end. The average farm woman might put up a thousand quarts of canned foods and preserves, and if that was average, it meant that larger families were canning into the thousands.

The garden might produce tomatoes, sweet corn, beans, beets, peppers, cabbage, carrots, cucumbers, squash, asparagus, rhubarb, potatoes, onions. There were strawberries, blackberries, raspberries, and half a dozen other varieties. There were cherries, pears, peaches, apples, grapes. A crop might be jellied or juiced or canned whole, or put in a five gallon crock to ferment like the cabbage, or spiced with herbs and pickled like the cucumbers, or buried in the root cellar like the carrots and beets.

As the hot summer day steamed to a close, the men would quit field work in the afternoon to tend to their other chores, and in the kitchen the cooking and canning would go right on until supper. Then came clean-up and perhaps an hour's rest doing chores like darning, and then to bed, for 5 a.m. would come along fast.

From the Civil War to beyond World War II, this schedule was standard for the farm woman, just as fieldwork and dairying were part of her husband's routine. During a two-day Farmers Institute at Pittstown in 1896, the evening session was held for women and their interests:

"Mrs. Mary R. Brown of Swedesboro read a paper on 'Education Needful for Success and Contentment on the Farm.' She said ignorance cannot succeed in agriculture . . . She showed the necessity of scientific knowledge in agriculture as in anything else, and thought that the principles of agriculture should be taught in our public schools; that the elements of natural philosophy and the mechanisms of machinery should be understood by all farmers.

"Boys who leave the farm with its horses and carriages and no days off do not better their condition when they get a position with its 312 days of labor and no picnics. They may gain a little socially; for this reason social life should be bettered on the farm in the country. In the country, loss of position or sickness does not result in almost immediate penury or starvation. Mrs. Brown was followed by Mrs. Helen S. Johnson of Cory, Pa., who delivered a very entertaining lecture on 'Home Hygiene.' "

Women tended to keep track of education and encouraged its formation and development at all times. When the Board of Agriculture undertook its regeneration in the 1915-22 period, it had Jason Hoffman, the county superintendnet of schools, on its by-laws committee. He helped the Board form its policies on education, and the Board helped him organize farmer help on school problems.

Transportation improvements made the one-room schools of the 19th century more accessible, during which women had become dominant as schoolteachers. They used their resources so well that during the 1920s one of those one-room schools might cover nine grades and teach not only reading-writing-reckoning, but philosophy, history, geography, literature, music and art as well to the older children.

Schoolteachers were accepted in the community with great respect and affection, and any teacher who wanted could spend every evening of the year dining with one student's family after another. Problems got hashed out in an open atmosphere; everyone knew what was happening, and when the school planned a special program for the holidays, there would be singing, dancing, recitations, and even a plump Santa during Christmas week.

When hard physical work and money were required for a community project, the men would do the largest share, while women were most active with the many smaller details and chores. For example, the all-male Board of Agriculture founded the feed co-op, which became the local Agway in the 1920, but the young woman who kept its books from going astray was an integral part of its success. (She later married one of the Board's most prominent men.)

Her generation of farm women were active in a time when opportunities were opening up for women because of the automobile. Normally a farm wife left the farm only infrequently, for Grange meetings, church, and shopping trips. Now young unmarried women began to get jobs in nearby towns as clerks, bookkeepers, and in many other posts. The farm community was such a well regulated family that many of them would walk and hitch rides on farm trucks to get into town to work.

Further, as women became more mobile, they began to see ways to influence the farm community, ways that men certainly did not have time for, and ways they were somewhat better at.

When the Board appointed a Women's Advisory Committe in 1938, these changes suddenly became more visible. Although they had only been appointed to help hire a home economics agent, the women behaved as energetically as the Board of Agriculture had when it got its first county agent. Within a year the advisory committee considered dental clinics, representation on state-level women's groups, and generally "crowding over the line" as Philander would have put it.

Almena Crane of Pittstown is one of the many women who found their opportunities growing. The county's Granges were proud of their record of voting for women's suffrage in 1920, and now women were taking on their full range of opportunities:

"I'd lived in the county several years before I became active in women's groups. I was aware there was a group allied with the County Board. At an annual Board meeting I observed a bit of controversy over the role women should play. Shortly after I was asked to become a member of this women's committee, and at about the same time they reorganized and became known as the Associated Women of the Hunterdon County Board of Agriculture.

"The committee began its activities by supporting the extension service. We were a little more independent than some of the groups in other counties and we felt the work carried on by

"Away with canning," says one expert to another. Almena Crane of the Associated Women holds some frozen goods as she discusses the modern technique of freezing with Hunterdon Home Agent Florence Walker. Freezing eventually replaced canning for the storage of most perishable items.

the extension and the County Board should reflect the needs of the county. So we often proposed meetings and programs that other counties were not carrying on.

"We became a very strong group. We had annual meetings for the women of the county. Throughout the year we conducted other sessions. I recall one at Stanton Grange when the overflow was so great the hall didn't hold them. We had to have babysitters for the children. This eventually became Homemakers Day. We had speakers on cultural topics, on homemaking, and on inspirational subjects. It was really looked forward to by a particular group of farm women who were not members of women's clubs or active in other women's groups."

Less than a decade after Almena and her husband, Robert, had moved to Hunterdon, following their graduation from Cornell, he died in 1942. Left with growing children and a farm the two of them had labored to rebuild into a modern operation, Mrs. Crane did not return to urban life. She took over managing the farm crop and poultry operation, continuing into the 1960s.

When the State Board of Agriculture honored her for "Distinguished Service to New Jersey Agriculture," her record showed she had earned the honor: the Executive Committee of the Hunterdon Board of Agriculture, the state Department of Agriculture's Rural Advisory Committee, Franklin Township School Board, National Farm Bureau Women's Committee, and Hunterdon Medical Center trustee.

Mrs. Crane travelled to Scotland in 1959 to represent the Farm Bureau at the World Convention of Countrywomen. The Northeast Poultry Producers named her Poultrywoman of the Year in 1956, and New Jersey named her Mother of the Year in 1955. Today she is perhaps best known for her years of work with the Hunterdon County Library.

Women like Mrs. Crane had begun working in the fields alongside their men and continued working alongside them in community service. When Elizabeth Grandin of Clinton found herself with several hundred acres of farmland left in legacy after World War I, she went to Cornell and became a scientific farmer. After Anne Stevenson of rural Califon had her first daughter in 1946, the next year she became part of the first North Hunterdon Regional High School Board, which she served until her daughter was grown.

When the quiet-spoken county welfare director, Rose Angell, became interested in a hospital for the county in 1943, she teamed up with a former public relations director, Louise Leicester, to germinate the idea and got the Board of Agriculture started on it. Marjorie Van Ness, who settled in Franklin Township in 1967, culminated her career as a horsewoman by becoming the first woman to sit on the state Board of Agriculture in its history four years later in 1971.

Mrs. Clifford Snyder, the former Melda Chambre, was the first woman to serve as president of the County Board of Agriculture, 1974-76, making Hunterdon the first in the state to elect a woman to that position.

Most farm women became homemakers for their brothers or husbands, but by the 1930s some had begun to find jobs in the towns as clerks and secretaries. Except, that is, for Ruth E. Ent, who became the homemaker for the entire county as secretarial assistant to the county agents, seeing that they kept their appointments and supervising the countless mailings of farm literature.

The Auxiliary Forces

Mrs. Melda Snyder was the first woman to serve as president of the County Board of Agriculture, from 1974 to 1976, making Hunterdon the first in the state to elect a woman to serve in that capacity. In addition, she was a director of the New Jersey Farm Bureau, president of the Board of Managers of Cook College, Rutgers University, vice president of the State Board of Agriculture, president of the American Association of University Women, and served on the Hunterdon County Planning Board. The County Board contributed generously to the Hunterdon Visiting Homemakers, which she helped organize and also served on its state board. Mrs. Snyder received distinguished service awards from local and state agricultural and educational organizations, and in 1978 received the Citizen of the Year Award from the Hunterdon Chamber of Commerce. Farm organizations were leaders in their recognition of women.

When Board president Clifford Snyder married Melda Chambre in the 1940s, he taught her farm management and she continued operating their 500-acre farm after his death in February 1967. She had worked in the Hunterdon County schools as a supervisor employed by the state for service in rural schools. These "helping teachers," as they were called, did much to foster the 4-H and extension activities. Sarah Strong, also a helping teacher and a farm girl from Ringoes, was outstanding in her service to the county.

While the accomplishments of some women exist on record, the equally important accomplishments of many will never be known because they were so subtle. "A farm wife can make or kill a farm operation, I've always thought," Ruth Ent of Sergeantsville declared when she retired from 42 years of work at the extension service a few years ago.

Yet, she never pointed out in interviews that she had just spent all those years as a farm woman who quietly kept things organized for the county agents through depressions, wars, milk strikes, and public controversies. And possibly had done as much as any county agent or Board of Agriculture man to keep that office a success. As the archetypal Philander Martenis commented, you can never tell what a woman is thinking if she doesn't wish you to know, and quite often it is something as good as your best thoughts.

The women on Hunterdon's present-day farms have all these traditions to draw on. The modern dairyman with his automated 200-cow barn and the crop farmer with his 800 acres to plow hardly seem to leave any room for a feminine influence, it would seem. That is, until you reflect that his wife keeps the books, works in the fields when he is sick, persuades him to take a vacation, and be the one person consulted when major decisions and risks are involved.

When *Working Woman* magazine interviewed Melda Snyder, the reporter discovered she held several college degrees and had a background as a coordinator of school systems. Yet, there she was driving farm wagons, going to an equipment dealer in Pennsylvania to get a machine part, spending evenings with the county Board and State Board of Agriculture. With all the wealth of opportunities, she chose farming. "I couldn't be happier living any other way," she said.

* * *

Bessie Barnes operated a 100-acre dairy farm with a herd of 20 pure-bred Jerseys owned by her mother. She adjusts the mechanical milker in this World War II photo. With a hired hand (if not off to war) for the heavier work, there was no reason why a woman couldn't run a farm successfully.

The vegetables and other food in this Grange exhibit at the Flemington Fair in 1949 are identified by their proper names and selected for evenness and quality. Judges examined each one and scored it and also scored the booth on attractiveness. Ringoes took second place. Special committees from each Grange designed the booths — the result, a potpourri of riches from the farm and garden. (Rutgers University.)

There had to be organizations not only for the farmer, but for the whole farm family as well. The Hunterdon County Agricultural Society, written about by Kenneth Myers in his history of the Flemington Fair, was one of these. Myers writes that the reorganization of the society in 1856 provided for an annual fair that included fruit, flowers and home department exhibits, as well as the usual farm exhibits. So the distaff side of the family was recognized early, and although the children were not mentioned often, being "better seen than heard" in the 19th century, they doubtless had more fun at the fairs than the adults. It followed, that when 4-H became strong in the county the following century, the fair would become its most prominent means of showing 4-Hers accomplishments to the general public.

But the organization that symbolized and served the farm family most deeply was the Grange, founded in Hunterdon in 1874. It is a simple organization. Local Granges combine to form a county Pomona Grange, while the county Granges form a state organization and the state Granges form a national Grange. Hunterdon has had 13 local Granges and a Pomona Grange. There are seven degrees of ritual qualification open to members with three of them given by the local Grange and the others handled by successively higher levels.

The National Grange was founded in 1867 in Washinton, D.C., by seven men, headed by Father Kelley of Minnesota. According to William J.S. Harvey, master of Hunterdon's Pomona Grange No. 3, it was designed to unite the farm families of the south with those of the north, "following the bitterness and hatred created by four long years of civil strife."

"The Grange is not a secret organization, rather a family, fraternal organization with secrets. Its ritual is based on the Holy Bible, and represents the oldest and noblest occupation known to man — Tillers of the Soil."

Ringoes Grange No. 12 is the oldest, being founded in 1874. Locktown No. 88 was formed the following year and Sergeantsville No. 101 in 1876. Kingwood No. 106 was founded in 1882, Oak Grove No. 119 in 1896, Spring Mills No. 120 in 1897, and in 1900 Grandview No. 124 and Riverside No. 125, Three Bridges, came into being. Hickory No. 133 of Jutland was founded in 1903, Stanton No. 148 in 1905, Whitehouse No. 159 in 1906, Mount Lebanon No. 212 of Anthony in 1927, and the Sidney No. 215, near Clinton, was formed in 1930.

The Grange functioned and continues to function as a support organization in agricultural and community affairs. Other organizations more

A farm could become nothing but mud and misery, that is until the distaff side began to assert its influence. Then it could become as well-dressed as city cousins, as this old photo shows. No doubt they're off to church or a picnic or courtship. (Eugene Brokaw Family Album.)

completely devoted to important projects undertook those projects knowing they would find whatever help they asked for from the Grange. That help would consist of an opportunity to talk to farmers at meetings, the opportunity to borrow the meeting hall for only the janitor's fee, and any other kind of assistance the Grangers might be able to organize.

In their 100-year history, Grangers have backed every major agricultural project in the county and almost every major community project. There have been thousands of dinners, picnics, watermelon and strawberry feasts held to raise money for worthy projects and to keep people informed on those projects.

The community effect has been incalculable — as incalculable as always having a friend around who wishes you the best and gives what modest help they can manage in any of a thousand ways, and always when it's needed most.

Grover Bodine and Jennie McBride, both from the Flemington area, pose for the photographer in a scene that gives lie to any notion that farmers spend all their time in overalls and calico. Church and social gatherings demanded more. Afterwards, the route home usually included a covered bridge, as effective a custom as mistletoe at Christmas.

The Auxiliary Forces

It was usual for the men who were the rural legislators, the Board of Agriculture Executive Committee and so on, to be Grangers as well. And when there were no other groups or general leaders to take on an important task, then the Grange went out and did it. "Our County Board of Agriculture was organized Nov. 14, 1885, by the Hunterdon County Pomona Grange . . . The Board met and adopted their by-laws and we trust effective work for the agriculturists of our county will be accomplished." Readington, Ringoes, Sergeantsville, Locktown and Kingwood Grange provided the Board of Directors for the new organization.

No last word can be said on Hunterdon's Granges. Though the farm community had dwindled severely by 1960, many Granges decided to continue in operation, some with just enough membership to keep going. They continue in the faith that their existence is an important and worthwhile community contribution, and, as in the past, they spend their greatest energies in cheerful socializing and giving their time to help other people and groups.

County Home Agent Florence Walker uses the microphone at the Flemington Fair as Lina Williams of Sergeantsville shows the crowd how the old woven chairs are recaned on a sample seat. Programs of the Home Agent, supported by the Board of Agriculture's Associated Women, stressed child care and homemaking in general. (Rutgers University.)

Linda Spencer of Lebanon is crowned Miss New Jersey Dairy Princess of 1965 by the outgoing princess, Kathleen Holmes of Toms River. The contest was created to publicize the quality of the state's dairy products at a time when farmland was rapidly being lost to development. Farm leaders endorsed the Farmland Assessment Act of 1964, and the dairy princess ceremonies symbolized farming as an important state industry.

X
Marketing the Product

The father of a Hunterdon County maid, newly proposed to by a young farmer, said to her: "Never marry a farmer. Regardless of the weather, it is always too hot or too cold, too wet or too dry." He might have added: and he always has trouble marketing his product.

The late Egbert Bush, president of the Hunterdon Board in 1915, observed in an unpublished essay that businessmen and unionized workers of his time were usually successful in getting special "advantages" from government to protect the stability of their businesses or the value of their labor. They worked together, too. "I can't pay my men good wages unless you favor my suit," a businessman would tell government. And special laws, special import prohibitions, special considerations would follow. As for farm-

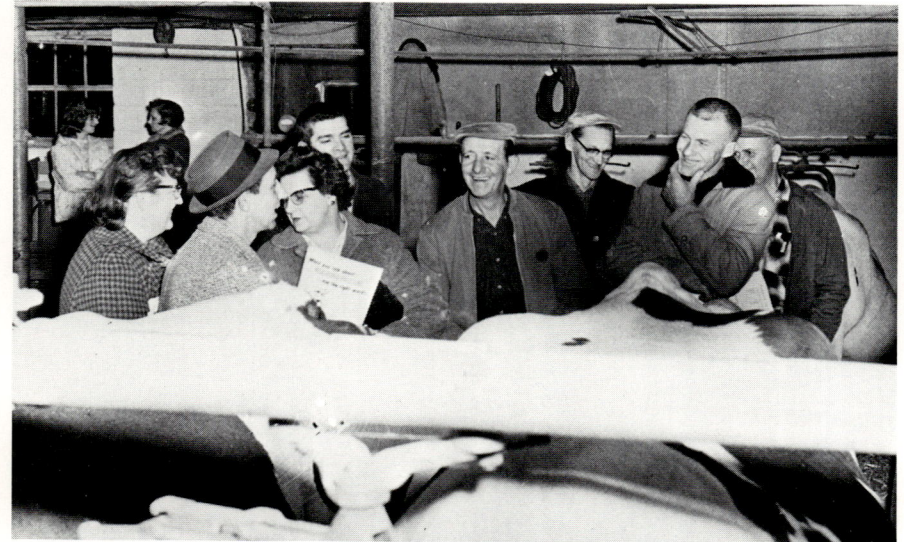

Host William Teets of Cokesbury rubs his chin as he listens to the lecture at a 1950s barn meeting, sponsored by the Hunterdon Holstein Association. Natalie Teets, his wife, is in the background, at left, talking with another woman. Isadore Fleming and Eva, his wife, are in the center, with Mr. and Mrs. George Harner at left. The County Extension Service also conducted such demonstrations.

ers, Bush noted:

"I am trying to show the disadvantages under which Farmer Gibson is laboring. I am trying to show that any industry so favored that it can make somebody else pay all its extra expenses must have very great advantages over one not so favored. And that is exactly the relation of the other great industries of today to agriculture.

"Imagine representative farmers gravely announcing they will have to raise the price of wheat and potatoes ten cents a bushel in order to meet the increased cost of labor. What a shout of derision would go up from the very men, who, in other industries, are doing the same thing without so much as drawing a facial muscle!

"Why all this difference? Why are the same tactics businesslike in the carrier and manufacturer and ridiculous in the farmer? Simply because the farmer has practically nothing to do with fixing the prices of his products, while the other parties have their prices largely under their control."

Then comes the tough part. Bush rejected as immoral the notion that farmers ought to create their own special niche in the politics of business — and get the same advantages. "I am not contending that farmers should have the power to fix the prices of their products. Human nature on the farm is much the same as human nature everywhere else — too selfish and grasping to be entrusted with anything like absolute power. I am willing to concede that if farmers had such power they might say to the hungry, 'Pay our prices or go without bread.' How all our finer feelings revolt! How all our ideas of right rebel against the very suggestion!

"But if such power in the hands of farmers would be so dangerous by what system of logic can we justify similar powers in the hands of other people? If the law of supply and demand is the only safeguard in fixing the prices of farm products, why should not that same law apply to all other necessaries of life?"

By this logic the too-successful powers that business and the working man wield are rejected as a meaningless prosperity that ultimately eats away the true health of the community and reveals an empty victory. Such idealism may seem fatally hampering in everyday practical life. But ideals weigh on a man's conscience and ultimately determine whether he feels prosperous or somehow doesn't feel satisfied.

It may even lead a farm person to make the traditional deprecatory remark, "Oh, farmers are too damned independent to ever organize!," when what he feels underneath is, "Maybe it's just as well that we don't."

But things have changed. They had to. If the the price is poor, the farmer cannot lay off his employees for a few weeks or months until times get better. He is locked in.

At the time the farmer plants his crop — during the fall for spring harvest or in the spring for fall harvest — he has no idea what the prices will be when he offers it for sale at harvest time. Meanwhile, he pays interest on his mortgage, he pays his taxes, he prepares the soil and he buys the seed, fertilizer, and the spray. Then he prays for rain and waits for the harvest. There is no turning back. He gets a large crop or a small one, but in the end he gets paid what the market offers.

Nowadays, some grain farmers can afford to build storage facilities and gamble on a higher price. However, this option is not open to the vegetable farmer or to the livestock producer. When his product is ready for the market, he must sell it. Oh, yes, he can withhold his pigs or his beef for a week or a month, but he must go on feeding them, and the increased growth is rarely justified pricewise.

In livestock raising, the gamble is always great. A farmer decides to have, say, ten sows farrow in the spring. They must be bred in the late fall so they will farrow in the spring. The new crop of pigs will not be ready to market until the following fall at the earliest. That's a year's gamble. At no point can be shut down the operation and not lose his shirt.

The egg producer is at only a slightly less disadvantage, as it only takes nine months from the day the eggs are set to hatch until the new chicken is laying eggs herself. If the market is too bad, he can sell the hens for meat. Here, again, he is caught, because if the price is bad, other poultrymen will be selling their birds for meat and that price will also go down. The man who plants an apple orchard must wait for five years for a reasonable crop.

As Arthur Danberry of Ringoes will tell you, the dairyman's problem is, in a way, unique and worse. Until recently, Danberry was involved since boyhood in dairying with his father on their farm near Ringoes. His grandfather was a dairy farmer in the county before him and the basic problem the farmer faces today has changed little.

There are really two problems: first, milk is bulky and perishable and has to be marketed every day, and, second, the fluid milk plant or cheese factory that the farmer has a contract with is his only outlet. He really is tied down. Compounding his problem is the fact that cows, by nature, tend to give more milk in the spring when the grass is green. Production falls off toward the fall and winter. If the farmer has a fluid milk market, he must attempt to produce milk evenly the year round and take a much reduced price for excesses over his minimum production. Holding this loss down requires that he be an expert cowman who understands herd health and watches each cow carefully.

For these reasons, the dairyman has probably felt more desperate and resorted to violence and strikes more frequently than have other farmers. Going on strike is not really a solution for him, however. The cows have to be milked and fed and the milk dumped in a ditch. Usually, then, the local health officer gets after him. Of course, the cows can be sold to a butcher, but it would take years and many, many thousands of dollars for the man to get back into the dairy business again. From the time a calf is first conceived until it becomes a cow and has a calf of its own and starts to milk takes the better part of three years.

The first milk strike took place in 1898. It lasted five days, but records show that it accomplished little. South Jersey dairymen, shipping mostly to Philadelphia, had formed an organization called Interstate in the 1880's. They bargained with their handlers, but they also owned some cheese factories that could take care of some of the surplus milk that the member produced. The Dairyman's League, which consisted mostly of farmers shipping to northern New Jersey and New York State, was formed in 1901. In 1916, the League headed up a strike in the New York milk market. Enos J. Perry, the Rutgers dairy specialist, recalls:

"But I remember back to the days in 1916 when the League headed up a strike in the whole New York milk market. I happened to be a county agent in Pennsylvania and I never want to go through another one of those. It was so serious and, in some cases, turned brother against brother. Some favored keeping the milk home and going on strike, while others were against it — and in the same family. It was a sad story."

The League strike lasted two weeks and some farmers did win a somewhat higher price, but they lost two weeks of milk. Then America entered World War I, at which time the government put a ban on strikes. It set up a "fair" price that farmers said favored the consumer. After the war, the League staged another 18-day strike that some dairymen considered a victory, although most felt it was a debilitating blow to the strikers.

Hunterdon faced another problem: farmers had first two, then three, co-ops from which to choose.

Arthur Danberry's father was one of the founders of United Milk Producers, adding a third group to Interstate and the League. He was county president for a number of years.

Each dairyman had to choose from two or three groups, all loyal to the farmer, all wanting his complete support. Ed Gauntt recalled clearly the desperation and uneasiness he met when he became county agent in 1927 and had to deal with three different organizations all waltzing with different farmers.

"Yes, the Philadelphia Interstate was a Philadelphia market and the Dairymen's League was New York and the United Milk Producers came in and took people who didn't think either one of them were doing a good job. I remember

A hungry calf expresses the pain of an empty stomach in the same way a human baby does — Waaaah! Because milk is too valuable, calves do not get to suckle from their mother's udder for very long after birth. They're given a pail with an artificial teat, containing milk mixed with liquid nutrients. This one, however, had progressed to drinking from a pail and nibbling on hay.

we used to get into some terrible situations. For example, a farmer near Stanton came in to see me one day and said I should have been at Lebanon last night. One of the UMP directors had called you a dirty skunk.

"Who was it? When he told me, I said, I guess I better go to the next meeting and find out what this is all about. I went to the next meeting and they called on me. I got up and said, I understand somebody called me a dirty skunk at the last meeting. I just came to find out what it was all about. This guy jumped right up and said, I called you a dirty skunk.

"I said, why? And he said, I found out that you thought I was keeping the money here and not turning it in to the Trenton office (of the UMP). You called the Trenton office to find out if I had turned the money in. Is that right? I said, that's absolutely right, but it wasn't my idea. One of your members came in to me, and said I'd like to find out if John is paying Trenton; will you call them? That's all I did; I called for one of your members.

"Then I said, now you've been condemning the Dairymen's League for being crooked, and you've been condemning the Philadelphia Interstate for being crooked, and now your members are accusing you of being crooked. You're all in the same boat, and I'm in the middle and you can call me a dirty skunk if you want to, but I just followed out the direction of one of your members. He finally apologized, but, oh, we had some great times."

When the Depression struck in the early 1930's, things got really tough. William Phillips of Milford said: "I have milked by hand for 90 cents a hundredweight. That's less than two cents a quart and that doesn't add up very fast." The New Jersey government, recognizing the extreme plight of the dairymen, decided to take some action by declaring a state of emergency and establishing a board that would fix the price paid the dairyman for his milk and what the handler could sell it for. Despite the general dis-

The daily ration of feed concentrate is dished out by dairyman James Spencer of Lebanon. A shallow concrete trough holds hay, sometimes silage, and the concentrate provides nutrients to balance out the diet. A metal cup near the cow's head delivers water when she presses her nose to it, and the separate stanchions keep the cows from wandering and overcrowding.

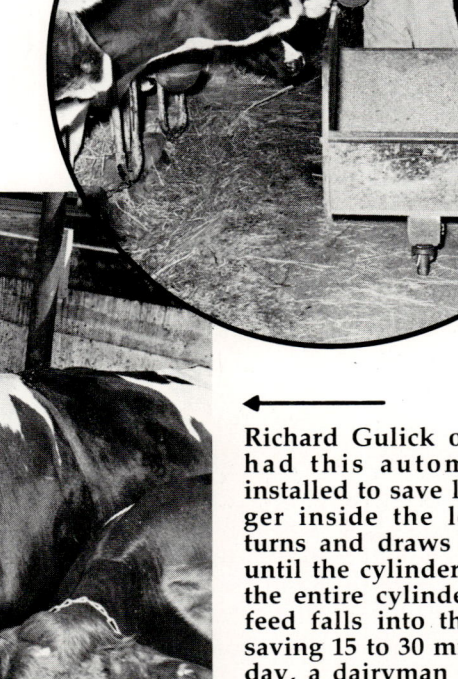

Richard Gulick of Flemington had this automatic feeder installed to save labor. The auger inside the long cylinder turns and draws feed through until the cylinder is full. Then the entire cylinder rotates and feed falls into the trough. By saving 15 to 30 minutes twice a day, a dairyman could expand his herd and perhaps do without a hired hand.

like by most farmers for government interference, the problems were so great that there was really no option and the co-ops supported it.

Former Hunterdon Assemblyman Wesley Lance of Annandale remembers the 30s and 40s in terms of the Milk Control Law:

"The statute said that for a two-year emergency period the state Milk Control Agency could fix the price of milk. During my early days in the Assembly, I was in a state of mortal fear that I wouldn't be able to have this renewed. A bill of this type could be passed more easily in a rural agricultural Senate. But in the Assembly, I would be faced with Essex County . . . "

Essex and Bergen counties and some other hard-nosed urban areas had sympathies to rural areas that extended as far as their direct and immediate benefits to them were concerned. Lance was able to convince his city cousin legislators that their consumers were benefiting from the control legislation, too. They had a good inexpensive supply of milk, rather than high prices and chronic shortages. Lance left no stone unturned and became very sensitive to urban issues in an effort to win the support of his city cousins.

During the war years, former Hunterdon State Senator Arthur F. Foran was director of the Milk Control Office. He did his job so well that when milk dealers brought civil court cases to try to bust the law, they failed. The law was renewed until the 1950s, when broader federal controls took over.

The state controls probably helped some. Hubert Schmidt, the historian, discovered the fact that between 1945 and 1965 farmers received on an average 10 cents a quart for their milk. Farmers stayed in business during the period of rapidly rising costs by becoming more efficient and increasing the productivity of their cows.

State control, however, faced the problem that there was no way to prevent a New Jersey dealer from buying out-of-state milk. New Jersey dairymen produced only about 25 per cent of the milk needed in the state. The Office of Milk Control set a price that the dealer had to pay Jersey dairymen for the milk he sold for fluid use and another price for so-called surplus milk, which, of course, existed to an extent the year round, but largely in the spring. However, the handler was free to buy milk from out of the state at a totally uncontrolled price and, after importing it, could assign fluid milk prices to the milk he purchased out of state, ending up with a "blend" just high enough to keep his producers from going broke. Obviously, this was enormously beneficial to the New Jersey dealer, who was buying in an open market and selling in a protected one.

A movement began to establish a federal order which would set a price to the producer for all milk sold in North Jersey, regardless of source, and eliminate this juggling of farmers' money. On this issue, too, New Jersey dairymen disagreed. Some wanted no federal control. Others would accept it if it covered New Jersey only. Some wanted one type of market order, others another. The New York producers who provided the bulk of North Jersey milk and the federal government wanted one order covering New York and New Jersey.

A committee appointed by the governor, in which Hunterdon's Lloyd Wescott was very active, sought for some compromise and, at a federal hearing which started in July of 1956, adjourned for Christmas and reopened the following February (the longest hearing ever), a compromise was worked out. New Jersey milk is now priced to the farmer as part of the New York-New Jersey federal order. This has brought a degree of stability, if no great prosperity, to the market.

During the time that the state order was working poorly and the federal order was being fought about, there were three strikes: one, called by the Guild, was led by a minister named Reverend Dorney and two by a more aggressive farm organization known as NFO, or National Farmers Organization, in which young dairymen like Terrence Hoffman of Califon were active. Given the nature of the milk marketing system, these produced limited effect. The farmer still remained at the mercy of the market as a whole.

Since the New Deal days, a number of federal programs have been started, designed to help all farmers, especially crop farmers and dairymen, cope with an abundant over-supply in some years and shortages in others. Essentially, these programs have taken the form of minimum prices below which the government will not let the products sell. The government will either buy and store the product or loan the farmer money so that he can store it himself, if he has the facilities. This does create a new set of problems. If there is a surplus in the hands of the government, it overhangs the market, keeping prices depressed as the government tries to get out

Marketing The Product

from under the frequent large holdings of farm products thus deny the farmer the high price he might get in a year of short supply. So, while the farmers accept the programs, they are not happy with them.

Without much question, farmers must be classed as the greatest optimists, one might even say gamblers, of all. Year after year they plant a field, set a batch of eggs to hatch, breed a sow to farrow, raise a heifer calf to become a cow, plant an orchard — believing that somehow there will be a profitable market when the time comes to realize it.

Government programs have helped farmers strengthen their position, but it has been entirely through their own efforts that they have become the most efficient agricultural producers in the entire world by a wide margin. One has only to recognize the part that agricultural exports play in the balance of trade to realize the importance of American farming to the nation and recognize the fact that the cost of food to the American consumer is by far the lowest in the world.

So one look at the history of farming in Hunterdon County as a microcosm of an enormous industry facing unique and challenging problems, but obviously able by its nature to attract the diligent and hopeful farm families who are the American agriculture.

* * *

Howard Fleming, father and son, show off their non-purebred Holstein "Joy" along side eight milk cans representing her week's production of milk. She produced 100 pounds of milk a day when this photo was taken in 1959 at the Fleming dairy in Califon. In other words, Joy supplied 50 families with a quart of milk a day. It was an unusual record, yet all farmers hoped for such surprises arising out of improvements in care and breeding.

Cows relax in their private lounge, called open-stall housing. This one, at the Wescott farm in Rosemont, was built in 1959 and has been studied by Rutgers dairy specialists toward perfecting the design for others to use. Cows are separated into groups according to their feeding requirements. Formerly, they were housed in long rows of stanchions, awaiting the milkman or the milking machine. Lloyd Wescott and Robert Manners of Ringoes experimented with the "milking parlor," into which the cow walked, was milked in several minutes, and then ambled to the open-stall lounge. Thus the cows are more comfortable and dairymen more efficient.

Marketing The Product

There's a farm down Wertsville Road outside of Ringoes that out-of-towners and schoolchildren probably know better than the average adult Hunterdon resident. Its owner is a very friendly man.

"Over the years we've had many thousands of people here to visit, and people from all over the world, too. I've never been one to seek publicity, but of course the college knows about us, the Extension Service, so we've showed our operations here to people from many countries of the world, many busloads of farmers, and busload after busload of school children — you know there are still people not too far from us that don't know what a dairy cow looks like.

"We'll run through and explain the operation — the dry cows, the milk cows, and of course we still have some pigs. Being from the 'old school' we still have some pigs and chickens and guinea hens and geese and ducks and swans and peacocks. The kids seem to enjoy it very much, not only their teachers; you can see the joy in their faces.

"Then when we're done around the barn, I show 'em our conservation practices — strip cropping, terraces, farm pond, the whole thing. I'll put these kids on a wagon — usually we use two of them because about 50, or 60 come in a busload. We'll put straw bales on, they'll sit on those, then we'll take a trip over the farm and I'll stop and explain the different types of crops, what they are, what they are utilized for, then get a back view of the farm, of the pond, and quite often we'll see deer and pheasants running.

"You know, I've done this for 20 years and often now, I'll be somewhere a good ways from home and someone will come over and tap me on the shoulder and say 'Aren't you Mr. Manners? Say, I was at your farm.'"

Robert Manners and his wife, Elsie, farm a dairy and crop operation with their grown son, Gregory. The story Manners tells of his career over the past three decades has many points in common with Hunterdon's remaining dairymen. The feelings about farming and its relation to the community he describes are like those of many other farmers in the county. Yet, he is the first to point out he is not a spokesman, and that his neighbor down the road might disagree with him completely on any of his notions.

Manners started his career in 1943 with 18 cows. "I haven't come far. I was born and raised just a mile up the road. I bought a bare farm. I lived up on my brother's because I was still single, ate there, would come down here to do my chores and milk the cows.

"I bought a tractor and a two-bottom plow and a harrow the first year, then gradually as we could, we added equipment and grew very slowly. We had a milking machine, and don't forget at that time it was quite modern. It was just on the tail-end of the horse era. In fact the man I bought the farm from had a sale of goods before I took possession and he still had two horses."

In the early 1950s, Manners saw where the future lay and that it was time to expand the old cow barn. His uncle, a "city cousin" with a doctorate in chemistry, owned the farm next door and it had a woodlot with a lot of good oak. "We went to the woods and cut the trees ourselves. We snaked the logs out with a tractor and loaded them by hand on a flatbed wagon. We took them to the mill, had them sawed, brought them here, stacked them in the wagon house to dry for a year. The addition we built on the barn made room for 60 cattle. We took the horse box stalls out of the old part, the old stanchions, and resurfaced everything."

That established the Manners farm as one of the modern dairies of the time. Five years later, in 1958, the barn burned to the ground. Meanwhile, milk prices had been stagnant for a decade and real estate taxes were climbing, as was everything else. Maybe it was time to move out of the state to farm; maybe it was time to get out of farming altogether; maybe it was time to rebuild — but to a different pattern to meet an increasingly harsh economic future.

"I went out and did a lot of work. I talked to the best dairymen, the best farmers in the community. I went to the college. I did a lot of traveling through many states to see what I wanted to do if I wanted to stay in agriculture. I loved my community, and I almost promised myself I couldn't leave it. My roots were too deep for that. Mr. Krueger, the extension engineer at Rutgers, helped put a lot of stuff on paper I had seen in other states."

W.C. Krueger was a man who could stand in front of a cowbarn with a farmer and as they talked, draw a finished plan of what he needed on the back of a milk check envelope. Of course, later the envelope sketch would be translated onto a bigger sheet of paper, but the finished barn looked just like the one on the envelope. He was the kind of man Hunterdon farmers wanted and appreciated.

"We wound up with an end product that he and I thought would do the job. At that time there were people that wanted to have my head checked, because the open housing we used was a no-no at the time. It was a dirty word; people really thought I should be checked out for making this drastic move."

Manners had correctly chosen a drastic move that was to be the wave of a more efficient future. No more stalls, and in the their place open areas for cows to circulate indoors in the winter, plus milking parlors where they are milked at high speed. This became the standard design in 1980, 22 years later.

"It wasn't easy for me to do. Don't forget, I was born and raised on a farm and I had farmed here 15 years or so with a stanchion-type operation. To make this 180 degree change, it was harder for me than it was for the cattle, I guarantee you.

"But it worked out exceptionally well. Of course, I doubled the number of cows — to ever get all that paid off, you have to increase the volume. That's part of the name of the game: efficiency. And it worked out."

The new barn brought Manners to the present. They have made other changes, though. They now farm over 700 acres of nearby land owned by "city cousins:" airline pilots, manufacturers, engineers, white collar men, the typical farm-owner of today.

"It's very near an impossibility to bring the true agricultural picture to an outsider who has not lived on a farm himself," Manners said. "There's so many variables that go into my occupation. You know, the weather, this can crucify me. I can put on everything the book says, all the knowledge I might have gained, the proper units of fertilizer to grow 100 bushels of corn. I can put on the proper kind of lime, I can have the most expensive and best tillage tools in the country.

"I can have the finest men in the world running that equipment. I can have the greatest harvesting equipment, but you know if that Good Man Upstairs doesn't give me the moisture I need, I'm dead as can be.

"Most of our lives we're tied up closely with the soil, and maybe that's why a lot of us are here. The nature of our work certainly puts us closer to the Maker. All our work is like this — you breed these cattle to the finest bull in the world, and you wait two years to see how the calf turns out, and it doesn't always turn out that she'a a top notcher. I know they talk about Atlantic City and Nevada, but you know we're the biggest gamblers in the world!

"If I walk out to the barn right now I don't know what I'm going to find — a cow down, a sick pig, a heifer being born backwards, the variables are so numerous it's impossible to list them all. And the return is not there. We don't have it built-in, as in industry, when you know your retiring day is coming, and your sick days, and all those other benefits. For us the money has to come out of profits and go into a savings account. For farmers, it's generally a checking account they work out of and they're glad at the end of the month there's enough there to cover.

"I think when I get out of the milk business and milk is a dollar a quart, I'll appreciate the fact that the man that produced it earns every single penny he gets. We're not just producing volume; we are inspected and reinspected and checked and double-checked, and there are very high standards. Yes, and it's a shame when the government allows those import gates to open up that they don't follow through and make sure the products that are imported follow these same high class standards. They don't.

"As to the government, I have to say they still have that quote-unquote cheap food policy, and there is no such thing if they are going to make these demands upon us. You know we follow all the rules and regulations that everyone comes along with — OSHA, the environmental people, all of them.

"There's nobody to tell people this. You know, when you go to the meat store and the grocery — I go maybe twice a year; I'm not much for shopping — but you walk down there and you see the price of some of these meats — holy jumpin' mackerel! They make your head spin, you know, and of course they're cussin only one guy: the guy that produced that. They don't know what he got for that meat, and they don't realize that the price more than doubled, and probably tripled since it left the farm."

"We're cats of a different breed and when we're gone it's going to be a sad day, because you don't only train a man to do farming. I think 90 percent of us are born at it, or deeply involved from early in life.

"As long as I'm here, I don't look for anybody to come up my lane, tap me on the shoulder, and thank me for being a farmer. But, you know, we pay a fairly high price in real estate taxes to have the privilege of farming this land. And we keep the air clean and the beauty and the charm of the community and the rolling hills of Hunterdon and all that. Most of the people who move here to Hunterdon will tell you that."

Though, as Robert Manners is quick to point out, you have to watch the newcomers all the time, because they often try to solve problems by passing laws at the township level which infringe on the ability of farmers to farm. Yet, Manners' family, like many, has made the best of it. Hunters, snowmobilers, even those who ride to the hounds, find permission to use his land when they ask, and he's happy to see the kind of development he finds in his neighborhood, if development has to occur.

"Your horse people have helped keep agriculture in Hunterdon in a very stable state. Oh, yes, I see these people across the road are subdividing their land with 10 and 12 acre lots so they can keep farmland assessment. They'll probably have a little horse barn and a little paddock and a couple acre horse pasture out back of the house. I really don't think that's why the farmland assessment law was put through. But, they've found a way around it, and, truthfully, I'd rather see five houses over there than I would 55."

These are some of the thoughts and feelings of one of Hunterdon's dairy farmers. A lot of hard work, a lot of bitter frustrations, and a lot of love. There is something to be said for living a mile from where you were born and never having to move to find change, because the world around you is changing so fast. And you find you can keep up. Sometimes with worry, sometimes happily, but always knowing you are free.

That's how it was 100 years ago. That's how it is now.

Three of Hunterdon's leading dairymen discuss free-stall housing and the abandonment of the old stanchion system for cows on a visit several years ago to the Burlington County farm of Lester Jones Jr. (left). The local men are, left to right, John Paulmier, Robert Manners, and Richard Gulick. The change was logical and convenient, but stanchions had been in use for so long that many farmers thought the new idea was iffy. So they talked with dairymen like Jones who pioneered the free-stall system.

XI
Horses In Hunterdon

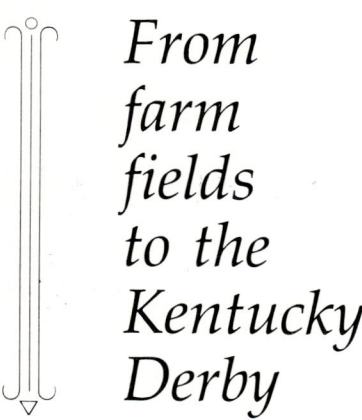

From farm fields to the Kentucky Derby

*Three things I never lend —
my 'oss, my wife, and my name.*

Robert Smith Surtees
Hillingdon Hall
1845

From the time of the earliest settlers in Hunterdon County, horses have held a special place in the thoughts, if not always the lives, of many people. In the 18th century, they were a necessary fixture in the daily life of virtually every family, as they served the dual purpose of field beast of burden as well as the only dependable form of transportation. Tax records as early as 1735 show that each farm had one or two horses, and most had four to ten which worked in teams of two for both travel and draft.

These early animals were described by historian Thomas Budd as "good serviceable" beasts, but they could hardly be described as elegant — or even mildly attractive. They came to the country as descendants of European imports primarily by way of New Amsterdam and New England, and although the Dutch are credited with having brought over some well-bred animals, the indiscriminate breeding of young America and difficult living conditions brought about a rapid decline of any good stock which may have reached the shores of the New World.

On the whole, the horses were a poor lot, and early records describe them as small, unkempt, fleabitten, dull, dirty, spotted and marked. Few stood more than 13 hands, or 52 inches, tall, the size of a medium pony today. All were poorly fed, given only the most rudimentary care, and consequently incapable of any hard or sustained work.

In the earliest years, horses, like all other livestock, grazed freely on open land, eating little grain or other feed. Some were restrained with hobbles or yokes, but most often they were branded or ear-marked with the rest of the farm

W.N. Burgess's East Lynne Stock Farm in Raritan Township in 1895 was the home of fine standardbreds. Today's owner, Richard Mannon, has restored the property and built a track near the river in front of the house. Fine harness horses are raised and trained at the facility.

animals and allowed to roam the empty lots. With barns small or nonexistent, most horses wintered outdoors, and the hair on the rangy animals was reported to grow so heavy that brands and markings could not be verified until spring when they shed their shaggy winter coats.

As land was cleared and life took on a routine of its own that involved more than the basic fundamental necessities of life, horses were one of the first to feel any real effects. They were put to work in the fields in increasing numbers since they could walk twice as fast as the plodding oxen used for the heaviest draft work, and this gave farmers time for harvesting more crops and building barns. As soon as practically possible, horses were given some care to help increase their strength and serviceability — they were fed grain or hay in the worst weather, and often had a barn roof over their heads to provide some shelter from the winter.

Even in those difficult times, however, Americans showed traces of their inheritance from European ancestors, and records show that good horses were held in high esteem. In 1774 John Lambert noted in his memo book that his "one

Eyd mare folded a valient mare Colt," a cause for joy in the family.

Improvements in the breeding of horses were noticeable earlier than for other livestock, with a rather primitive form of selective breeding. Early New Jersey law required unconfined stallions to be at least 14 hands, or 56 inches, tall, and, although not strongly adhered to until several decades later (about 1730), farmers usually left only their best male foals whole, practicing their own form of selective breeding. These "best" were not often any too good, though, according to the comments of European visitors.

If a farmer did have an exceptional stallion for that day he could exact a price from others wishing to breed to this stud. In 1782 Demarr Ford of Readington Township commanded £3 for the use of his stud "Farmer," and in 1805 Jonathan Moorhead from the Flemington area was charging $10 to guarantee a foal to clients. But this was not the only money to be made in the horse business in the 18th century — harness and saddlery businesses began to appear as early as 1737, and "horse geers" were prominently listed in probate inventories, showing its value, as well as that of horses. However, harness businesses were often combined with other trades, such as a local Kingwood tavern keeper who could also handle what little saddlery business there was in the area.

Veterinarians and farriers were also part-time occupations, as horseshoes were a rarity and veterinary medicine was still a combination of folklore and trial and error. Medical science of the period is exemplified by the Hankinson family of Amwell Township, who, in 1788, swore by the process of using pieces of cloth soaked in vinegar solution and fastened in the ears of the horse as a cure for the "dum stagers," whatever that may have been. Another home remedy included the breathing of the smoke of burning leather "or any other stinking thing" to help cure the "Niagary horse Disorder." Bleeding was also a common cure-all for many afflictions.

Interest in breeding better quality horses increased steadily, and as the 1700s drew to a close more affluent "gentlemen farmers" began to import higher quality stock and dabble with the breeding of finer, larger road animals to which they gave exceptional care to increase their performance, appearance, and consequent worth. One European horseman commented, however, that the American penchant for equating biggest with best in many fields did little to add to the quality of early selective breeding. In 1793 Joseph Capner from near Flemington was recorded as

The horse-drawn mail coach, which traveled between Whitehouse and Flemington in the late 1800s, is a good example of the working road horse of the era. Harness, including fly nets, was made entirely by hand at local saddlery shops.

practicing some breeding of horses as a sideline to his real business, sheep, and others around the county were following the same path.

The prevalence of horses for transportation, combined with the gradual improvement of roads near the end of the century, provided real interest in the breeding of good road horses, and stallions were selected almost solely for their road qualities, rather than their pulling and work abilities. Farmers cared little about the pedigree of their draft horses, but not so with road and riding horses.

Lighter wagons and carts gradually replaced heavy farm wagons necessary to negotiate the early trails, for as historian J.D. Schoepf wrote in 1783, "To go afoot is an abomination to the American, no matter how poor or friendless." An increasing number of horses in the early and mid-1800s were also shipped and driven from the west and midwest, including Iowa, Nebraska, Kentucky, Ohio and Michigan, and "car horses" were brought out from the cities when street cars were electrified. Tavern yards throughout the county, from Lambertville to Clinton and Frenchtown to Readington, became the scene of loud and enthusiastic sales and auctions on a regular basis. Prices fluctuated between $120 and almost $200 for good stock, but "Indian ponies" and western ranch horses were reported to be cheaper than better bred horses known to come from Ohio and other midwestern areas.

This preoccupation with fine road horses and lighter carts led quite naturally to the beginnings of horse racing in the county, and the number of chance meetings and "brushes" along the road that developed into informal speed contests began a steady rise which was to lead to one of the most popular sports in the county, as well as the nation — harness racing. The kindling of the competitive spirit in these early farmers spread rapidly as the elements of basic survival became easier to achieve, and it was rumored that at the time "every farmer had a fast horse." The trotting turf in more developed areas of the country became the closest thing known to organized sports of the day, and formal road races with increasing rules and regulations were a rising form of entertainment. Courses began to spring up, particularly along the Old Trenton Road, Route 31, which was dotted with taverns. As travellers moved from inn to inn, tavernkeepers often sponsored horse races to attract clients, and informal betting was not unknown.

It was during this period that writer Hubert Schmidt notes that "people had great affection

A chance meeting, or "brush," on a lonely country road, as depicted in this Tom Beecham print, provided the opportunity for many informal trotting races throughout the county in the mid-1800s. Vehicles with two or four high-spoked wheels were early predecessors of today's bike-wheeled sulkies.

and pride in the trotters and pacers they drove to church and public events." Numerous stud advertisements in local newspapers indicated rising interest in good animals and many stallions often had fancy names and long pedigrees — some possibly more imagined than real.

New Jersey was developing quite a name for itself in the standardbred racing circles, and several good studs were stabled periodically in the area. They were advertised as "celebrated running horses," "full blooded," "imported turf horses" with an occasional one touted as both a "field and road horse." As far back as the early 1800s the standardbred became the darling of the Hunterdon County area. If thoroughbred speed racing can be called the sport of kings, harness and standardbred racing is the sport of the common man. Standardbreds became the most coveted road horses of the day due to the speed and style they displayed while still performing the necessary duty of carrying the family to town, church or visiting.

The Old Trenton Road was not the only area sporting a strong interest in horse racing. Competition in the rather "racey" community of 19th century Ringoes was extremely stiff, particularly down the main street from town to church. Residents were said to have risen up in fierce opposition to the suggestion that the church be moved into the village, because this would cut out the favorite race meeting on Sunday mornings to and from church.

It was into this competitive horse-oriented society near Amwell that one of Hunterdon and the nation's great sports heroes was born. Hiram Woodruff, born and raised in old Hunterdon County in an area which has since been reassigned to Ewing Township, Mercer County, was touted and worshipped as "the king of America's trotting turf" and "America's master reinsman." Brought up in a family of horsemen, Woodruff was put astride the legendary turf horse "Topgallent" when a boy of ten years, and it was a natural progression that led to the winning of his first race four years later.

During his 30-odd years as the nation's top reinsman, Woodruff raced trotters in the saddle, hitched to high two-wheeled sulkies and to four-wheeled wagons, all with equal success. It was not for many years that the low bike-wheeled racing vehicles of today came into vogue, along with the variety of harness, training aids and miscellaneous paraphernalia of formalized racing.

While road and racing horses were getting care out of proportion to their usefulness on farms,

Pacer "May E. Gratton," driven by Earl Pittman, set a track record of 2:01¾ at the Flemington Fair in 1933. The outrider helped drivers in the event a horse was a "bad actor" and got out of line or the driver was thrown from the sulky.

Draft horses like Al Dodge's prize-winning heavyweight team still gather at the Flemington Fair for horse pulling contests. Although some are used for occasional farm chores, most undergo special training for such competition.

and were becoming a status symbol and recreational item, good draft animals were still the backbone of the farming community, and were taking over an increasingly large amount of field work. The horsedrawn planter and cultivator were developed at this time, and it was these patient, plodding equines that allowed the time and expense of keeping and raising higher class road and carriage horses. Draft horses did receive some glory in occasional pulling and plowing contests, but the first state fair in 1840 emphasized racing horses, both thoroughbreds and standardbreds, making but small mention of some imported brood mares of a draft breed.

This rising horse population caused an increase in saddle shops, and by the early 1800s every village had at least one harness maker of its own. The shops were busy with a full load of harness repairs and new saddle and harness orders. The price of a good saddle, handmade in 1805, was advertised to be $17, and pride in high quality workmanship was increasing rapidly.

Medical attention and education had progressed little, though, with newspapers often printing copies of purported cures, few of which had even a pseudo-scientific basis. In 1826 the Hunterdon *Gazette* recommended a cure for spavin, a disease of the bones, which featured angleworms fried in butter as a key ingredient.

The first Hunterdon County fair in 1856 offered county residents the opportunity to parade their champions in all three categories of work, road and show horses, but the special attraction was the new race course built as soon as there was a permanent fairgrounds. This trotting track remained a focal point at the fair for more than 100 years, with few breaks in the yearly week of racing during fair week. Fancy carriages and buggies were also valued possessions as roads continued to improve, and the 1878 fair was reported to have special exhibits for vehicles of several categories. But it was harness racing that brought out the spectators and lent the real excitement and holiday atmosphere to fair week. The 1858 fair offered a mere $30 first prize and $20 second prize to the fastest trotting horse, but by 1865 divisions included $200 for the fastest pacer and $300 for the fastest trotter.

"Doc" Harris and his famous team of brown mares, "Kate" and "Rose," put on a one-man horse show in front of the grandstand at the Flemington Fair. The team delighted fairgoers from 1907 to 1935, when one of the mares died.

The track was also open for training during the year, and Flemington was part of a six-track New Jersey-New York-Pennsylvania racing circuit, lending it a certain air of respectability. However, it could not really compete with the large New York and metropolitan area tracks on the "grand circuit."

One of the best-known drivers and trainers to occupy the fairgrounds' stables was Tom Berry, who came to Flemington about 1909 shortly after his arrival in this country from England. He remained in Flemington for 18 years, during which time his training ability and racing wins brought many owners and their horses to Hunterdon County to train at the fairgrounds. When Berry left Flemington for Hanover Farms Stables in New York in 1927, he had more than 40 horses from as far as Ohio and North Carolina under his care and training.

By the mid and late 1800s breeding was beginning to hit its stride in Hunterdon in draft, road and racing breeds, but the most prosperous and interesting was breeding for the racing turf. Early racers were strictly trotting horses, meaning they stride forward in a gait moving diagonal pairs of legs — left front and right hind or right fore and left hind. But breeding of a speedy relative, the pacer, was also being perfected rapidly. These pacers move by striking forward simultaneously with both legs on the same side, the right fore and hind, then the left fore and hind, in a rocking kind of gait.

Of the several stock farms which prospered in the county near the end of the century, East Lynne Stock Farm, which still stands on Route 31 outside Flemington, was one of the best known. Owned by gentleman farmer W.N. Burgess, the farm consisted of "225 acres of grassland — well watered, divided into convenient fields by heavy post and rail fence — capable of supporting a large amount of grazing stock in good condition." Facilities included a training track where trainer Charles Johnson broke and gaited youngsters before taking them to early races. Many good horses were said to have been bred by Burgess, but his best known nationally and his personal favorite was "Lynne Bel," referred to as "the fastest stallion ever bred in New Jersey" in his day. Burgess commented that the colt was "the only one that he ever owned which a good price did not tempt him to part with," — and with good reason. Lynne Bel ran first at Belmont Park in New York, second in the Kentucky Derby in 1895, and piled up numerous records for the next six or seven years of his racing career before being put out for permanent

LYNNE BEL, 2.10 1-2

SIRE OF 5 IN 2.15 LIST AND OTHERS, ALL ON HALF-MILE TRACKS.

EAST LYNNE STOCK FARM, FLEMINGTON, N. J.
GREAT CHANCE FOR SMALL BREEDERS. THE FAST STALLION

Lynne Bel, 2.10 1-2

Dam Vashti (dam of 2) by Bayonne Prince, 2.21¼, by Kentucky Prince (sire of dams of 128). 2d dam Luella by Mambrino Pilot.

FREE SERVICE FOR 1909

LYNNE BEL will be bred during the season of 1909 free of charge to mares approved by me, with the stipulation that when the foal is weaned the owner of the stallion and the owner of the mare shall each offer a price for same, and the highest bidder will take the foal at the price named. Mares will be kept from April 1st to October 1st on pasture at $5 per month. Balance of year in box stall with feed at $10 per month.

Here is a grand chance for owners of good mares to breed to a royal stallion without the investment of a dollar. Lynne Bel was one of the fastest, gamest race horses of his day, and he is in the best form of his life. He never sired a bad-looking colt or one without speed. I intend to give him the best possible chance this year, hence the above remarkable offer. Send for application blank and further particulars. No responsibility for accident or escapes.

W. N. BURGESS, Prop., East Lynne Stock Farm, Flemington, N. J.

stud in Hunterdon County.

The contribution of "Lynn Bel" and Burgess to racing history in the county did not stop with their winnings. In 1909 the horse was put up for free stud service to approved mares, with the stipulation that when the foal was weaned "the owner of the stallion and the owner of the mare shall each offer a price for same, the highest bidder taking the foal at the price named." The offer allowed owners of good mares in the area to breed to a top stallion without investing a penny, and to see the product of the union before having to feed and care for the youngster. As "Lynne Bel" was known to be a strongly built and strikingly handsome animal in addition to his speed, many fine horses were bred through this generous offer.

After a slight drop about 1900, the county horse population remained steady for the first two decades of the 20th century. Through 1917 agriculture flourished in the area primarily due to the efficient use of horses and many rural families remained dependent on the animals. New machines early in the century mainly transferred tasks from man to horse or put horses to better use. Teams of three or four horses were often used for hauling, allowing more to be carried to market.

Racing continued at the fair, but with limited success particularly after parimutuel betting was licensed at larger tracks in 1940. Better accommodations and larger purses drew entries and spectators to licensed tracks, but the fair continued to hold meets until 1970, when automobile racing replaced harness racing. But it was the invention of the tractor and its increasing use in the 20s which dropped the bottom out of the equine market in the area and brought about the rapid displacement of the horse in agriculture — a decrease which was to continue until sometime past the middle of the century.

There were some rather half-hearted attempts to revive draft horse breeding in the county in recent times and some farmers have held on to teams, primarily out of nostalgia for the old days. During the war, though, one county oldtimer, who used to farm in the Round Valley area, recalls going back to using his horses for hauling and plowing, especially when it looked like the tractor might get stuck. A good team of horses is much like a fine piece of equipment, he mused, when they are working well and smoothly together. Parts were always available, and gasoline, which was scarce, was no problem.

Donald Alpaugh of Lebanon Township recalls the days when his father could purchase a good

Until 1970 harness racing was a source of entertainment and excitement at the Flemington Fair, and for several years horses and autos shared the track. However, softer footing for the horses had to be graded from the track before autos could run on it. The trouble outweighed the interest after several years.

In the 1940s and especially during World War II, horses provided a cheap and dependable source of work and transportation. Flemington farmer John Bartles never traveled except by horse, while others used teams to fill in when tractors needed repair or gasoline in the time of rationing. (U.S.D.A. Photo by Forsythe.)

working team from Dvoor's Flemington auction for $300 to $400, and they used two teams to farm the family's entire 150 acres. Today, Alpaugh might pay $5,000 for a team. He maintains two pairs on his farm, primarily for hauling, but sometimes for training for the pulling contests at the fair. He admits, however, "I just love to plant corn with a team, and if I could compete economically with mechanized farmers I would use horses for all my field work." Just for old times' sake, he does set aside about 30 acres of corn to plant each year with his team.

But it was not the working farmer or the race horse trainer who brought about the horse's return to prominence in Hunterdon County — it was the pleasure rider, the show competitor, and the racing breeder, all looking for convenient and hospitable land to practice their hobby or business. And it is this group of horsemen who have helped retain the open fields and rolling hills and agricultural atmosphere of the county.

In the late 1950s and early 1960s, the horse population and industry in the county hit bottom with only 516 horses reported in 1959. However, by 1974 the number had more than tripled to 1,381 and a real surge was under way in all aspects of the equine industry.

Hunterdon Horses and Mules
1850-1981

year	horses	mules
1850	7,793	182
60	9,421	463
70	9,520	689
80	9,673	740
90	10,075	599
1900	8,661	202
10	8,961	152
20	8,058	247
30	4,121	157
40	2,949	114
59	516	
74	1,381	
78	2,181	
81	4,000 (approx.)	

Source: Hubert Schmidt, *Rural Hunterdon*

Standardbred breeding, always popular to some degree, grew rapidly, largely because of the Standardbred Sire Stakes program launched in 1976 as an offshoot of the 1961 Department of Agriculture horse breeding and development program. Financial rewards for raising high quality horses have made equine pursuits attractive and realistic for more and more people until today the horse industry is a $350 million economic asset to the state.

Robert Tucker, a leading harness horse breeder in the county, moved to Lebanon Township in 1965 after combing northern New Jersey for more than two years for an acceptable location to establish a breeding farm. Today he has expanded his operation to include four farms totaling approximately 850 acres, where three top-ranked studs stand and more than 400 horses are stabled at one time or another during the year. Tucker attributes the standardbred's popularity over the thoroughbred flat racing horse to the fact that harness horses are still "the sport of the working man. They are easy to work and play with," he explains, "and if an owner wants to he can actually get up in the sulky and exercise and train his own horse." In addition, stud fees, although rising, are a fraction of those demanded for quality thoroughbred stallions. There are many owners who can keep one or two horses in their backyards and race on a limited scale without the high monetary investment involved in thoroughbred racing.

At one time trotting ponies were popular in Hunterdon, which sported a track on Route 31

Saddle breds, popular show horses even at the 1935 fair, are still favored for their flashy movement and elegant style. Fanciers in Hunterdon County today breed and show these striking animals trained both for saddle and harness.

just south of the South Branch of the Raritan River. Richard Fear, who bought a few Shetland ponies for company on his 100-acre farm in Alexandria Township, accidentally almost made a full-time business out of breeding racing ponies until the economy and expense of traveling to widely spread tracks "kind of took the fun out of the sport," which was mainly a hobby for most competitors.

But race horses were not the only breeds to prosper in Hunterdon. Show and pleasure mounts, which the Department of Agriculture estimates make up 50 percent of the equine population, continued to increase as more and more people found the hobby a relaxing or interesting way to fill leisure hours. Hunterdon's horse population, which is estimated to be about 4,000, is topped by only two other New Jersey counties, and breeds include Standardbred, Thoroughbred, Appaloosa, Tennessee Walking Horse, American Saddlebred, Hanoverian, Quarterhorse, Arabian, Trakhaner, Morgan, Pinto, Palimino, numerous types of ponies, and even a few scattered donkies.

The county's location, almost equi-distant between top show centers in the metropolitan New York and Pennsylvania areas, is a primary reason many serious competitors have located in the county. George Morris, who has long held a top position in international horse circles, located his training center, Hunterdon, Inc., in Franklin Township in the early 1970s, and his widespread clientele is drawn from all parts of the country. But it isn't just the big-time establishments which

Unable to work like draft horses or run like race horses, show and pleasure horses gained popularity as a hobby as autos rose to prominance and horses were taken off the road. This competitor in the fair infield shows good form by early 20th century standards.

International rider and trainer George Morris chose Franklin Township for his training center, Hunterdon Inc., which attracts large clientele from across the country. The open rolling hills and central location between New York and Philadelphia make the county ideal for training show hunters and jumpers and their riders. (Hunterdon County Democrat.**)**

are prominant, for smaller family operations are also mushrooming throughout the county. It is a rare weekend when several horse shows are not competing for county entries and pleasure horses cannot be seen in trailers heading to weekend trail rides, gymkanas and various get-togethers.

A natural outgrowth of this increasing interest in horses and related activities has been the formation of organizations for practically every aspect of the sport. In 1949 the Delaware Valley Horse Club was one of the first formed and is still unique in the state. Dr. Welling Howell, long a well-known veterinarian in Hunterdon, recalls the infant stages of the organization growing out of informal gatherings of kids in his office. "They were mistreating their horses out of a lack of knowledge rather than maliciousness, and really needed some information and guidance," he explains. Today the group owns ten acres of land in Delaware Township "bought entirely with nickels and dimes from members. We don't want to go big-time and A-rated," emphasized Howell. "We want to keep the group for the backyard horse and rider." Consequently entries for the organization's show are a nominal $12 for the entire day's classes as opposed to many shows which cost $12 or more per class.

The Hunterdon County 4-H horse clubs, founded in the 1950s, have also been instrumental in educating youngsters to the joys and responsibilities of horse-keeping. Today there are nine clubs throughout the county, and they include more than 180 members, making it one of the largest parts of the 4-H program. The Eastern States Dressage Association, formed several decades ago, was another forerunner in equine sports. Led by Lazelle Knocke of Readington Township, the group was one of the first in the country to organize and promote the primarily European activity, dressage, which stresses the basic gymnastic development of the horse and his movements to their highest degree. Although still seen and practiced in its best form in Europe, dressage associations have grown from Hunterdon County roots to include dozens of clubs and many thousands of members across the country.

One of the most recent developments in county equine organizations is the formation of the New Jersey Bred Hunter Association in 1974. Led by Joan Brown of Centerville, the group is the first in the nation to establish a registry for half to full thoroughbred hunter-type horses foaled in the state or sired by a stallion standing at stud there. Financial awards from the New Jersey breeding program provide hunter breeders with an incentive and opportunity to show their animals in hand and encourages improvement of breeding stock. The final goal, according to Mrs. Brown, is the development of horses of Olympic caliber — good-tempered, sound, sure-footed, heavy weight, with stamina, speed and weight-carrying ability.

With this increasing range of equine activities and organizations, horses continue to play a large part in the growth and development of Hunterdon County particularly due to the wide variety of businesses surrounding the animals. Feed stores, fence companies, tack and saddlery shops, trailer companies and building contractors are all supported by equine activities. In addition, jobs provided include race track personnel, trainers, grooms, exercise boys, farriers, veterinarians, and private barn help. All are necessary sidelights providing income for thousands in the county.

Extension Service figures show the slow eco-

Riding to the hounds, long a tradition in Europe and the U.S., came formally to Hunterdon County with the forming of the East Amwell Hunt Club in 1962 by William Read (with the trumpet) and others. Affiliated with the organization is the pony club which has been instrumental in teaching youngsters good riding and horsemanship practices. (Kurt Herrmann.)

nomy of the early 1980s has had its effect on the horse business — the construction of large facilities and indoor arenas, which began to dot the countryside in increasing numbers in the 60s and 70s, has been lagging, and the cost of feed is still rising. However, horses have become so much a part of the life-style of many in Hunterdon County, with horse farms preserving land which would otherwise have gone for development, and mounts filling the spare time of many residents, the equines have pretty much assured their continued prominance for many years to come.

Horses like "Stoddard," driven here by Bill Paulmier of Stockton, are an expensive but pleasant hobby. Although sometimes kept as status symbols, they also provide owners with relaxing and entertaining hours on weekends and add to the rural atmosphere of Hunterdon.

Standardbred breeding is a fast-expanding part of Hunterdon's booming horse industry today. Hundreds of equine babies are born each year at Robert Tucker's four farms in Lebanon Township. (Kurt Herrmann.)

Afterword

By Phillip Alampi
State Secretary of Agriculture

One of the strengths of New Jersey's agricultural industry is the willingness of our farmers to try something new and to see the potential for long-range benefits. Even as far back as 1781, when the New Jersey Agricultural Society was founded, New Jersey farmers recognized the value of organization, of working together, of learning from each other, to try to better themselves to make a better tomorrow.

Hunterdon County farmers have proven themselves to be major contributors to the development of New Jerwey's agricultural industry, as this book indicates. Proudly, they continue to play a major role in the Garden State, demonstrating the innovative thinking that typifies the New Jersey grower.

During a recent 15-year period, no less than 40 percent of our state's farmers changed the kind of crop grown or the type of livestock raised on their farms. What does this mean? It means that contrary to what some may have thought, New Jersey farmers are not set in their ways, but are unfettered by any "it-was-good-enough-for-granddad-so-it's-good-enough-for-me" philosophy. They have responded remarkably to changes in the market, changes in the needs of the consumer, and changes that affect production costs. It should also be noted that science has brought many advances to agriculture because farmers have asked for -- have demanded -- the research and technology needed to help them keep up with the changing times.

I remember when Dr. Larsen of Denmark was brought to this country on a grant by the Hunterdon County Board of Agriculture, and Enos Perry first demonstrated artificial insemination at Peter Van Nuys' farm in Somerset County in 1938. That was when I was teaching vocational agriculture at Woodstown High School in Salem County, and I brought some of my students along to see this amazing scientific breakthrough. It was exciting for all of us who were there, because it was new and it was being tried out for the first time right here in New Jersey. The result was a unit built on the Lloyd Wescott farm to centralize the bull studs.

Agriculture has scored many such dramatic firsts in New Jersey. It is said that we in the urbanized northeastern United States experience social and economic changes about 10 years before the rest of the nation. In other words, we in New Jersey are seeking solutions to problems long before midwestern and western farmers even know they have a problem. By the time they do, they are ususally in a position to borrow from the pages of our book.

By the time the Hunterdon County Board of Agriculture was organizing, New Jersey had already been officially classified as an urban state by the U.S. Census Bureau, for in 1880 more than half of the state's population lived in the cities.

Since that time, New Jersey has grown to be the most densely populated state in the nation. Yet, we are still able to boast that about two-thirds of the state is either agricultural or forested. Additionally, food and agriculture is the state's second largest industry, and cash receipts from farm products alone now total more than half a billion dollars.

How does one account for this? How can agriculture continue to prosper and flourish in this urban enviroment wedged between New York City and Philadelphia? Strong agricultural leadership and a unique agricultural organization that is the envy of many other states have together contributed to agriculture's continued position of prominence in the Garden State.

Long before there was a state Department of Agriculture in New Jersey, there was a state Board of Agriculture, created by the legislature in 1872. From the start, the state Board of Agriculture was authorized by the legislature to appoint its own secretary. Then, in 1916, when the New Jersey Department of Agriculture was organized, the legislature authorized a new, eight-member state Board of Agriculture to serve as the policy-making body for the department. The members of the board were elected at the annual State Agricultural Convention by the delegates who represented county boards of agriculture, farm organizations, agricultural societies, the State Agricultural College, the State Experiment Station, and the New Jersey State Grange. The names of the board members were certified to the Governor, who then issued commissions. Again, the state Board of Agriculture was empowered by the legislature to choose its own secretary.

Even after the constitutional convention of 1947, the delegates to the annual state Agricultural Convention retained their ability to hold the State Board of Agriculture. To this day, the delegates annually select two farmers by majority vote to recommend to the Governor for appointment to the state Board of Agriculture with the advice and consent of the state Senate.

The state board also retains statutory authority over the county boards of agriculture as provided by the legislature in 1887, and the state board, with the approval of the Governor, appoints the Secretary of Agriculture, for an indefinite term. The Secretary of Agriculture serves as a member of the Governor's cabinet and is the principal executive officer of the New Jersey Department of Agriculture. Since the creation of the department in 1916, there have been only four secretaries to the board.

In 1956, when I was interviewed by then-Governor Robert Meyner for the positon of state Secretary of Agriculture, I was asked to name the most critical issues facing New Jersey agriculture. I told him without hesitation: farmland preservation and marketing improvement. Were I asked the same question today, 25 years later, my answer would still be the same, although I might add a third related issue: the right to farm.

The fact that the same issues need attention today does not mean that nothing changed in New Jersey agriculture. On the contrary, agriculture has seen dramatic changes in the last 25 years, many of which are chronicled in this book. It's just that there are some issues which are timeless in that they will always be the subject of concern within the agricultural industry.

Land use and marketing were important issues for our nation's earliest farmers. In fact, our nation's western borders probably never would have developed to the point they have today if the pressures of urbanization in the East had not urged farmers, trappers and others to seek out more spacious land. Well, there is no more land today than there was then. There are, however, many more people in the world who need the food and fiber grown on our farmlands. There are also greater demands upon the land for more diverse uses. It is because we have come to recognize our farmland as our most precious, non-renewable natural resource, that land use continues to be an important issue for our state.

Marketing also continues to be of great importance to New Jersey agriculture, because of the dramatic changes that have occurred in our society in recent times. Can you imagine trying to tell a livestock farmer in Hunterdon County 200 years ago that one day, livestock would be marketed electronically via a computerized bidding system?

New Jersey sits on the doorstep of one of the greatest consumer markets in the world. Fifty million people -- nearly one-fourth of the nation's population -- live and work in the 10 northeastern states. Nearly two-thirds of the United States population is within a 24-hour drive by truck, which means New Jersey farm products arrive "fresher by miles." Harnessing this vast market, and with the aid of modern technology, going beyond our immediate territory into the foreign market, is quite a challenge. But with every challenge comes excitement, and in New Jersey, a willingness to meet that challenge, to experiment, and to succeed. In Hunterdon County farmers that spirit has shone through time and time again, and I am sure will shine on and on for many years to come.

OFFICERS OF THE HUNTERDON COUNTY BOARD OF AGRICULTURE

Presidents
Joseph Bodine, Flemington, 1913-14.
David W. Buchholz, Pittstown, 1979-
Egbert J. Bush, Stockton, 1915-17.
John T. Cox, Readington Township, 1886-88.
Arthur Danberry, Ringoes, 1971-74.
Henry Fisher Jr., Sergeantsville, 1964-66.
E. M. Heath, Locktown, 1901-08.
James Lane, Readington, 1909-12.

V. R. Matthews, Ringoes, 1889-1900.
John Middleton, Frenchtown, 1967-69.
Philip Mowery, Lambertville, 1961-63.
John Paulmier, Stockton, 1977-78.
William Phillips Jr., Milford, 1953-60.
Burris Snyder, Pittstown, 1918-20.
Clifford E. Snyder, Pittstown, 1921-52.
Melda Snyder (Mrs. Clifford E.), Pittstown, 1975-76.

Vice-Presidents
Orville Barrick, Pittstown, 1979.
William Bellis, Copper Hill, 1915-16.
Theodore Blew, Franklin Township, 1980-
H. F. Bodine, Flemington, 1894, 1909.
Dr. N. B. Bolieu, Jutland, 1893.
David W. Buchholz, Pittstown, 1977-78.
Alvah Bush, Readington Township, 1922.
George Bushfield, Stanton, 1912-14.
Fred Clucas, Oldwick, 1980-
W. W. Conover, Flemington, 1895-96.
John T. Cox, Readington Township, 1897-98, 1903-04.
H. E. Deats, Flemington, 1908.
J. S. Dilts, Three Bridges, 1918-19.
Theodore (Dory) Dilts, Three Bridges, 1924-47.
William Dubon, Pittstown, 1901-02.
Henry Fisher Jr., Sergeantsville, 1963.
J. B. Fisher, Sergeantsville, 1889-92.
Isadore Fleming, Califon, 1969-70.
William S. Goddard, Jutland, 1964.
Arch Gulick Jr., Lambertville, 1953-58.
John C. Haynes, Annandale, 1920-21.

E. M. Heath, Locktown, 1900.
Harold Holcombe, Lambertville, 1965-68.
William Kinney, Asbury, 1965, 1967-72.
James Lane, Readington, 1899.
John Middleton, Frenchtown, 1966-69.
Philip Mowery, Lambertville, 1960.
W. H. Opie, Readington, 1910-11.
John Paulmier, Stockton, 1973-76.
William Phillips Jr., Milford, 1951-52.
Joseph Prall, Flemington, 1906.
William Prostak, Lebanon, 1975-76.
Newton B. Rittenhouse, Sergeantsville, 1886-87.
Charles F. Runge, Frenchtown, 1977-79.
Paul M. Smith, Pittstown, 1962.
Melda Snyder (Mrs. Clifford E.), Pittstown, 1971-74.
Richard Stevenson, Califon, 1959.
Margin Stout, Milford, 1963-64.
William Teets, Lebanon, 1961-62.
Frank Trout, Pittstown, 1905-07.
Lloyd B. Wescott, Rosemont, 1948-62.

(Note: Since 1950 there have been both first and second vice-presidents.)

Secretaries
H. F. Bodine, Flemington, 1889-92.
Percy W. Bush, Stockton, 1921.
William W. Case, Baptistown, 1893-1909, 1917-1920.
Roscoe DeMott, Three Bridges, 1911-1916.
E. M. Heath, Lockton, 1886-88.
Jack Rinehart, Franklin Township, 1972-79.
Charles F. Runge, Frenchtown, 1980-
Patricia Runge, Frenchtown, 1979-80.
Richard S. Schomp, Stanton, 1921-52.
Fred Totten, Ringoes, 1953-71.

Treasurers
W. A. Drinkwater, Whitehouse, 1918-20.
Charles W. Eichlin, Frenchtown, 1974-
Blanche Hoffman, Flemington, 1963-72.
I. H. Hoffman, Baptistown, 1892-1901.
E. E. Holcombe, Mount Airy, 1887-91.
John Hudnett, Neshanic Station, 1932-62.
John Middleton, Frenchtown, 1973.
John Tine, Stanton, 1921-31.
Rev. F. J. Tomlinson, Pittstown, 1902-16.
Joseph William, Sergeantsville, 1886.

HUNTERDON COUNTY MEMBERS, NEW JERSEY BOARD OF AGRICULTURE

(Asterisk denotes the person served as president or vice-president while on the eight-member board.)

1924-32	Clifford E. Snyder, Pittstown.**	
1925-26	David H. Agans, Three Bridges.	
1934-38	Richard S. Schomp, Stanton.*	
1939-43	James C. Weisel, Rosemont.**	
1944-48	Charles H. Cane, Rosemont.*	
1952-56	Lloyd B. Wescott, Rosemont.	
1958-62	Leslie M. Black, Stockton.	
1966-70	Oscar J. Grossman, Frenchtown.*	
1969-73	William H. Plenge, Asbury.	
1971-75	Mrs. Eugene Van Ness, Flemington.	
1976-80	Melda Snyder (Mrs. Clifford E.), Pittstown.	

CITATIONS FOR DISTINGUISHED SERVICE, NEW JERSEY BOARD OF AGRICULTURE

1951	William J. Lauderdale, Lambertville.
1961	Almena D. Crane, Pittstown.
1966	Lloyd B. Wescott, Rosemont.
1969	Charles H. Cane, Rosemont.
1969	James C. Weisel, Rosemont.
1970	Fred H. Totten, Ringoes.
1974	Richard S. Gulick, Ringoes.
1976	Stanley L. Douglass, Pittstown.
1977	Marjorie S. Van Ness, Franklin Township.

GOLDEN EGG AWARD, STATE DEPARTMENT OF AGRICULTURE SERVICE TO THE INDUSTRY

1957	James C. Weisel, Rosemont.
1957	Charles H. Cane, Rosemont.
1964	Oscar Grossman, Frenchtown.
1965	Alois C. Schlott, Frenchtown.
1973	Abe Berkowitz, Lambertville.
1973	Edward J. Hilton, Stockton.

New Jersey and Hunterdon Agriculture: *A Chronology*

1781   New Jersey Society for Promoting Agriculture, Commerce and Arts formed (forerunner of N. J. Agricultural Society).
1828   John Deats, blacksmith near Stockton, patents famous Deats Plow.
1840   New Jersey State Agricultural Society incorporated.
1840   35,510 chickens in Hunterdon County.
1864   Rutgers is awarded Morrill Land Grant funds, starts course in agricultural science.
1870   Approximately 13,000 Hunterdon cows producing about 600,000 gallons of milk. (See 1970 production)
1871   Holstein breed introduced in Hunterdon.
1872   State Board of Agriculture established.
1874   First Hunterdon grange established, Ringoes No. 12
1880   Hunterdon poultrymen adopt kerosene incubator.
1880   155,000 hen chickens in Hunterdon.
1880   U.S. Census Bureau officially calls New Jersey urban for the first time.
1881   Hunterdon's first creamery, Sergeantsville.
1886   Hunterdon County Board of Agriculture founded.
1887   State law establishes county boards of agriculture.
1892   Joseph D. Wilson of Stockton sends day-old chicks to Chicago by train; first long distance shipment of chicks in U.S.
1893   Farmers Alliance picnic draws 5,000 people in Hunterdon.
1898   First milk strike.
1901   Dairyman's League founded.
1910   Hunterdon population 33,569 people.
1912   Hunterdon Poultryman's Association founded.
1912   Rutgers organizes extension service.
1913   State law authorizes farm extension agents under Rutgers control for all counties.
1914   World War I begins.
1914   Smith-Lever Act provides federal support for county agents.
1915   Chestnut blight.
1915   Hunterdon County Board of Agriculture reorganized.
1915   State Board of Agriculture reorganized.
1916   New Jersey State Department of Agriculture established; Alva Agee named first Secretary of Agriculture.
1916   Smith-Hughes Bill provides federal aid for agricultural education in high schools.
1917   U.S. enters World War I.
1917   First Rutgers farm demonstration held in Hunterdon.
1918   First Hunterdon 4-H clubs formed.
1918   Flu epidemic hits county.
1919   Hunterdon begins dairy herd improvement program.
1919   Farm club established at Flemington School.
1919   American Farm Bureau Federation formed with 12 states; New Jersey Farm Bureau founded.
1920   Hunterdon population 32,885.
1921   Hunterdon Board opens co-op feed store.
1921   Board establishes permanent relationship with Flemington Fair Association.
1922   First annual Hunterdon farm auto tour.
1922   First annual Farmers-Businessmen Picnic.
1923   Mount Airy 4-H dairy club formed.
1923   Kerr Chickeries, Frenchtown, ships 3.5 million baby chicks.
1923   First annual county corn show.
1923   John Van Doren's cow selected top state producer.
1925   William B. Duryea succeeds Alva Agee as State Secretary of agriculture.

1926 The Battle of Jutland.
1927 2,605 farm families in Hunterdon.
1927 Edwin A. Gauntt appointed first Hunterdon extension agent.
1928 Feed co-op absorbed by GLF (Agway).
1929 First Hunterdon egg-laying contest.
1929 Stock Market crash.
1930 First successful U.S. egg auction, Flemington, Aug. 1.
1930 Hunterdon population 34,782 people.
1931 Poultry added to Flemington Egg Auction.
1932 State Milk Control Board established.
1933 Federal Agriculture Adjustment Act (AAA).
1934 Livestock added to Flemington Egg Auction.
1934 Dwight Babbitt succeds Edwin Gauntt as Hunterdon extension agent.
1934 Famed *Rutgers* tomato variety perfected.
1935 Hunterdon soil conservation program begins.
1936 Hunterdon farmers contract to produce "canhouse" tomatoes for Campbell Soup Co.
1936 B.F. Ramsburg named first fulltime Hunterdon 4-H agent.
1937 Willard H. Allen appointed as third State Secretary of Agriculture.
1937 Extension Service marks 25th anniversary.
1937 New Jersey establishes soil conservation districts.
1937 Researchers learn that light stimulates chicken pituitary gland, thus enabling hens to lay eggs year round.
1937 Miss Geneva Wolfe named first Hunterdon home demonstration agent.
1938 New Jersey establishes Certified Fresh Egg program.
1938 Nation's first artificial breeding co-op for dairy cattle.
1938 Hunterdon Board appoints Women's Advisory Committee (later Associated Women of the Hunterdon County Board of Agriculture).
1938 Delaware Valley Farmers Co-op founded.
1939 First artificially sired calf born, Stanton, Feb. 15.
1939 Hunterdon Board Associated Women formed.
1940 New Jersey Agricultural Society is revived.
1940 Hunterdon population 36,766 people.
1941 Pearl Harbor attacked, Dec. 7.
1941 Hunterdon War Board established, Harold Everitt chairman.
1944 County Fire Block system introduced.
1949 Fund drive begins for Hunterdon Medical Center.
1950 Hunterdon population 42,736 people.
1951 Groundbreaking for medical center.
1953 Hunterdon Medical Center officially opened, July 3.
1953 New Jersey chickens produce 2.7 billion eggs; demand for eggs starts rapid decline within a year.
1954 2,204 farm families in Hunterdon.
1955 Almena Crane (Mrs. Robert) named New Jersey Mother of the Year.
1956 Phillip Alampi named State Secretary of Agriculture
1959 1,480 farm families in Hunterdon.
1959 William McIntyre succeeds Dwight Babbitt as third county extension agent.
1963 New Hunterdon Extension Center building opened, Oct. 26.
1964 Voters approve Farmland Assessment Act to stabilize farm taxes.
1970 Approximately 13,000 Hunterdon cows producing 16,420,000 gallons of milk. (See 1870 production.)
1971 Blueprint Commission on the Future of New Jersey Agriculture appointed.
1973 Blueprint Commission makes its report of 13 recommendations.

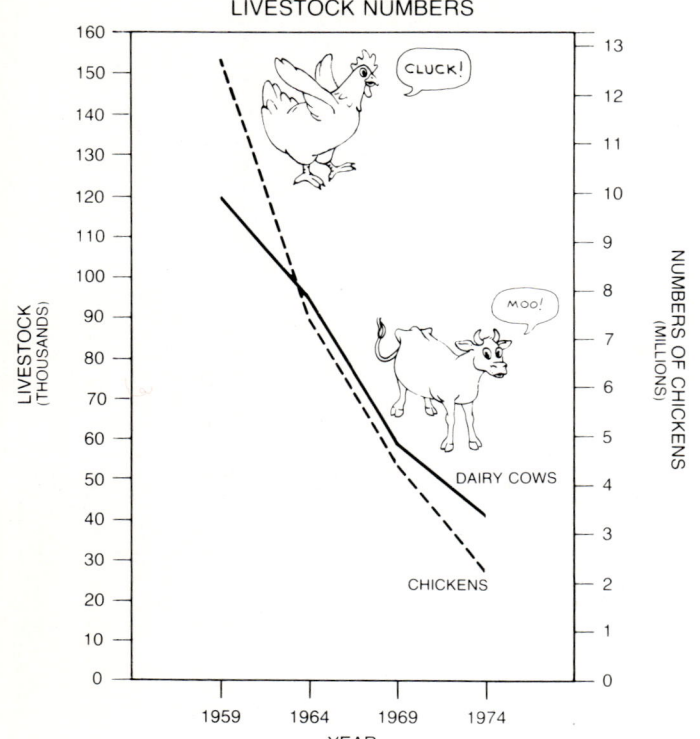

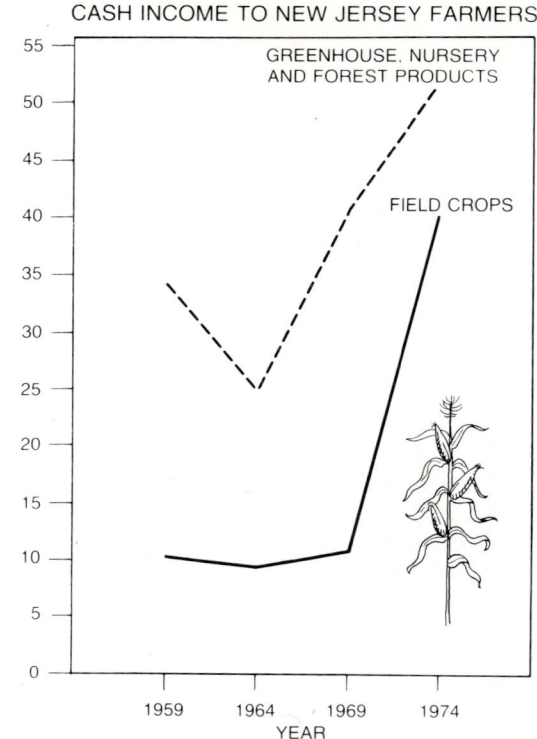

The three graphs illustrate the story of farming in New Jersey and Hunterdon County over the past several years. Above, dairy and poultry farming are seen as declining in terms of the numbers of livestock and chickens, while field crops and nursery products have risen to dominance just as dramatically. Below, gross income is compared to net profit. Farmers have had to invest larger and larger amounts of "risk" capital, but their net income has remained comparatively fixed.

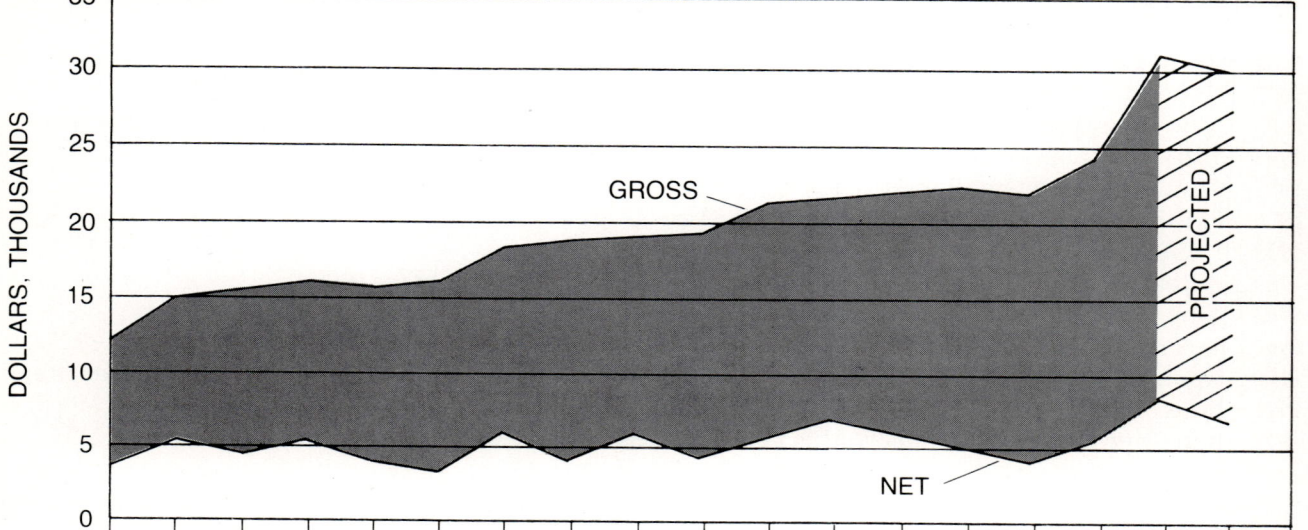

Source: New Jersey Crop Reporting Service

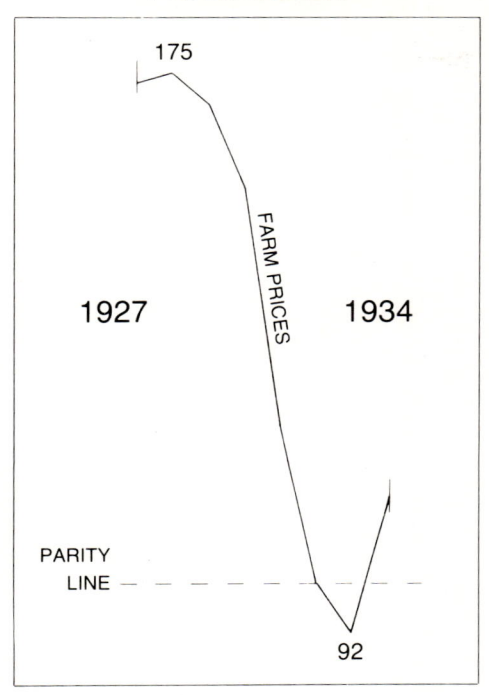

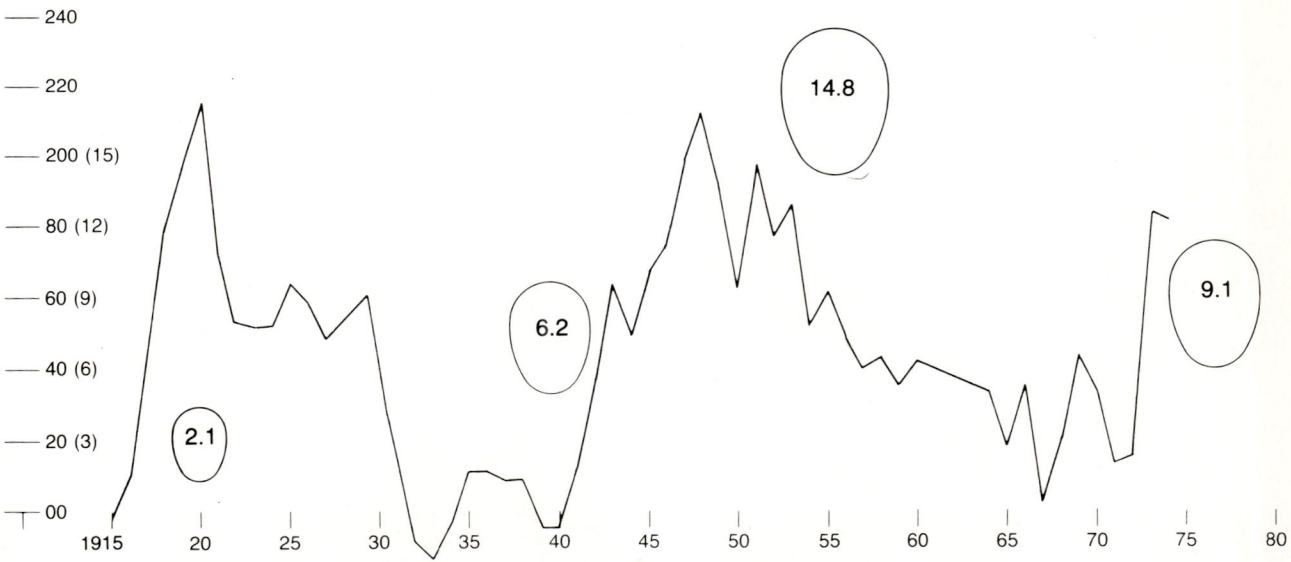

The jagged line shows how much farmers received for their eggs and poultry from year to year, using 1915 as a base of 100. Thus, $100 worth of eggs and poultry in 1915 was worth $215 in 1920. In 1933, $100 worth of eggs and poultry was worth $87. The numbers in the eggs represent the millions of dozens of eggs produced in Hunterdon County. Instability was a permanent feature of the market, but it produced "super" bargains for housewives over the years and continues to this day. Buying a dozen eggs for $1 in 1980 is roughly equivalent to purchasing an automobile for $500! Family farmers with flocks averaging 500 hens or less produced most of the country's eggs into the 1950s.

Source: New Jersey Crop Reporting Service

Bibliography

BOOKS

Alexander B. Allen, *Where Town and Country Meet* (Flemington, 1909).

Thomas Bailey, *The American Pageant* (Boston, 1966).

Murray R. Benedict, *Farm Policies of the United States, 1790-1950* (New York, 1966).

Henry Steele Commager, *Living Ideas in America* (New York, 1951).

Contagious Diseases of Domesticated Animals (USDA, Washington, 1881).

John T. Cunningham, *This Is New Jersey* (New Brunswick, 1953).

_____ , *Garden State: The Story of Agriculture in New Jersey* (New Brunswick, 1955).

_____ , *New Jersey: America's Main Road* (New York, 1966).

Clarence B. Fargo, *History of Frenchtown* (New York, 1933).

Charles M. Gardner, *The Grange — Friend of the Farmer, 1867-1947* (Washington, 1949).

W.A. Henry and F.B. Morrison, *Feeds and Feeding Abridged* (Madison, Wisc., 1926).

The History of the New Jersey Agricultural Society, 1781-1940 (Trenton, 1947).

The History of East Amwell (Flemington, 1976).

Thomas F. Hunt, *The Forage and Fibre Crops in America* (London, 1920).

Orville Merton Kile, *The Farm Bureau Through the Decades* (Baltimore, 1948).

John W. Lequear, *Traditions of Hunterdon* (Flemington, 1957).

David Edgar Lindstrom, *American Farmers and Rural Organizations* (Champaign, Ill., 1948).

Richard P. McCormick, *New Jersey from Colony to State, 1609-1789*, Historical Series, Vol. 1 (Princeton, 1964).

_____ , *Experiment in Independence: New Jersey in the Critical Period, 1781-1789* (New Brunswick, 1950).

George Scudder Mott, *The First Century of Hunterdon County, New Jersey* (Flemington, 1878).

New Jersey: A Guide to Its Present and Past. Compiled and written by the Federal Writers' Project. (New York, 1939).

Dimitry T. Pitt and Lewis Hoagland, *New Jersey Agriculture: Historical Facts and Figures.* State Department of Agriculture, Circular No. 339 (Trenton, 1943).

Franklin M. Reck, *The 4-H Story: A History of 4-H Club Work* (Ames, Ia., 1951).

Diana L. Reische, *U.S. Agricultural Policy* (New York, 1966).

Hubert G. Schmidt, *Rural Hunterdon: An Agricultural History* (New Brunswick, 1945).

_____ , *Some Hunterdon Place Names* (Flemington, 1959).

_____ , *Agriculture in New Jersey: A Three-Hundred-Year History* (New Brunswick, 1973).

Jean Wilson Sidar, *George Hammell Cook: A Life in Agriculture and Geology* (New Brunswick, 1976).

Mary B. Sim, *Commercial Canning in New Jersey: History and Early Development* (Trenton, 1951).

James P. Snell, comp., *History of Hunterdon and Somerset Counties, New Jersey*, 2 vols. (Philadelphia, 1881).

Ray E. Trussell, *Hunterdon Medical Center: The Story of One Approach to Rural Medical Care* (Cambridge, Mass., 1955).

Twenty Years of Community Medicine: A Hunterdon Medical Center Symposium (Frenchtown, 1974).

Peter O. Wacker, *The Musconetcong Valley of New Jersey: A Historical Geography* (New Brunswick, 1968).

Harry B. Weiss, *Country Doctor, Cornelius Wilson Larison of Ringoes, 1837-1910* (Trenton, 1953).

_____ , *The History of the New Jersey State Board of Agriculture, 1872-1916* (Trenton, 1949).

_____ , *The New Jersey Department of Agriculture, 1916-1949* (Trenton, 1950).

_____ , *New Jersey State Grange, 1873-1954* (Trenton, 1955).

_____ , *Life in Early New Jersey* (Princeton, 1964).

Williams' New System of Handling and Educating the Horse, Together with Diseases and Their Treatment (Claremont, N.H., 1879).

Carl Raymond Woodward, *Agriculture in New Jersey* (New York, 1930).

_____ , *The Development of Agriculture in New Jersey, 1640-1880* (New Brunswick, 1927).

_____ , *Ploughs and Politicks* (New Brunswick, 1941).

_____ , and Ingrid Nelson Waller, *New Jersey's Agricultural Experiment Station, 1880-1930* (New Brunswick, 1932).

The Yearbook of Agriculture (USDA, Washington, 1936-present).

REPORTS, PAMPHLETS AND OTHER MATERIALS

Annual Reports, New Jersey State Board of Agriculture, 1886-1915 (Trenton).

Annual Reports, Hunterdon County Agricultural Agent, 1934-40 (Flemington).

Capner Family Papers, Hunterdon County Historical Society (HCHS).

J.L. Connet, *Flemington, N.J.* (Flemington, 1898).

Calvin Danberry Farm Account Book, January 1, 1931, Danberry Family, Ringoes.

Directory, New Jersey Agricultural Organizations, New Jersey Department of Agriculture (Trenton, 1977).

Grandin Family Papers, HCHS.

William J. S. Harvey, *The Grange: Hunterdon County's Heritage* (Flemington, 1964).

Highlights of the 1976-77 Annual Report. New Jersey Department of Agriculture (Trenton).

Hunterdon County Agricultural Society Collection, HCHS.

Idle Farms in Hunterdon County New Jersey, Circular 227 (Trenton, 1932).

Kerr's Guaranteed Lively Chicks, 1924 (Newark).

Kerr Poultry Manual (Frenchtown, 1944).

Joseph G. Knapp, *Seeds That Grew: A History of the Cooperative Grange League Federation Exchange* (Hinsdale, N.Y., 1960).

Minutes, Hunterdon County Board of Agriculture, 1915-present, HCHS.

Kenneth V. Myers, *The Flemington Fair Story* (Flemington, 1978).

Hubert Schmidt, *Flax Culture in Hunterdon County, New Jersey* (Flemington, 1939).

Serving Hunterdon One Hundred Years, 1854-1954: A Picture Story of Our County and Hunterdon's First Bank (Flemington, Hunterdon County National Bank, 1955).

The Secret of Affluence (USDA, Washington, D.C., 1976).

Clayton H. Stains and Karl H. Frederick, eds., *Plain As Day: An Information Booklet.* Flemington Auction Market Cooperative Association. (Flemington, 1958).

Sutphen Wilson Daybooks, Sergeantsville, 1877-80, 1880-85, 1891-1901, 1901-22. Louis V. Kovi Collection.

Jerry Zyck, *Fertile Furrow, 50 Long Years* (Trenton, 1966). A brochure published on the occasion of the Golden Anniversary of the New Jersey Department of Agriculture.

Index

Agans, David, 14, 17, 18, 92
Agriculture Adjustment Act (AAA), 40-41
Agway, 35
Alampi, Phillip, 75 *ill*
"Alice" (bull), 121
Allegar, Mrs. Luella, 53 *ill*
Allen, Major Edward, 160
Allen, William, 51 *ill*
Alles, Clarence, 23, 156
Alles, Linton, 75
Alpaugh, Donald, 196
Amerman, D.W., 121
Amwell Township, 2
Anderson, John, 141
Angell, Mrs. Rose, 60
Apgar, Sylvanus, 24, 116, 119
Artificial insemination, 52-53, *ff*120
Auction Market (Flemington), 38, 93 *ill*, 94-96
Babbitt, Dwight, 44, 45 *ill*, 57, 58 *ill*, 99 *ill*, 118
Babbitt Report, 45-47, 49, 57
Baker, H.J., 27, 28
baler, 145 *ill*
Barnes, Bessie, 174 *ill*
Barrick, Orville, 146 *ill*
Barry, Tom, 49
Bartles, John, 197
Bartles, Walter, 58 *ill*
Barth, Violet, 52
Bastedo, Raymond, 33, 34, 51
Battle of Jutland, 31-32, *see* Meaney
Bauer, Walter & Theodore, 162 *ill*
Baylor, John, 140
Bean, Edward, 99 *ill*
Beattie, Dr. Jack H., 123
Beaudette, Dr. F. R., 91 *ill*
Beecham, Tom, 191 *ill*
Bill, Louise, 68
Bellis, H. D., 116
Bender, Carl, 144
Berkowitz, Barney, 119
Berkowitz, Dora, 119
Berry, Tom, 194
"Betsey the Golden Guernsey," 125
Black, Leslie, 105
Blue Cross, 59
Blueprint Commission, 81
Bodine, Grover, 176 *ill*
Bodine, H.F., 84-85
Bodine, Sen. Samuel, 64 *ill*
Bond, Charles C., 116
bootlegging, 18
Borjesson, Thomas W., 116
Boss, Nelson, 119
Briggs, Robert, 140
Britton, Harry, 140 *ill*
Brokaw, Eugene, 19

Brokaw, Mrs. Shirley, 162 *ill*
Brown, Joan, 201
Brown, Mrs. Mary R., 171
Buchel, Joe, 163
Budd, Thomas, 188
Bull rings, 118
Burd, Charles, 71 *ill*
Burd, Frank E., 5
Burgess, W. N., 189 *ill*
Bush, Alvah, 21
Bush, Egbert T., 14, 16, 20, 39, 169, 178
Bush, Percy, 18
Bushfield, George, 64 *ill*
Businessmen-Farmers Picnic, 51, 57
Butkewicz, Nick, 56 *ill*
Campbell Soup Co., *ff*49
Cane, Charles, 36 *ill*, 61, 91, 93 *ill*
Capner, Joseph, 190
Case, Howard, 109, 116
Case, W. W., 17, 155
Case, Willette, 50 *ill*
cattle auction, 119
Cerney, Louis, 24
chicken thievery, 33-34, 90-91
chickens, *see* Chap. VI
Columbia University, 17
combine, 151 *ill*
Conover, Breve, 29
Co-Op, 34-39
Cornell University, 13
Corwin, Dr. E.L.H., 61
Cox, Herbert, 27 *ill*
Cox, H.R., 140
Cox, John Tunis, 15
cows, *see* Chap. VII
Crane, Almena, 172 *ill*, 173
Crane, Robert, 53, 56 *ill*, 57, 59
Cray, Andrew, 91
Cray, J.S., 15
Cripps, Russell, 1
Cronce, Arthur, 10
Crouse, Paul, 49 *ill*
Crutchfield, Nancy, 54
Curtis, Frank, 55 *ill*
Dairy Herd Improvement Association, (DHIA), 116
Dairymen's League, 24, 39, 180
Dalrymple, Frank, 64 *ill*
Dalrymple, John, 58 *ill*
Dalrymple, Marie, 68 *ill*
Delaware Valley Farmers Cooperative, 73
Danberry, Arthur, 26, 41 *ill*, 72, 133, 179
Danberry, Calvin, 46 *ill*, 133
Davis, C.V.N., 121
Davis, Mrs. William, 97
Davis, William, 42

Deats, Hiram E., 15, 116, 127
Deats, John, 127
DeBoer, Roy, 80 *ill*
De Jonge, Max, 86 *ill*
DeMott, Donald, 99 *ill*
DeMott, Roscoe, 15
Denmark, 120-122
Dilts, J.D., 27
Dilts, Shirley, 52
Dilts, Spencer, 17
Dilts, Theodore (Dory) H., 11, 20, 22, 26, 29, 34, 37, 41, 48, 57, 68, 116
Douglass, Stanley, 116, 120
Drenning, Bruce, 79
Dodge, Al, 193 *ill*
Drinkwater, W. A., 17
Driscoll, Gov. Alfred, 63
Duckworth, H.D., 130
Duke, Dr. F. Bennett, 122
Dunbar, Rev. Edward, 54, 64 *ill*
Duryea, William, 50 *ill*
Dvoor, Jacob, 119
East Lynne Stock Farm, 194-196
Edgar, George, 121
Egeter, Roy, 170 *ill*
Ellis, John T., 115
ensilage (or silage), 135, 147
Ent, Ruth, 77, 174
Eby, Claude, 144
Espelle, J.J., 16
estate tax, 78-79
Everitt, Doris, 157
Everitt, Harold, 35, 58, 118 *ill*, 120
Everitt, Roger, 158 *ill*
Exxon Research and Engineering Center, 24
Davidson, Barbara, 158
Falkenberg, Jinx, 90 *ill*
Farm Bureau, 18
Farmers Union, 39
Farmland Assessment, 75, 77-79, 149-150
Fear, Richard, 199
fertilizer, 3, 139, 148
Finkle, Joseph, 56 *ill*
Fisher, Henry, 80 *ill*
Flaherty, Dorothy, 68 *ill*
Fleming, Howard, 183 *ill*
Fleming, Isadore & Eva, 178 *ill*
Flemington Fair, 21, 30, 115, 160-161, 175
Flemington High School, 15, 17, 23, 39, 134
Foran, Sen. Arthur F., 182
Ford, Demarr, 190
4-H, 49-51, 155, 163 *ill*, *see* Chap. IX
Frank, Mrs. Werner, 106 *ill*
Frazee, Eugene, 77 *ill*
Frazee, John, 117 *ill*
Fredericks, Ernie, 1
Fulper, Norman, 49, 147
Funck, Frank, 21, 22

Future Farmers of America (FFA), 39, 157 *ill*
Garrison, Carlton S., 140
Gauntt, Edwin Armour, 27, 28-43, 44, 91, 93 *ill*, 180
Gebhardt, Phillip, 51
Glass, John, 39
GLF (Grange-League Federation), 21, *see* Agway, 35
Gobel, Adolph, 24
Goddard, William, 77 *ill*
Gottshall, Newton, 93 *ill*
Grandin, Elizabeth, 173
Grange, The, 12, 175-177, *see* Chap. IX
Grossman, Oscar, 66, 73, 105
Grossman, William, 93 *ill*
Gulick, Arch Jr., 48
Gulick, Richard, 81 *ill*, 181 *ill*, 187 *ill*
Gutzwiller, Mrs. Max, 170 *ill*
Hageman, Mr. & Mrs. Albert, 49
Haines, Joseph T., 116
Hammell, Mrs. Anna, 117 *ill*
Hamilton, Dr. Jack, 123
Hamp, Mrs. Charles, 53
Harner, Mr. & Mrs. George, 178 *ill*
Harper, Harold, 99 *ill*
Harris, "Doc", 194 *ill*
Hartpence, Earl, 76, 141, 148
Harvey, Wm. J. S., 175
Haver, Alvah, 37, 49, 58 *ill*, 63
Haver, Jennie, 53
Haynes, John C., 17-18, 21-22
Henderson, Dr. J. A., 121
herbicide, 149
Higgins, Mrs. Ellsworth, 77 *ill*
Higgins, Mrs. Geneva Wolfe, 53 *ill*
Hill, David, 133
Hill, Everett, 153
Hitler, Adolph, 57
Hitz, Ralph, 49
Hockenbury, G. W., 112
Hodulik, Robert, 58 *ill*
Hoffman, Blanche, 60, 71
Hoffman, Jason, 15, 171
Hoffman, Gov. Harold G., 55 *ill*
Hoffman, Terrence, 182
Holcombe, Charlie, 141
Holcombe, Harold, 141
Holstein-Freisian Association, 22, 24
"Home Demonstration Agent" ("Home Agent," "Home Economist," "Extension Home Economist"), 54
Hoppock, William, 116, 119
Horn, Edna, 76
Horn, John J., 21, 22
Howell, Dr. Welling, 200
Hudnett, John, 11, 49
Hunt, Walter, 58 *ill*
Hunter, John, 79
Hunterdon County *Democrat*, 51, 141

hybrid corn, 139 *ill*, 140-141
insecticides, 148
Irwin, Bill, 49 *ill*
Jakimer, Richard, 163
Japp, George, 99 *ill*
Johnson, Charles, 194
Johnson, David, 39
Johnson, Mrs. Helen S., 171
Johnson, John, 17
Johnson, Seward, 49 *ill*, 64 *ill*
Jones, Alben E., 93 *ill*
Jones, Lester Jr., 187 *ill*
Kelley, Father, 175
Kerr Chickeries, 86
Kerr, Richard, 86
Keuls, Harry, 49
King, Fred, 164 *ill*
King, Dr. Thomas L., 164 *ill*
Kingman Brothers, 122
Kinnamon, William, 58 *ill*
Kinney, Russell, 49 *ill*
Knight, Walter, 163
Knocke, Lazelle, 201
Komisar, Samuel, 112 *ill*
Kram, Malcomb, 163
Krueger, W.C., 185
Kugler plow, 5
Kuhn, W.S., 15
Kuster, Ernest, 153
Kunkel, Otto, 152
Lamont, Wm., 64 *ill*
Lachenmayr, George, 99 *ill*, 105, 107 *ill*
Laire, Hugh, 10
Lambert, James, 116
Lambert, John, 189
Lambert, Susan, 158 *ill*
Lance, Wesley, 64 *ill*, 74, 182
Larison, Dr. C. W., 132
LaRowe, Hart, 116
Larsen, K.A., 121
Lauderdale, William, 20, 37, 41, 44 *ill*, , 48, 61
Lawrence, Wilmer, 93 *ill*
Lenni-Lenape, 2
Leicester, Louise Bonnie, 50, 64 *ill*
Lewis, Harry, 89
Lindbergh, Charles, 57
Locandro, Rober, 81 *ill*
Losch, John, 80
Losche, William, 81
"Lynne Bel", 194, 195 *ill*
McAghon, Justin, 69 *ill*
McBride, Jennie, 176 *ill*
McCandless, Thomas, 116
McCrea, Mrs. Cora, 53 *ill*
McIntyre, William, 44, 77 *ill*, 78 *ill*, 121, 144
McKinney, LuAnn, 163
McNutt, Waldo, 61, 64 *ill*
mail coach, 190 *ill*

Manning, Paul, 49 *ill*
Manners, Robert, 184, 187
Mannon, Richard, 189 *ill*
"Martenis, Philander," 165-168
Matthews, Fred, 89
Matthews, V.R., 12-13
Meaney, Beatrice, 31
Medical Center (Hunterdon County), 60-64
Milk Control Board, 39-40
Merrill, Leland G., 75 *ill*
Meyer, Fred, 122
Middleton, John, 80 *ill*
Miller, George, 124 *ill*, 146
minimum price law, 40
Moorhead, Jonathan, 190
Moreau, D.H., 22, 26
Moreau, Mrs. D.H., 53 *ill*
Morris, George, 199, 200 *ill*
Moskowitz, Joseph, 64 *ill*
Mowery, Philip, 78 *ill*
Mulhocaway Farm, 122 *ill*
Myers, Kenneth, 175
Neilson, Marius, 113 *ill*
Nemeth, Gazi, 57
Nevius, J.M., 121
New Deal, 47
"Niagary Horse Disorder", 190
Nichol (State Police Captain), 33
Nichols, Ray, 163
Nief, Ed, 93 *ill*
North Hunterdon Regional High School, 24, 65, 70
Oehme, George, 1
Oley, Warren, 92
Oliver, Charles, 158
Opdyke, Stacey, 102 *ill*
Oster, Jacob, 99 *ill*
"Paclamar Astronaut," 125
Paulmier, Bill, 202 *ill*
Paulmier, John, 187 *ill*
Parker, George, 80 *ill*
Pauch, James, 114 *ill*
peaches, 130-132, *see* Chap. VIII
Pearce, Mrs. George, 83 *ill*, 104 *ill*
Perrine, David, 147 *ill*
Perry, Mrs. Beth, 161
Perry, Enos, 118, 120, 180
Philhower, Harry, 21
Phillips, William Jr., 119
Phillips, Mrs. William Jr., 170 *ill*
Phillips, Mrs. William Sr., 170 *ill*
Phillips, William, 11, 69, 119, 123 *ill*, 135, 170 *ill*
Pittman, Earl, 192 *ill*
Pomona Grange, 175
Porter, Frederick K., 19
Princeton Survey of State and Municipal Government, 54
"Progress Oral Premier", 120 *ill*
Pyatt, George, 1

Pyatt, Harold, 1
Pyatt, William, 1
Ramsburg, B.F., 50, 133, 157
Rapp, William, 99 *ill*
Read, William, 201 *ill*
Reading, Frank, 26
Reading, John, 2
Reed, Dr. Douglas, 123
Repair, Nate, 153
Rinehart, Alfred, 4
Rinehart, Arthur, 134, 143, 148
Rinehart, Jack, 150
Rinehart, John, 4, 134
Rinehart, John Alfred, 21, 135 *ill*, 142*ill*
Rinehart, John Emmett, 21
Rinehart, Robert, 150
Rittenhouse, W. E., 16, 58 *ill*
Roland, Walter, 20
Rozzo, E.J., 89 *ill*
Runyon, A.J., 86
Rutgers Research Farm (Beemerville), 144
Rutgers University, 13, 15, 89, 100
Saums, Mildred, 169 *ill*
Schanzlin, Hans, 122
Schellenberger, George, 146 *ill*
Schick, Herman C., 14, 118, 119
Schick, Herman L., 10
Schmidt, Hubert G., 1, 57, 111, 182, 191
Schoepf, J.D., 191
Schomp, Eloise, 35
Schomp, Richard S., 11, 21, 28, 29, 35, 37, 44 *ill*, 50, 52 *ill*, 61, 122
Schwartzkopf, Col. H. Norman, 24, 32, 39
Schomp, Roy, 116
Scott, Bill, 5, 6, 8, 9
Scott, Charley, 5, 6, 8, 9
"sexing," 90
Sexton, Lamar, 99 *ill*
Sharer, Eugene, 58 *ill*
sheep, *see* Chap. IX
Skillman, Mrs. Craig, 53, 53 *ill*
Slamp, Barney, 58
Sliker, Samuel H., 29 *ill*
Smith, Chester, 6, 27
Smith, Edna, 171
Smith, Frank J., 156
Smith-Hughes Bill, 17, 156
Smith-Lever Act, 156
Smith, Liz., 154 *ill*
Smith, Martin A., 22
Snyder, Burris, 16, 19, 21
Snyder, Clifford E., 11, 19, 21, 24, 26, 29, 35, 41, 44 *ill*, 60, 66 *ill*, 68, 75 *ill*, 79, 91, 115, 116, 121, 122, 173
Snyder, Melda, 20, 53, 79, 150, 173 *ill*, 174
soil conservation, 47-48
Sorby, R.S., 58 *ill*
soybeans, 138

Spencer, James, 181 *ill*
Spencer, Linda, 177 *ill*
Standardbred, 198
steam moguls, 135 *ill*
Stevenson, Anne, 173
Sperling, Russell, 10
Stains, Clayton, 58 *ill*, 93 *ill*
Stem, Herbert, 64 *ill*
Stevenson, Ann, 59
Stevenson, Richard, 57, 119
"Stoddard," 202 *ill*
Stout, Howard, 119
Stout, Margin, 115, 123 *ill*, 136 *ill*
Strong, Sarah, 53 *ill*
Strouse, Harold, 49
Stryker, James, 116
Suydam, Wallace, 44 *ill*, 49, 93
tattooing (of chickens), 91
Tax Reform Act, 79
terracing, 47
Teets, Darlene, 158 *ill*
Teets, David, 119
Teets, Fred, 119
Teets, Natalie, 178 *ill*
Teets, William, 178 *ill*
Tharp, Charles, 24
Tharp, Sherman, 17, 156
Thompson, Charles, 72 *ill*
Thoreau, Henry, 109
Timm, Alex B. Jr., 48
Tine, John, 11, 18, 21
"Topgallent," 192
Totten, Fred, 17, 45 *ill*, 115, 118, 140
Traub, Jerry, 99 *ill*
Treiber, Max, 99 *ill*
Trimmer, Bert, 1
troopers, 31-34
Trussell, Dr. Raymond, 62
Tucker, Robert, 198, 203 *ill*
Ulrich, Martin, 49
Van Doren, Fred, 118 *ill*, 119
Van Doren, H.S.O., 88
Van Doren, John, 116, 118
Van Lieu, Beulah, 160
Van Ness, Marjorie, 173
Van Nuys, P.O., 121
Van Pelt, Herbert, 49 *ill*, 61
Van Zandt (farm equipment dealer), 137
Velehradsky, Henry, 23
Voegtlen, W.C., 118 *ill*, 119, 121
Volkmar, John, 58 *ill*
Wagner, Walter, 129 *ill*
Wagner, William, 48, 117 *ill*, 118 *ill*, 119
Wais, Dick, 30
Walker, Florence, 172 *ill*, 177 *ill*
War Board, 58
Weber, Mrs. Samuel, 43 *ill*
Weider, Orville, 170 *ill*

Wiese, Kurt, 82 *ill*
Weisel, James, 36 *ill*, 64 *ill*, 90 *ill*, 93 *ill*
Welsh, Frank, 18, 20
Wescott, Lloyd, 9, 57, 60, 64 *ill*, 68, 108 *ill*, 122, 146 *ill*, 148, 161 *ill*, 182
Wettstein, Calvin, 76, 79 *ill*, 123 *ill*, 153
Whetherby, John, 99 *ill*
Wilson, Arthur, 119
Williams, Frances Anne, 164 *ill*
Wilson, Arthur, 120
Wilson, Harold, 10
Wilson, Joseph D., 85
Wilson, Lester, 10
Wilson, Sutphin, 128 *ill*
Wirtz, Paul, 99 *ill*, 100-103
World War I, 13, 14, 16, 144
Woodruff, Hiram, 192
Woodward, Howard, 99 *ill*
Wooley, Charles M., 93
WOR Radio, 52
Wortman, Mrs. Vernon, 53
Yorkwin (winter wheat variety), 140
Zyck, Jerry, 90 *ill*

In appreciation . . .

The industries, businesses and financial institutions listed on these two pages have provided underwriting funds to the Hunterdon County Board of Agriculture. These funds have helped the Board keep the sales price of "As Ye Sow" at a moderate cost. The Board is deeply grateful for this generous cash assistance which is enabling it to provide a quality publication to the widest possible audience.

The American Agriculturist Foundation, Inc., Ithaca, N.Y.

Selected Risks Insurance Company, *serving New Jersey agriculture since 1926,* Branchville, N.J.

Durling Farms, *a Hunterdon County tradition for 100 years,* Whitehouse, N.J.

Agway, Inc., Syracuse, N.Y.

Don Shuman Associates, Realtors, *a Hunterdon County institution,* 130 Main Street, Flemington, N.J.

Flemington National Bank and Trust Company, Flemington, N.J.

Kuhl Corporation, *equipment for the poultry and egg industry since 1908,* P.O. Box 26, Flemington, N.J.

Agway Petroleum Corporation, Harrisburg, Pa.

Circle Diner, *restaurant and cocktail lounge, where you'll always meet a friend,* Rte. 202-31, Flemington, N.J.

New Jersey Agricultural Fair, Flemington, N.J.

Hunterdon County National Bank, P.O. Box 410, Flemington, N.J.

Flemington Fur Company, 21 Spring Street, Flemington, N.J.

Johanna Farms, Inc., *country fresh dairy products, citrus juices, yogurt and spring water,* Flemington, N.J.

The Large Foundation, 117 Main Street, Flemington, N.J.

Agway, Inc., Harrisburg, Pa.

Hunterdon County Democrat, P.O. Box 32, Flemington, N.J.

Town & Country Bank, *keeping a beautiful area growing . . . beautifully!* Rte. 202-31, Flemington, N.J.

Stonegate Standard Bred Farms, Inc., *Robert A. Tucker, president and owner,* Glen Gardner, N.J.

The Farmers' Reliance Insurance Company of New Jersey, *over 100 years of insurance service,* Lawrenceville, N.J.

Hunterdon, Inc., *George H. Morris,* Pittstown, N.J.

DISCARD

630
Ko   c. 1

Kovi, Louis V
As ue sow

DATE DUE

MAY 5 '83			
MAY 17 '83			
JAN 0 2 200?			

GAYLORD   PRINTED IN U.S.A.